Problems and Solutions
in
Small Business Management

Problems and Solutions
in
Small Business Management

The Editors of *Small Business Forum*
The Journal of the Association of Small Business Development Centers
Published by the University of Wisconsin—Extension

UPSTART PUBLISHING COMPANY, INC.
The Small Business Publishing Company
Dover, New Hampshire

Published by Upstart Publishing Company, Inc.
A Division of Dearborn Publishing Group, Inc.
12 Portland Street
Dover, New Hampshire 03820
(800) 235-8866 or (603) 749-5071

Neither the author nor the publisher of this book is engaged in rendering, by the sale of
this book, legal, accounting or other professional services. The reader is encouraged to
employ the services of a competent professional in such matters.

Library of Congress Cataloging-in-Publication Data

Problems and solutions in small business management / the editors of Small Business
    Forum, the journal of the Association of Small Business Development Centers.
        p.   cm.
    Includes index.
    ISBN: 0-936894-71-7
    1. Small business--United States--Management--Case studies. I. Forum (Madison,
Wisconsin)
HD62.7.P75 1995
658.02'2--dc20   94-38328
                                                                                      CIP

Chapter illustrations by David McLimans, © 1995. Used by kind permission of the artist.
Cover design by Joni Doherty, Northwood, NH.

Printed in the United States of America
10 9 8 7 6 5 4 3 2 1

For a complete catalog of Upstart's small business publications, call (800) 235-8866.

Table of Contents

"My Company is Growing Very Fast. What Should I do Now?"

Robert M. Schramm, Ed.D.

This case study is about a man who owns a tire distribution business who asks, **"My Company is Growing Very Fast. What Should I Do Now?"** Six years ago, Jack Hayes started his company with $1,000. Now he has a busy, $1.5 million company that is experiencing a cash crunch and growing pains. In addition to having more employees and computer equipment than he ever dreamed he would have, Jack also has more debt than he ever thought he would have.

Is his business going to really take off now — or is it going to go up in flames? What should he do? Six experts offer their suggestions: George M. Dawson, Philip P. Friedlander, Jr., Jon R. Ryan, Timothy M. Baye, David H. "Andy" Bangs and William A. Delaney.

"Convince Us You Can Solve Your Cash Flow Problems."

Robert Gruber and Catherine Stover

Bankers have increased their pre-lending requirements and now are much more likely to require well-researched business plans than they did a year ago. And, as many business owners have already found out, lenders are even asking established businesses to prepare plans when loans come up for renewal. Our case study is about a fifteen-year-old business whose bank note is due in six months. Unfortunately, the firm is experiencing cash flow problems, and the loan officer is nervous.

With responses by: Herbert E. Kierulff, Dean Treptow, Aaron Caillouet, Alvin J. Williams, Steven K. Lacy, Susan G. Macy, and Donald T. Nicolaisen.

"I Know I'm Relying Too Heavily on Two Key Customers. But What Can I Do?"

Catherine Stover

Quality Honey Distributors, Inc., a packer/distributor, is experiencing a dilemma that is all-too-familiar for many small-business owners. The owner asks, **"I Know I'm Relying Too Heavily on Two Key Customers. But What Can I Do?"**

Even though her business is profitable and her sales are increasing, owner Jan Staple knows she is in a vulnerable position. She knows that she has to increase her customer base. But with all the demands on her time that she is currently juggling, how is she going to be able to take on additional work?

Five experts offer their suggestions on how Jan should focus her marketing efforts: Kenneth J. Cook, Mark Stover, Paul Dunn, Alfred L. Whiteman and Rachel Sager.

"How Ethical Can I Afford to Be?"

Catherine Stover

In "How Ethical Can I Afford to Be?" you will not find a consensus in our experts' responses. As a matter of fact, this case shows a wide range of ways to approach this complex issue.

Five experts address this thorny problem: William Taylor, G. Medford Smith, Denis Collins, Arthur Freeman, and Richard J. Delacenserie.

"What Should I Do With My Problem Employees?"

Catherine Stover

In a small business, mastering the product or service may be the *easy* part — and the hard parts are managing problem employees, finding affordable health insurance, and doing all the things to protect the business from liability lawsuits.

This case study, for example, is about a CPA firm's senior partner who doesn't know what to do with two of his employees. One of the partners has become rude and difficult, and one of his new hires has become a rising star who may just leave the firm.

Seven expert commentators offer a range of specific suggestions: Lawerence L. Steinmetz, Gareth S. Gardiner, David N. Campbell, Debra A. Hunter, Edward M. Pickett, Sally Helgesen, and Mary Rowe.

"I Want to Hire a Top-Level Employee. How Do I Go About It?"

Catherine Stover

This case study is about an owner of a software development company who asks, **"I Want to Hire a Top-Level Employee. How Do I Go about It?"** Kim Williford, Ph.D., knows that she can no longer do everything: she needs to find a vice-president to handle the financial operations. For the first time, she is in the market to hire someone who can significantly change her company.

She is reluctant because she has made hiring mistakes in the past. In fact, she believes that her worst management mistakes in the history of her business have been in hiring.

The following experts offer their suggestions: Roger J. Plachy, Jim Johnson, Michael W. Mercer, Ramzi B. Baydoun, John W. Jones, Debbie Berk, Julie M. Buchanan, David A. Lord and Edward M. Pickett.

Quality Improvement: Too Much? Too Little? Or, Too Late?

David S. Krause and Catherine Stover

"Quality Improvement: Too Much? Too Little? Or, Too Late?" is about a manufacturing firm that has implemented a quality-improvement program. Like many American businesses, this one is trying to decide if the long-term benefits of improved quality will be worth the short-term costs of equipment and employee training, while their future hangs in the balance.

The eight responses from nationally-recognized professionals provide a very insightful and thorough examination of what the owners could do next: Norman Richard, Randall Hackbarth, Ronald Heilmann, William Golomski, Pat Wolf, Judy Jorgensen, Dennis Poeschel, Paul Woerpel, and Thomas Davis.

"I Want to Sell My Business. Where Do I Begin?"

Donald Reinardy and Catherine Stover

Ben Logan was apprehensive about the process of calculating a price for his business. What determines value? Are future projections more important than past earnings? Are valuation formulas accurate? How does one prepare a business for sale?

Four valuation experts present four different perspectives on Ben Logan's situation. Taken all together, they offer a multi-faceted look at a complex process.

Responses by: Theodore F. Gunkel, Leonard J. Sliwoski, Bradley Van Horn, and W. Michael Donovan.

"Should I Sell My Business to My Son?"

Donald Reinardy and Catherine Stover

In **"Should I Sell My Business to My Son?"** Ben Logan's mixed feelings about his 29-year-old son's management abilities rise to the surface — and add to the complexity of his situation.

Ben Logan wants to do three things simultaneously: sell his business quickly, keep his family happy, and secure his own financial future. Are these goals compatible? Where should his priorities lie? Our expert commentators — a second-generation family business owner, a professor of organizational inquiry, a management consultant, an accountant, and a family business consultant — offer an interesting range of perspectives.

With responses by: James R. Hayes, Dennis T. Jaffe, Eric G. Flamholtz, Robert Gurber and John L. Ward.

Resources for Small Business

Introduction

A tire distributor from the Midwest told me that he was worried about becoming a victim of his own success. His business was growing fast—maybe too fast—and he knew he needed to shift gears and get back in control. After starting with $1,000 six years ago, he now has a $1.5 million company, and more employees, computer equipment, and debt than he had ever dreamed of. So, where should he begin, and who can he talk to?

If you own a business or are a student of business, you know that there is more than one place he could start, and that there is more than one "right" answer. The hard part is separating the symptoms from the problems, and deciding which issues need attention first.

That's why in the case of this tire distributor—and in the other stories you'll find in this book—we asked at least five different experts to tell us what they would do in a particular business situation. We know that it can be very helpful to see a range of solutions to a problem. After reading a variety of perspectives, you can take the next step, which is to decide where to begin.

Six months after we published the tire distributor's story and accompanying advice (which you will find in Chapter 1, p. 1), we received a letter from him. It was like hearing from a good friend. He said,

"I would like to share a few changes that have occurred since the article was published. I began to write a detailed business plan for the next three years, concentrating on reducing expenses. It seems to be working—net profits are up eight percent. After careful consideration, I decided not to buy the second location, and to concentrate on Eastern Tire. At long last, business seems to be rolling a bit smoother now and I can finally say, 'I may be out of wheel trouble.'"

I hope that you will enjoy—and benefit from—the case studies in this book. It is a collection of the most popular ones that originally appeared in the *Small Business Forum* during the last five years.

The *Forum* is a national business journal published by the University of Wisconsin-Extension. Our goal is to provide useful, important information for small-business owners. You can reach us by calling 608-263-7843, e-mail us at wilson@admin.uwex.edu, or write us at 432 North Lake Street, Madison, WI 53706-1498.

I had a hand in writing most of these case studies. And I honestly can't tell you which part I enjoyed most—talking with the business owners, finding the experts, or hearing from the people who have read and used the information given at the end. I am glad that Upstart Publishing has put this collection together, so that it could become available to more people—like you.

Welcome to our case studies!

—Catherine Stover
Senior Editor, *Small Business Forum*

Chapter 1

"My Company is Growing Very Fast. What Should I Do Now?"

Robert M. Schramm, Ed. D.

David McLimans

I t was a typical Thursday night dinner at the Hayes household: the family was there, the meat loaf was there, and tires dominated the conversation.

Bill was telling his son, Jack, not to worry about their $50,000 business loan. "Just wait till our busy season. We'll be okay. Besides, everyone gets a big loan sooner or later. You're not rich until you owe a million dollars."

"Dad, we may get rich sooner than we think."

Carol Hayes, who had been hearing tire stories for nearly 30 years, said, "You've worried a lot about the business for the last few weeks. What's going on?" She frowned. Ever since her husband joined her son's business, they did nothing but talk about tires. Lately, however, the conversations had become more strained.

"I don't know, Mom. It's just that it's been growing so fast, and we have all this debt, and some days I feel like I don't know what I'm doing running a tire distributorship."

"It's just a temporary cash crunch. All businesses go through them," said Bill.

Dr. Schramm is an associate professor in the College of Business and Economics at the University of Wisconsin-Whitewater.

1

It's just that it's been growing so fast, and we have all this debt, and some days I feel like I don't know what I'm doing running a tire distributorship.

"Well I'm sick of hearing you guys carry on about it. Why don't you get an outside opinion?"

Jack looked at his mother. "What do you mean?"

"I mean you should get your financials together and write down what happened each year and then give it to someone. Get an opinion about it. Who knows? Maybe everything's okay. Or, maybe you should be doing something differently. All I know right now is that I'm sick of hearing you complain about it."

Jack said, "Maybe she's right."

Bill shrugged. "Might not hurt."

"I'll think about it."

Here is what Jack Hayes wrote several weeks later:

The History of Eastern Tire and Supply Company

In 1989, at the age of 20, I decided to start my own business. Because I had worked summers at Liberty Tire Distributor (where my father, Bill, was a partner) I decided to sell tires.

While working at Liberty Tires, I learned that most tire dealers didn't like to deal in the used trailer tire market. There was a demand however, for used semi-trailer tires due to the shipping transportation requirements of many carriers. Many companies ship goods in a trailer that rides on a flatbed train car. The companies then contract a carrier to take the trailer full of goods off the train, hook the trailer to a truck and deliver the goods to the buyer. Shippers like UPS and Santa Fe Railway require the tires on the trailer to have at least 1/8" tread depth for safety reasons. If a tire on the trailer is bad, it is not cost effective to purchase a new tire just so the trailer can sit on a railway car and be driven a short distance. For this reason, shippers are constantly searching for cheap used trailer tires with a minimum of 1/8" tread depth. I had found my niche. I would become a used trailer tire dealer.

First, I needed start-up money. I asked my parents to lend me $1,000 to get started. With this money I bought a van for $400 and on March 14, 1989, Eastern Tire and Supply was started.

Next, I needed a business office. One of my friends who owned a trailer dealership offered to let me store my inventory and use his phone for $100 a month. At first, I was strictly a used tire broker. I went to local tire dealers and asked if I could purchase their used tires for $2 - $5 each. As I said before, many dealers weren't interested in the used trailer tire business and were happy to dispose of the tires for a small profit.

Tires come in three basic categories: used, retread and new tires. Used tires are worn tires that have not been altered. Retread tires are bald tires that have been put through a process which bonds newly treaded rubber to the bald tire surface. New tires are purchased directly from manufacturers such as Goodyear and Cooper Tires.

There is a great variance in the prices of the different tire categories. The following table illustrates ranges for the general costs, sale prices and cost of goods sold of a standard 1000 x 20 trailer tire.

	Used	Retread	New
Cost Range	0-$20	$60-$80	$130
Sale Price Range	$35-$50	$79-$105	$154
Cost of Goods Sold	0-40%	76%	84%

I was ready to go; I had a van, a business office and an inventory of 10 used tires (approximate value $40). I remember writing to my girlfriend and telling her that if things went as planned, I would be a millionaire in a couple of years. That prediction proved to be harder to achieve than I ever anticipated.

Over the next two months, I made 10 to 15 phone calls and three to four personal visits each day without a nibble. Then, I stopped by Dependable Truck and Trailer and the manager, Ben Walters, asked if I had any 11.00 x 22.5s. (My entire inventory was the most popular tire, 10.00 x 20.00.) I didn't even know what an 11.00 x 22.5 tire was, but I said, "Yeah, I can get them for you by the end of the day." As soon as I left I called my dad to ask what an 11.00 x 22.5 tire was. Before the end of the day, I had purchased five such tires for $5 each and sold them to Ben for $35 each, a net profit of $150. I've still got that first invoice to remind me of the golden rule of wholesaling: persistence pays off.

I still had a lot of free time on my hands so I continued to cold-call customers and stop by personally from time to time. I enjoyed talking to these guys and I was eager to learn as much about the business as I could. They seemed just as eager to take me under their wing and teach me the ropes. As I got to know potential customers, I saw my sales slowly increase. The trailer tire business is a small field where everyone knows each other. Once word got out that I was a "good guy" who could be trusted, small orders began to come my way. By July, I was selling an average of 20 tires a week for a net profit of $600. My only other expenses were gas for my van, $25 a week for the office rent and $25 a week for my parents' loan. I was on my way.

Eastern Tire and Supply Company
Consolidated Income Statement and Cost Analysis

For the fiscal years ended June 30

	1995 $	% of sales	1994 $	% of sales	1993 $	% of sales
Net Sales	$1,344,055	100.0%	$1,411,491	100.0%	$1,311,865	100.0%
Cost of Sales:						
Beginning inventory	62,557	4.7	58,366	4.1	65,190	5.0
Purchases	897,417	66.8	902,793	64.0	868,658	66.2
Auto and Delivery	14,634	1.1	1,820	0.1	15,152	1.2
Salaries and Wages	80,119	6.0	16,908	1.2	{	{
Misc. shop costs	6,808	0.5	89,818	6.4	15,601	1.2
Ending inventory	(113,040)	(8.4)	(62,557)	(4.4)	(58,366)	(4.4)
Total Cost of Sales	948,495	70.6	1,007,148	71.4	906,235	69.1
Gross Profit	395,560	29.4	404,343	28.6	405,630	30.9
Operating Expenses:						
Salaries and wages	134,584	10.0	150,453	10.7	171,128	13.0
Advertising	7,006	0.5	11,283	0.8	10,487	0.8
Depreciation	14,000	1.0	20,693	1.5	22,031	1.7
Insurance	23,934	1.8	24,513	1.7	18,199	1.4
Rent	40,250	3.0	42,000	3.0	35,000	2.7
Taxes	75,198	5.6	59,272	4.2	48,481	3.7
Telephone	12,011	0.9	14,286	1.0	11,444	0.9
Utilities	6,099	0.5	5,873	0.4	7,318	0.6
Other	43,660	3.2	55,271	3.9	51,706	3.9
Total operating expense	356,742	26.5	383,644	27.2	375,794	28.6
Operating Income	38,818	2.9	20,699	1.5	29,836	2.3
Other Income (Expense):						
Interest income	6	0.0	82	0.0	—	—
Interest expense	(6,457)	(0.5)	(11,860)	(0.9)	(15,092)	(1.2)
Other income	—	—	—	—	693	0.1
Income before income tax	32,367	2.4	8,921	0.6	15,437	1.2
Income Taxes	10,034	0.7	2,657	0.2	867	0.1
Net Income	$22,333	1.7%	$6,264	0.4%	$14,570	1.1%

Note: Some totals do not add up, due to rounding of numbers.

Six months after my first sale, Eastern Tire was beginning to show some small, but consistent profits. I used these profits to branch out into the retread and new tire market. Unlike the used tire market, retreads and new tires were not readily available, so I began to purchase a small inventory of tires. In February 1990, my total inventory consisted of 25 retread tires, 12 new tires, and four rims and wheels. The total value of my inventory was approximately $3,000, or, in other terms, all my profits thus far.

Then my office was broken into and all the inventory stolen. It was back to ground zero. But this time I had the accounts to fall back on that I didn't have when I started. Nonetheless, the loss put me in a cash bind. If I replenished my inventory, I couldn't afford to buy insurance to protect myself from another

Eastern Tire and Supply Company
Financial Analysis

	For the fiscal years ended June 30			Robert Morris Associates Averages for the 12 months ended March 31, 1992[1]	
				All Sizes Column	
				Services	Retailers
	1995	1994	1993	Tire Repair	Auto & Home Suppliers
Liquidity					
Current Ratio (x)	1.3	1.2	1.3	1.4	1.7
Quick Ratio (x)	0.8	0.9	1.0	0.7	0.6
Working Capital	$71,563	$46,182	$59,047	—	—
Pretax Operating Cash Flow	52,818	41,392	51,867	—	—
Leverage					
Capital Structure:					
Long-Term Debt	49.2%	55.9%	72.3%	—	—
Shareholders' Equity*	50.8	44.1	27.7	—	—
Total	100.0%	100.0%	100.0%	—	—
Debt to Equity (x) *	4.3	6.1	8.7	2.3	2.1
Times Interest Earned (x)	6.0	1.8	2.0	1.6	1.9
Profitability					
Operating Margin	2.9%	1.5%	2.3%	1.9%	2.5%
Net Margin	1.7	0.4	1.1	1.1	1.4
Pretax Return on Equity *	42.6%	21.8%	48.5%	6.4%	10.7%
Pretax Return on Total Capital	21.6	9.6	13.5	—	—
Pretax Return on Assets	8.1	3.1	5.0	2.4	3.4

* *Shareholder loans included in stockholders' equity.*
Pretax operating cash flow is defined as earnings before interest, taxes and noncash charges.

[1] *Reprinted with permission from the Annual Statement Studies, 1992 edition, copyright Robert Morris Associates 1992.*

Interpretation of Statement Studies Figures: RMA cautions that the Studies be regarded only as a general guideline and not as an absolute industry norm. This is due to limited samples within categories, the categorization of companies by their primary Standard Industrial Classification (SIC) number only, and different methods of operations by companies within the same industry. For these reasons, RMA recommends that the figures be used only as general guidelines in addition to other methods of financial analysis.

loss. If I bought insurance, there wouldn't be enough money left to replenish my inventory. The only solution was to locate a more secure storage area to reduce the possibility of theft. So I replenished my inventory with used tires first, and, because I couldn't risk another loss, I delayed purchasing new tires, retreads, rims and wheels until I could find a more secure storage area.

I asked if I could rent office space from Capitol Tire, a medium-sized new passenger tire dealership. They had no interest in truck or trailer tires although it seemed to be a natural supplement for their business. Because my business niche didn't conflict with the passenger tire market, they agreed to rent me 1,000 square feet of storage space and an office for $200 a month.

Locating my office in Capitol Tire not only provided safety for my inventory, but I gained a considerable amount of knowledge simply by being around other tire salesmen. This knowledge helped me realize that I still had a lot to learn about the business. It seemed the only way to learn was to ask questions. No books have been written about succeeding in the glamorous world of tire sales.

Knowledge is obtained through your own experiences and those of others. So I asked question after question after question. I learned the most from application questions. What tire was appropriate for a cross country driver, a gravel hauler or a local trucker? What were the main differences between tire manufacturers? How should I determine the correct sale price of the used and retread tires? I also attended technical classes offered by Goodyear and Cooper to learn how tires are manufactured.

At this point Eastern Tire and Supply began to take the shape of a real business, with accounts receivable, accounts payable and all the worries and headaches that go with them. One of these accounts in particular almost destroyed my budding enterprise. In order to sell new tires, I would borrow from tire dealers and pay them after I was paid. Things worked fine with small accounts, but then I landed my first big account. One customer started buying $5,000 worth of retread tires a week. For six months the customer paid within 30 days and things were fine. Then I realized the customer hadn't paid for a while, but I was still filling his orders. Before I knew it, he owed me $25,000, which meant I owed my suppliers $19,000! I called him daily but he never returned my calls. I also notified him by mail and stopped by his office, all to no avail. Finally, I hired an attorney to sue the customer, but my attorney couldn't ever find the guy to serve his papers. By the time my lawsuit would come to court, I would have to declare bankruptcy anyway. I was desperate.

Once again I asked my dad for help. As I mentioned, the trailer tire business is a small field and everyone knows everyone. I don't exactly know what Bill did, but two weeks later the customer sent me a check for $12,500. One month later, I received the balance of the account and an additional $1,000 to cover attorney fees. I was back in business. I must admit that the experience put a scare in me. For the first time, I began to realize that eventually, I may need some *experienced* help. But I couldn't afford it yet.

As my accounts grew, I finally began to take things seriously. I wanted to expand. But how?

Meeting Kenny Forester, owner of Goddard Truck and Tire Service, was the answer. Kenny had mentioned that he wanted to retire in a couple of years. One thing led to another and before I knew it, Kenny offered to sell me his business. I told him I didn't have the money. He said, "That's okay, you can pay as you go."

I never even looked at Kenny's tax statements. I knew Kenny had two service trucks in good condition and two major accounts that purchased $5,000 to $8,000 per month in tires and service. Those accounts alone paid Kenny's asking price of $625 per week salary and $50 per week for stock options. In addition, approximately 90 percent ($27,000) of Goddard Truck and Tire Service's accounts payable was owed to Eastern Tire. This meant I would not be under immediate pressure to pay money out to other dealers.

Kenny was tired of worrying about the business. He wanted to get out but needed a steady income for two years. I'm not one to look a gift horse in the mouth, so I bought his company in February 1991.

Goddard Truck and Tire Service included two service trucks, two jacks, a lift, a compressor, two workers plus Kenny, his accounts, and most importantly his experience. I kept Goddard as a separate company on the books for a year because it was already incorporated. In August 1991, I finally asked my accountant to look at the business. As the August tax statements show, the purchase of Goddard Truck and Tire Service tripled my accounts receivable and doubled my assets. On the down side, I now had three employees to worry about, $39,427.89 in long-term debt and $30,791.37 in accounts payable.

The deal proved to be a springboard for Eastern Tire and Supply's expansion. The infusion of new equipment, personnel, and accounts resulted in immediate profits. Kenny could handle the new and old accounts while I began to branch out into the service field. Until now, I had been strictly a sales organization. It made sense to offer tire service as well. With two trucks and three new employees, I could start a 24-hour road service and offer repair and replacement services to my current customers.

An average service call yielded a 35 percent profit compared to the 16 to 24 percent profit on retread and new tire sales. In addition to increasing my profit margin, the new service area opened more doors to new accounts, which in turn yielded increased tire sales volume. By August 1991, my tax statement reflected an established business. I held an average of $16,137.68 in inventory (50 percent used, 40 percent retread, and 10 percent new), was

As my accounts grew, I finally began to take things seriously. I wanted to expand. But how?

I began to realize that I was making a common entrepreneurial mistake: I was beyond my managerial expertise. Each new account created new problems.

Eastern Tire and Supply Company
Statement of Monthly Revenues and Expenses for July, 1989

	July 1 - July 31	PCT
Income:		
Sales	$2,700.00	100.0
Cost of Sales:		
Beginning Inventory	40.00	1.5
Purchases	400.00	14.8
Auto and Delivery	300.00	11.1
Ending Inventory	(40.00)	(1.5)
Total Cost of Sales	700.00	25.9
Less Operating Expenses:		
Rent	100.00	3.7
Total Expenses	100.00	3.7
Operating Income or (Loss)	1,900.00	70.4
Other Expense:		
Loan	100.00	3.7
Total Other Expense	100.00	3.7

selling over 3/4 of a million dollars in tires and services, and employed one sales representative and two service technicians. It was time to move into my own building.

It was obvious I had outgrown my 1,000 square foot storage area at Capitol Tire and I was beginning to become a competitor with my new service offerings. Purchasing my own building was the next step, but as usual, I lacked the funds. A $5,206.67 per month operating profit was hardly enough to convince banks I deserved a substantial loan, so it seemed a partnership offered the best solution. I found a 5,000 square foot building located on the south side of Chicago for $208,000. My father offered to put a $50,000 certificate of deposit down as collateral, and then he and my brother agreed to buy the building with me as real estate partners on a 9½ percent five-year adjustable mortgage. Eastern Tire rented the building from the partnership for the amount of the mortgage, $1,755 a month. In effect, the partners only paid if Eastern Tire couldn't and *Eastern Tire always paid the rent.* In the end, the partners will own a $208,000 building in exchange for our signatures. On the other hand, Eastern Tire was able to establish a new location offering substantially more space for expansion.

In November 1991, I began to realize that I was making a common entrepreneurial mistake: I was beyond my managerial expertise. Each new account created new problems. I had to deal with personnel issues, insurance issues, credit problems and a host of other activities. I was simply beyond my capacity as a manager. I had to slow my expansion or take in an experienced partner to expand the business even faster.

Once again, the answer was found inside the family. My father knew the business inside and out and he had experience as a partner in his venture at Liberty Tires. With his experience and knowledge in the business, I could triple Eastern Tire and Supply's business in a couple of years. So in November 1991, Bill Hayes bought 50 percent of the business for no money and a promise of future growth. Thinking back, this was a risky deal. Okay, I was selling two years of hard work for the potential of future business. But I knew my dad was an expert salesman and he had helped me with advice and money whenever I needed it. Bill knew the tire business and could deal with people. I *needed* his experience if I was to continue growing at such a fast pace.

The business started to grow beyond my wildest dreams, and so did my expenses. Bill tripled the accounts receivable within a year. The problem this created was the need for

Eastern Tire and Supply Company
Consolidated Balance Sheet

	For the fiscal years ended June 30,		
	1995	1994	1993
Current Assets:			
Cash and cash investments	$(13,888)	$14,601	$28,487
Accounts receivable, net	217,013	165,519	159,728
Inventory	113,040	62,557	58,366
Prepaid income taxes	2,400	—	—
Prepaid interest	3,550	2,763	6,894
Other current assets	729	—	—
Total Current Assets	322,844	245,440	253,475
Property and Equipment:			
Leasehold improvements	23,935	—	—
Machinery equipment	20,407	15,744	11,545
Furniture and fixtures	707	—	—
Vehicles	97,779	81,654	81,353
Total Property and Equipment	142,828	97,398	92,898
Less: Accumulated depreciation	65,237	51,237	37,294
Net Property and Equipment	77,591	46,161	55,604
Other assets	435	435	—
Total Assets	$400,870	$292,036	$309,079

	For the fiscal years ended June 30,		
	1995	1994	1993
Current Liabilities:			
Accounts payable	$186,082	$161,530	$171,316
Accrued expenses	26,573	12,045	{
Notes payable - equipment	28,592	23,844	22,245
Federal income tax payable	10,034	1,286	623
State income tax payable	—	553	244
Total current liabilities	251,281	199,258	194,428
Notes payable - equipment	504	13,636	35,879
Shareholder loans	42,352	29,636	26,806
Notes payable - bank	73,145	38,250	46,975
Shareholders' Equity:			
Common stock	5,000	5,000	5,000
Retained earnings - beginning	12,455	6,192	(8,379)
Less: Treasury stock at cost	(6,200)	(6,200)	(6,200)
Net income	22,333	6,264	14,570
Total Shareholders' Equity	33,588	11,256	4,991
Total Liabilities and Shareholders' Equity	$400,870	$292,036	$309,079

The business started to grow beyond my wildest dreams, and so did my expenses.

Eastern Tire and Supply Company
Statement of Assets, Liabilities, and Equity Income Tax
August, 1991

<u>Assets</u>

Current Assets:		
Cash and Cash Equivalents	$(2,200.05)	
Accounts Receivable	20,000.00	
Inventory	20,000.00	
Loan Receivable - Goddard	2,000.00	
Loan Receivable - Escrow G.T.	<u>5,000.00</u>	
Total Current Assets		44,799.95
Property and Equipment:		
Vehicles	11,691.00	
Current Year Additions	<u>1,468.00</u>	
Total Cost	13,159.00	
Less Accumulated Depreciation	(4,910.00)	
Net Property and Equipment		8,249.00
Other Assets:		
Deferred Interest - Auto	853.98	
Deposits	<u>375.00</u>	
Total Other Assets		<u>1,228.98</u>
Total Assets		$54,277.93

<u>Liabilities and Proprietor's Equity</u>

Current Liabilities:		
Accounts Payable - Trade	$14,212.56	
Notes Payable	6,763.12	
Notes Payable - Morton Grove	10,000.00	
Notes Payable - Bill Hayes	<u>11,000.00</u>	
Total Current Liabilities		41,975.68
Proprietor's Equity:		
Proprietor Capital-Beginning	11,180.45	
Withdrawals - Personal	(3,499.51)	
Withdrawals - Taxes	(7,068.00)	
Withdrawals - Medical	(135.00)	
Withdrawals - Contributions	(50.00)	
Current Year Net Income or (Loss)	<u>11,874.31</u>	
Total Proprietor's Equity		<u>12,302.25</u>
Total Liabilities and Proprietor's Equity		$54,277.93

additional personnel, equipment, and inventory to maintain quality service. The service area now requires seven people plus a foreman to free up Bill and me to handle sales calls. We also hired a part-time secretary to handle the paperwork. For the fiscal year ended June 30, 1995, our personnel expenses and payroll taxes, including officers, clerical and shop personnel, amounted to $231,503.

Inventory has ballooned from $62,557 to $113,040 in the same time frame, and new computer equipment was needed to keep pace with all the orders. New tire equipment was also needed for the service area. Finally, we had

Goddard Truck and Tire Service, Inc.
Statement of Assets, Liabilities, and Equity-Income Tax, August, 1991

Assets
Current Assets:

Cash and Cash Equivalents	$(4,734.64)	
Accounts Receivable	61,671.06	
Inventory	20,482.00	
Prepaid Interest - Bronco	3,527.59	
Prepaid Interest - Auto	694.90	
Total Current Assets		81,640.91

Property and Equipment:

Machinery	2,354.00	
Vehicles	31,753.00	
Current Year Additions	15,697.38	
Total Cost	49,804.38	
Less Accumulated Depreciation	(26,903.00)	
Net Property and Equipment		22,901.38

Other Assets:

Deposits	2,504.00	
Total Other Assets		2,504.00
Total Assets		$107,046.29

Liabilities and Stockholders' Equity

Current Liabilities:

Accounts Payable - Trade	30,791.37	
Loan Payable - Ford Motor CR	18,595.55	
Accrued Taxes	2,080.45	
Federal Income Tax Payable	16.00	
Total Current Liabilities		51,483.37

Long-Term Debt:

Loans Payable Shareholders	6,630.93	
Notes Payable	32,796.96	
Total Long-Term Debt		39,427.89

Stockholders' Equity:

Capital Stock Issued	5,000.00	
Retained Earning-Beginning	9,017.47	
Current Year Net Income or (Loss)	2,117.56	
Total Stockholders' Equity		16,135.03
Total Liabilities and Stockholders' Equity		$107,046.29

outgrown our 5,000 square foot building in just two years. It was time to move for the fourth time in five years.

I happened to be driving by a vacant tire distributor when I saw a "For Sale" sign out front. I called the Realtor and found that the Small Business Administration (SBA) had been holding the building for two years and was anxious to sell. The asking price was $180,000. We offered $140,000. It looked like the deal would go through. Then, the day before we took a last tour through the building, vandals broke in and stole the car lifts, the copper tubing for plumbing and everything else of value. The SBA didn't want to spend the money or effort needed to repair the building. We offered to buy the building "as is" for $100,000. The SBA accepted. The bank gave us a 120 percent of the purchase price, five-year adjustable rate mortgage at a $7^{1}/_{2}$ percent interest rate. We added $40,000 to the $20,000 check from the bank, fixed up the building and moved in.

Many experts say experience and capital are two requirements for successful start-up businesses. My business was no exception. Eastern could never have grown so quickly without the capital and knowledge resources acquired during its expansion.

Eastern Tire has passed through the infamous first five years when most new business ventures fail. Current profits (1.7 percent) are not as dismal as they appear in the December State of Revenues and Expenses. Bill and I take home a middle-income salary and we are trying to sell the old building.

For the first time since starting the business, I was forced to take a long-term $50,000 loan to cover expenses. I have also established a $25,000 credit line at a local bank. We tried to work the traditionally slow season, (December through February) to our advantage by purchasing a large inventory of tires for $54,500 that would normally cost $58,000, a $3,500 savings. This purchase in conjunction with the other expenses has caused a temporary cash crunch. On March 10, I signed for an additional $50,000, 90-day loan at $6^{1}/_{2}$ percent to cover excess inventory costs and moving/building repair expenses. We believe we can sell the tires by the June 10 deadline and make a nice profit on the inventory.

Bill and I believe that we should continue to take risks and look for expansion possibilities. We are currently negotiating the possible purchase of a tire dealership outside of the Chicago area. However, this may create new challenges due to lack of geographic control over the operation.

In five to ten years, I would like to broaden the business focus into retread manufacturing. The equipment for this type of operation will cost approximately $300,000 to $500,000. Our current building does have sufficient space to house the potential operational growth.

Bill tells me, "You're not rich until you *owe* $1 million." If our plans materialize, I may be a rich man very soon. I just hope the tires keep selling so I can afford it! ∎

What advice would you give Jack Hayes? *We asked six experts to offer advice and suggestions.*

The family has been feeding the business and not the other way around.

You Will Be Out of Business in Two Years If You Don't Change Now

George M. Dawson

Author of Borrowing for Your Business: Winning the Battle for the Banker's "Yes," *Mr. Dawson is a financial consultant to small businesses in San Antonio, Texas. In the expert commentary published below, he is playing the fictional role of Jack's brother.*

Dear Jack:

What does it take to get your attention? Mom sent me your write-up on Eastern Tire. Should you be worried? I'm scared silly for you. You and Pop are born salesmen and the customer always comes first. Pop thinks success equals debt. You think success equals assets. And you are both wrong. Success is financing your business growth with excess cash flow from profitable operations.

I'm 500 miles away and not in the day-to-day operations, but my money is with you. The family has been feeding the business and not the other way around. If you and Pop don't change how you operate, Eastern will be out of business in two years, and he doesn't have much of a pension.

My vacation is in two weeks. We will be heading downstate and bringing the kids. I want to hold a family conference with you and Pop. Bottom line, as you business types say: either change the way the business is run or pay me out.

Your history of Eastern was your typical enthusiastic style of jumping around from subject to subject. You really bright people skip talk.

I may be the dull older brother teaching business management and history at a small state university, but those who don't learn from history will repeat it. Half of businesses that fail are profitable and owe income taxes, but they run out of cash. Eastern is suffering from "cashless profitability."

You must plan better and get control of the profitability of Eastern Tire. You lost money in 1992. You had another below-average year in 1994, and the improvement in profits in 1995 was due as much to lower interest rates, lower depreciation charges and a reduced advertising budget as it was to an improvement in your gross margin.

In fact, since your breaking through the million dollar sales level in 1992, after Pop came on board, Eastern's sales have gone nowhere.

You must manage the flow of cash in and out of the business. In the last two years, your cash balances have dropped $41,000 (Has your banker started bouncing checks yet?) while your visible debt load increased $63,000. And $10,000 of that debt increase is money I lent you to put in the business. That loan came on top of my investment two years ago in your first building.

You and Pop are so afraid of losing a sale that you let your customers walk all over you. You have over $51,000 more in receivables than last year and on declining sales. Do you use the credit approval and collection procedures I recommended after that $25,000 scare several years ago?

At our meeting, we will need to talk about replacing Doolittel and Sitzmore, your accounting firm. While your cost of goods sold has remained relatively steady as a percent of sales, the specific expense allocations have changed substantially from year to year, so it is hard to see what is really going on. And you should be getting a statement of cash flows, besides the Balance Sheet and the P&L.

Your accountants are not being of much help to you. They don't show how Eastern's business is divided between direct business sales and service/repair or the mix of used, new and retread sales. You should be managing your gross margin on each of these business markets. It's hard to tell if your inventory levels are okay or not without knowing the mix of your sales, but clearly inventory is too high.

Statements every six months are too infrequent for a business of your size. What expenses are in your accruals and when are they due? Do you know, or will it be a surprise?

We also need to go over some business arithmetic. Your "good deal" on tires saved you $3,500 or six percent for six months. If the bank charged you more than 12 percent, you lost money. And that doesn't even consider the 36 percent average annual excess inventory carrying cost. It also was a business risk you shouldn't have taken. I hope those are standard, popular, high-demand trailer tires.

Order a credit report on Eastern and see how many of your suppliers report you as "slow pay" ... because you are. And that won't help when you need to borrow more money.

You have done well to work down the equipment debt to finance companies (Do you always have to buy the newest and the best?), but you haven't made much progress on the bank business debt. When a borrower starts overdrafting, expect to hear from your loan officer. (I hope your accountants have your financials up to date.)

The first concern is clearing the bank overdraft ($14,000). Next fund the Federal tax liability ($10,000). The IRS is not at all understanding. While your $25,000 line of credit can fund these on an emergency basis, you should really do this with "permanent cash" created by shrinking the $50,000 of excess inventory and the $51,000 in slow receivables.

The credit line is for short-term purposes. Did you listen when the banker explained that she expects the line to be cleared for 30-60 days each year? You also need to bring down your trade payables by at least $25,000 to improve your credit rating.

I am very unhappy with the new building purchase. How could you have outgrown 5,000 square feet with two years of flat sales? Now you have another long-term asset financed by a five-year balloon note and a vacant property on your hands. Balloons in the real world either lose their air or pop. This is high-risk financing for a borrower. You need to replace the note on the new building with a long-term fully amortizing mortgage.

You have grown your business to the size where a cash flow projection model should be put together and installed on your new computer. The distribution business is pretty fundamental and we can either build this model together or one may be available through your trade association—or we can find someone there in town to help you with it.

I am tremendously proud that my brother, the entrepreneur, in six short years has gone from a one man, one van, $100 overhead shop to a dozen people and $1.3 million in sales.

However, I have a responsibility to Marilyn and the kids to invest our money soundly. Right now your business is too risky for me to remain comfortable with my investment without a solid commitment from you and Pop to controlled growth and professional management for Eastern.

Jack, you have a "Ready. Fire. Aim." approach. You prefer to be out in the field with customers instead of with "the numbers." As I see it, you have three choices: learn how to manage the business, hire someone to be your

You and Pop are so afraid of losing a sale that you let your customers walk all over you.

business manager, or be prepared to go back to one man, one van.

See you in two weeks,

George M Dawson

George M. Dawson

Do You Know What You're Doing?

Philip P. Friedlander, Jr.

Mr. Friedlander is the National Tire Dealers and Retreaders Association's executive vice president. He is also president of the Tire Dealer Service Corporation, a for-profit subsidiary; executive secretary of the Tire Retreading Institute; and managing trustee of the NTDRA Insurance Trust.

Dear Jack:

We are glad you decided to join the Association and to take advantage of our services.

In the coming weeks, you will find many opportunities to benefit from NTDRA membership. In the meantime, I want to respond to your question "What should I do now?"

You know, Jack, you were fortunate to begin your business in the 1980s. The 1990s are already different. Knowledge, planning, and a more systematic approach will be necessary.

I note that you became a tire dealer at the age of 20. You did not indicate any *business education* that you have pursued in the last five years.

Can either you or Bill read and understand an operating statement? For example, are you aware that your current ratio (which is the relationship between current assets and current liabilities) is 1.3? The acceptable range is 1.65-2.00. When you operate below the acceptable range, you are at risk in your ability to pay debts when due and will have increased difficulty in borrowing funds.

My question is: Did you know that? If not, you need to understand the definition and meaning of these key operating ratios. You should seriously consider taking courses at your university, not only in the understanding of operating statements, but in several other areas, particularly marketing.

Your current ratio is 1.3. The acceptable range is 1.65-2.00. Did you know that?

As a further guide, I am enclosing the section on "Interpretation of the Key Operating Ratios" from NTDRA's *A Practical Approach To Improving Tire Dealer Profits*. This should add dimensions to your businesslike approach to your tire dealership.

My first advice to you, then, is to take courses to fill in your business education. NTDRA offers a wide variety of seminars at its annual convention. For example, this year in the commercial tire business there will be three seminars sponsored by NTDRA's Commercial Tire Management Council. One of these will present results of a commercial dealer survey. Successful compensation and incentive programs for outside sales personnel will be discussed as well as model compensation programs.

Another seminar sponsored by the Commercial Tire Management Council will focus on dealers gaining a better understanding of fleet customers and their needs. This seminar is based on research by *Modern Tire Dealer* magazine and will provide help in establishing fleet maintenance programs.

The one seminar that should be a must for you, which is also sponsored by the Commercial Tire Management Council, will focus on determining "true costs" of operating a commercial business. This seminar will provide an analysis of benchmarks commercial dealers can use in measuring their own dealership operating costs. The results of a study on this will also be presented.

In studying your business history and your growth, I believe *you need to develop a business plan* and then use this as a guide to operate your business. This plan should be formal and written. It should spell out your goals for a period of time and describe the activities and action that will take you there.

In the planning process, you should precisely state the business you are in; i.e., commercial new tire sales, commercial retread sales, used tractor sales. Since you operate service trucks, you would add the word service to your identification.

Your business plan needs to identify and analyze the changes occurring in the commercial tire business and in the economy. It should also reflect the competitive structure in your trading area.

Determining your sales potential is a difficult task, but it's particularly necessary as you consider further expansion.

Have you at this point already said,"I don't know how to develop and use a business plan— and even if I did, I don't have time."?

Hold on. Developing and using a business plan is increasingly important to you.

For specific and detailed guides, I refer you to NTDRA's textbook *A Practical Approach to Improving Tire Dealer Profits*, and specifically to Chapter 1: "How to Develop and Use a Business Plan." The basic forms for preparation of a business plan are available in a companion workbook provided with the NTDRA textbook. It has eight separate forms which can help you.

While your letter focused on financial portions of your growth, you provided little to give me confidence that you have a carefully designed marketing plan, or that you have done any market research, which is even more important because you're thinking of expanding in the Chicago area. For example, you need to measure the impact of direct selling on your current and future commercial tire business.

With the steady shift to radial truck tires, cost of inventory and turnover will affect your cash flow and your ability to pay for your purchases in a timely fashion. The significant problems that are affecting the trucker have to be weighed when you count on your trucking customers' ability to pay you in a timely fashion. The industry recognizes that opportunities continue to exist in the commercial tire business, but an understanding of your competitors' need for modernization of new service equipment and training of personnel in the proper and safe mounting and demounting of truck tires are all demands you must face. The NTDRA also has help available in several of these areas.

This would be a good time to comment on the truck retreading business. Today, the overall quality is good; the pricing is very competitive, and like other areas of the tire business participating in a manufacturer's system, shop inspection by NTDRA's Tire Retreading Institute is important. Analysis is important in advance. Is this a reasonable niche for you in the future?

I want to return to the question of analyzing your competition. As outlined in NTDRA's textbook, Chapter 4 (Gaining and Keeping a Competitive Advantage), here are some of the questions you should address:

- In your market (and in your potential new market) who are the principal players selling in the market area?
- How much market share and dollar sales do they enjoy?
- Can you determine their strengths and weaknesses?
- Are there any recent new entries or withdrawals from the market?

- Do you have any advantages over your competitors in price, service, reputation, etc.?

You, of course, need a market strategy. With your current size and financial strength, it is doubtful that you can achieve the "lost cost" position through sufficient and efficient use of economies of scale. A low cost/low price/good profit strategy probably is not your best bet at this time. If I were you, I would focus on a strategy designed to capture a small but profitable portion of the market.

It is important, if you adopt the strategy of specific market niches, that this be combined with competitive pricing and with special emphasis on customer service.

Remember earlier, when we noted you should analyze your strengths? Now is when this comes into play.

One dealer we know believes his principal strength is customer service. His analysis shows that he is strong in repeat customers. He finds ways to go the extra mile either through his fast service or his convenient location.

We know of another dealer who has established a program of preventive maintenance for small fleets. They call in advance for checkups.

More and more we are seeing dealers who also develop an understanding of what business they are in, and listen to what customers want, and then deliver it.

I've enclosed exhibit 4-1 from the chapter "Gaining and Keeping a Competitive Advantage" in NTDRA's textbook. This competition evaluation form gives you an easy method to evaluate your competition both at your current location and at any new business. Jack, you need to use this before you go much further in your purchase plans.

Have you looked at improving your inventory turnover and, therefore, improving your cash flow? What steps are you taking to do this?

Without attempting to discourage your positive view and your enthusiasm for expansion, I am concerned with your apparent failure to look at market changes. You borrowed $50,000. You purchased advanced inventory (as is the practice) in the industry. Did you look at market *need*? Some truckers are having a difficult time. Your competition in your area is very strong. Maybe you need to be more analytical in making these decisions. What happens if you can't sell and *collect* the funds for this purchase in that 90-day period?

It is my feeling that you need to do more to make your current business more stable and profitable. If I were you, I wouldn't consider further expansion without development of a business plan, market and competitive analysis,

In your market (and in your potential new market) who are the principal players? Can you determine their strengths and weaknesses?

A Practical Approach to Improving Tire Dealer Profits
Interpretation of the Key Operating Ratios

Ratio	Acceptable Range	Higher than Range	Lower than Range
Current ratio	1.65-2.00	Solvent condition. Too high. May mean uninvested cash or excessive investment in receivables or inventories.	Risk of inability to pay debts when due. Probable difficulty in borrowing funds.
Acid-Test ratio	0.70-1.00	Safe liquidity position. Could mean inadequate investments in inventories or equipment.	Very dangerous position. Could lead to involuntary bankruptcy.
Average life of accounts receivable	42 to 48 days	Poor credit and/or collection policies. Risk of bad debts is high.	Restrictive credit and collection policies may inhibit sales growth.
Inventory turnover	4.5 to 7.0 times	Inadequate stock of merchandise. Lost sales. Heavy purchasing and handling costs.	Overstocking. Inability to move obsolete goods. High storage and financing costs.
Asset turnover	2.4 to 3.5 times	Strong sales growth. Leasing and ready access to supplies may be reason.	Low sales level for asset base. Heavy investments in inventory and/or fixed assets.
Rate of return on assets	9 to 12 percent	Strong profits. Efficiency and productivity high.	Low profits. Strong competition. Possible internal problems.
Turnover of owners' equity	6 to 10	Strong leverage. Economies of scale. Large size company.	Failure to leverage debt. Possible excess retention of retained earnings. Small size company.
Rate of return on owners' equity	15 to 20 percent	Excellent combination of efficiency, productivity and effective management. Good competitive position.	Lack of efficiency. Strong competition. Internal and inventory problems. High wage and/or operating costs.
Debt to owners' equity	1.6 to 2.8 times	Indication of "trading on the equity." High debt could lead to pressures if profits decline.	Conservative position. Inadequate capital may cause lost opportunities.

Ratio	Acceptable Range	Higher than Range	Lower than Range
Rate of gross profit	Varies by size, type, and method of distribution.	Firm selling prices. Low costs of merchandise. Aggressive management.	Discounting. Strong competition. High product costs. Poor inventory management and control.
Rate of net operating income	3 to 6 percent	High rate of gross profit with good expense control. Retail emphasis.	Low rate of gross profit and/or high operating expenses. Wholesale emphasis.
Rate of net income	2+ to 5 percent	Well-run, efficient organization. Strong customer base.	Sales problems. High costs. May be due to lack of promotion or external factors.
Sales per invoice	$150-$200	Emphasis on multiple sales. Aggressive sales management. Wholesale.	Excessive low value transactions. Missed sales opportunities. Retail emphasis.
Average invoices per employee	1,000 to 1,100	High level of employee productivity. Company-wide sales awareness.	Weak sales effort. Inadequate stocks of merchandise. Lack of "get-up-and-go."
Sales per $1 of wages	$5.30-$8.80	Wholesale. High productivity. Efficient organization.	Retail emphasis. Low productivity. Small company.
Wages/ Sales ratio	11.5-19 percent	Labor intensive. Retail emphasis. Low productivity. Small company.	Wholesale emphasis. Efficiencies of scale. Large scale company.

and for you personally, increased business education.

Jack, come to our convention and see the equipment, and attend the seminars (we have 18 choices this year). Use NTDRA's *A Practical Approach to Improving Tire Dealer Profits* and accompanying workbook.

While at the convention, Jack, you should go to Bank One's booth where you will be able to learn about Bank One/NTDRA's new program which can provide a credit line of up to $100,000 but with rates as low as prime plus 1, and 36-month equipment purchase loan program at 8-3/4 percent.

As I said in the beginning, use your new membership in NTDRA. Serving dealers like you is what we are all about.

Sincerely,

Philip P. Friedlander, Jr.

NTDRA
A Practical Approach to Improving Tire Dealer Profits
Workbook Forms

Chapter 4–Gaining and Keeping a Competitive Edge

Evaluation of Competitors

Instructions List your four leading competitors in the spaces marked "Company." Then, evaluate each of your competitors on a scale of 1 - 5 (1 being worst and 5 being best) on the factors described below. There is room on the bottom for additional comments.

Evaluate each of your major competitors on the following scale:
1. Worst. Very poor. No threat.
2. Below Average
3. Average
4. Above Average
5. Best, Excellent

COMPETITORS

COMPANY: _____ _____ _____ _____

Estimated Sales

Est. Market Share

Quality Advantage

Price Advantage

Cost Advantage

Service Personnel

Sales Force

Distribution

Reputation

_____

_____

Seriousness of
Competition

COMMENTS:
_____
_____
_____

Seven Critical Areas Need Your Immediate Attention

Jon R. Ryan

Mr. Ryan is the director of the Small Business Development Center at the Eastern Iowa Community College District, where he has worked extensively with small businesses whose exceptional growth creates problems. Previously, he was a commercial lender for ten years.

Dear Jack:

I enjoyed our conversation regarding the exceptional growth of your company and your expectations for continuing successes. Your enthusiasm and energy are commendable. Quite obviously, the entrepreneurial spirit drives you! You are to be congratulated on your successes so far.

But your worries about the rapid growth, expanding debt and long-term prospects of your business are very legitimate. Your father's offhand remarks about the "joy" of owing a million dollars have helped trigger your own warning systems—and justifiably so. I was pleased to hear you express some trepidation. That great entrepreneurial spirit is wonderful, but a dash or two of caution can be invaluable.

As I told you, I am leaving for two weeks of special training tomorrow. Thus, I need to offer some quick suggestions for you to consider and act on while I am gone. When I return, we can discuss them in greater detail and plan the next action steps as well.

As we discussed, there were some decisions that brought you to your current situation— decisions that might better have been done differently. You did many, many right things, but to establish a foundation of understanding, let's review a handful of problems.

First, you grew the beginning company with almost no capital and then grew into the next levels by borrowing, rather than by generating profitability. Second, adding your father as a full one-half partner brought you knowledge and experience, but no cash. And third, like Topsy in *Uncle Tom's Cabin*, you "just growed." That is, you acted first, prior to any planning, as opportunities presented themselves. You have now reached the point where your entrepre-

neurship needs to be melded with some management activities to ensure the organized growth and continuing success of the business.

Let me give you seven suggestions that will, I hope, enable you to gain better control of Eastern Tire.

First, create a cash flow projection for the next 12 months, and on a monthly rolling basis continue it—forever! Be certain to carefully compare each month's actual income and expenses to the projections. Your part-time secretary needs to go full-time to help with accurate bookkeeping, to keep a handle on cash flow and (an area I will discuss more in a minute) to work your accounts receivable. From what you told me, she can handle these tasks, given her background and education. The relatively nominal cost for her extended hours will be more than made up for in improved receivables collection and accurate, current information on the financial workings of Eastern Tire.

This leads me to a second suggestion: go to school. You need to bone up on accounting and how various financial activities affect the business. Also, some courses in general management, marketing and personnel would be valuable. If you are like most of my hard-charging entrepreneurial clients, sitting still in a classroom for a long time doesn't appeal to you. Let me recommend some of the short-term classes offered by the SBDC. You will not only learn valuable skills from "real world" business-experienced instructors, but have the chance to meet other business owners. The networking opportunities are a great way to share knowledge and hard-won experience. I will forward the next semester's schedule to you as soon as it is back from the printer.

While I am gone, as my third suggestion, have your secretary review the aging of your accounts receivable. You need to know who owes you what, and for how long. Remember the scare you received when one big account nearly stuck you for $25,000? It can happen again—quickly! You should review your accounts receivable with your secretary on a weekly basis from here on out. The first step is to review where you are right now and take immediate action—personally—to collect anything that looks troublesome.

We can have your secretary work with one of our SBDC counselors to establish a credit evaluation program for your customers. She will learn collection techniques and how to develop a system for efficiently collecting. Be certain your sales staff follow the rules we set up for credit selling. And be especially careful of your sales approach and your dad's sales approach! You will be tempted to offer credit to make a sale without carefully evaluating credit worthiness.

The 31 percent increase from 1992 to 1993 in accounts receivable is one of the reasons that you had to take out a loan.

These activities will help you get a handle on your rapidly mushrooming accounts receivable. The 31 percent increase from 1994 to 1995 in accounts receivable is one of the reasons that you had to take out a loan.

Another major problem is the increase in your inventory, up over 80 percent in 1995 from 1994 levels. As the fourth step, I suggest that you evaluate your inventory by size, type and manufacturer. Try to determine from actual sales figures (do not just guess or "go by feel"!) what your best sellers are. The Pareto Principle (or 80-20 rule, as it is often called) is probably noticeable here. That is, 80 percent of your sales comes from just 20 percent of the types of tires you carry!

Look at ways to minimize inventory by dropping non-productive lines. And be sure to do this review based on *profitability* of sales lines, not just volume. Consider which lines to drop, and get those tires moved out quickly, (or pay for restocking) to cut down on your borrowing.

My fifth suggestion is to evaluate expenses. When a business has "just growed," in my experience, some expenses have crept in, or gotten out of hand, and some thoughtful evaluation and pruning can generate fairly significant savings. Start with equipment and vehicles currently being purchased. Can you improve cash flow by leasing? Review each expense line, in detail, with an eye to minimizing cost and improving cash flow. Do you track advertising, for instance, to see what does and what does not work? Abandon the ineffective and concentrate on the areas that perform. Can you cut telephone costs by switching carriers or buying special business packages? And, what *really* constitutes the expenses in the "other" category? Is there room to cut? We can review this together when I return, but you should spend some time on this as soon as possible.

As a sixth activity, I suggest you begin to think about an advisory board—professional and business people who can offer you insight and practical advice. Your accountant is a good place to start; she is very capable and experienced and will help you consider implications of your financial decisions *before* you make them. And I believe your dad's golfing buddy—the retired banker from Peoria—would be a good addition. Perhaps you know someone in a related field, such as the car business or specialty retailing, who would be a good candidate. And one of my SBDC clients is a founder of a successful interstate trucking company—a tough business, as you know. She can offer lots of hard-earned knowledge from her very similar experience in growing a company very rapidly. These people can give you great advice; use them!

And finally, Jack, you need to do some formal planning. That means you write down who you

I suggest you begin to think about an advisory board.

are as a company, where you are as a company, where you're headed and how you are going to get there. I know how much you dislike this "paperwork" stuff. Okay. Just dictate your thoughts into that little hand-held recorder you use to keep track of your day's activities. Talk to it, telling it what you want the company to do and to be. Cover the areas on the enclosed business plan outline—the marketplace, the competition, the personnel and equipment needs, etc.—then have your secretary type it up and we can discuss it in detail when I return, along with your cash flow projections.

You're at a turning point, Jack. Acquiring that second location might be the worst thing you could do right now. Or, with some alterations in the way you do things now, it could be a great opportunity. But first, let's get a firm grip on some of these potential problem areas. We don't want your efforts and successes to be jeopardized by moving too quickly. Let's stop, together, and think, plan and act a bit more slowly than you have been. It's okay to catch your breath here! And, as you know, here at the SBDC we are ready and eager to help you continue your successes.

Best wishes.

Sincerely,

Jon R. Ryan

Take the Time to Learn More About Managing Your Business

Timothy M. Baye

An associate professor at the University of Wisconsin–Extension, Professor Baye has helped hundreds of small-business clients address growth management issues. He is also an engineering project analyst and is currently preparing to publish a small-business financial planning software system.

Dear Jack:

I was pleased to have the recent opportunity to meet with you and your father. Your financials and your business history have helped me to understand your situation. Your story was interesting and very familiar. I work with many clients who own fast-growing businesses. In many ways, your situation is very common.

Although you and your father would like to discuss how to continue this growth, I would like to first offer a brief analysis of your business's current financial situation.

The 1995 fiscal year saw a drop in sales of over $67,000, or 4.8 percent, as compared to 1994. Although the overall sales decreased, your efficiency in generating profits increased. Your *gross profit margin* grew by 2.8 percent, your *operating profit margin* (earnings before interest and taxes) grew by 93.0 percent and your *net profit margin* grew by 325 percent. This implies that you have been very effective in squeezing out as much profit as possible from your sales. Your investments in machinery, vehicles and lease-hold improvements have increased your firm's productivity. With the exception of the drop in sales, most of your other activity numbers look fairly good.

When reviewing your balance sheet, I am a bit more concerned. Your negative cash balance will not sit well with your commercial lenders for long. They may be patient, but they will not cover you forever.

Your trade receivables and inventory numbers are high. Your sales-to-receivables ratios are 6.19 in 1995 and 8.53 in 1994. Both of these numbers are lower than the average industry sales-to-receivables ratio found in the lowest quartile of the Robert Morris Associates data.

You stated that your current receivables balance is about average. Traditional average receivables collection period is determined by dividing accounts receivables by 365 days. Using this technique, your collection periods were 42 days in 1994 and 58 days in 1995. However, since you are open five days per week, I prefer to use the alternative method. This method uses the ratio of accounts receivables divided by average daily sales. Calculating in this way, your collection periods were 30 days in 1994 and 42 days in 1995. This approach appears to represent the nature of your business more realistically. The additional 12 days (16 days using the traditional technique) has had a significantly negative impact on your cash flow and subsequent cash balances. Considering the sales decrease and the receivables increase, it is easy to identify a major source of your cash flow difficulties.

Although your inventory turnover numbers are much better than the industry averages (implying that you do a good job in matching your inventory to demand), recent changes in this ratio cause me some concern. In 1994, you had an inventory turnover of 16.1. In 1995, this number had dropped to 8.3. I hope this is not a sign of a lapse in your inventory management practices.

Finally, your debt-to-equity ratio is about twice your industry average. This indicates that you have acquired most of your assets through borrowing. I can understand why the bank was a bit nervous about your fast growth. The negative sales trend, your cash and trade receivables balances and your debt-to-equity relationship *should* have caused your lender some concern.

Although you and your father wish to continue your rapid growth, I would suggest that you first take a step back and think about improving your current position. I also recommend that you understand your situation better before you continue pursuing rapid growth. Specifically, I suggest the following:

Address your cash crunch problems immediately. Rather than attempting to sell your building, consider leasing it. Give some additional attention to your trade receivables. I have enclosed some articles from the *Small Business Forum* on managing collections and inventory ("Managing Collections Without Giving Away the Store," "Managing Inventory," by Karl Borden). Please read these thoroughly and follow the author's advice. You need to return your average accounts receivables collection period to that "magic" 30 day (or less) number.

Keep up your good work on watching your margins and interest payments. Your heavy debt load and your low interest payments imply that you have not been paying any interest on your loans to shareholders. This is probably not a very good personal financial management policy, but it has helped your business's cash flow. Continue to look for productivity improvements over the next year. Keep a close eye on that gross profit margin. You are doing better than the industry average. However, the temptation to attempt to capture more market share through price reductions will quickly erode your margins and your profitability.

Improve your marketing skills. Hone your skills as a marketer. Many young businesses rapidly increase sales regardless of the customer. When a firm is young and aggressive, any sale will do. However, this approach generates a few clients who pay late and sometimes not at all. Servicing these types of clients is also commonly difficult.

It is wise to target profitable customers, rather than to target customers that are easy to sell to. I suggest that you review your customer files in order to identify what products you sell to

In 1994, you had an inventory turnover of 16.1. In 1995, this number had dropped to 8.3.

whom and compare this to your accounts receivables aging reports. This process should help you identify the "more profitable" customers, based upon the products you sell and the average collection periods by customer group. This type of research will not only help you in identifying the more profitable market segments within your current geographic area, but it will also increase your ability to identify and qualify future sales prospects.

Focus on your existing geographic market for the next 12-18 months. Strengthen your hold on your market share and attempt to build cash reserves to fund future growth. When you have built your cash reserves to assist in financing expansion, you should also have greatly improved your "profit-based" marketing management skills.

Plan for the future. Your case is a classic growth-by-networking, hard work, and seat-of-the-pants management. It is obvious that your tenacity, your father's connections and your ability to identify profitable opportunities have served you well. However, you are now entering into the next vulnerable stage of your own development as a manager. The transition from entrepreneur to professional manager, although difficult, is essential if you are to maintain control of this business. You can begin this process by taking the time to plan your firm's future. The planning process will teach you more about your current business than you ever thought you could know. It will also help you understand how to identify new profitable business opportunities and help you direct and focus your business's growth.

As you grow and approach that "one-million-dollar-in-debt" mark, the ability to identify highly profitable business opportunities, and also have the resources and ability to take advantage of those, slows down. Systems put in place to help "establish" the firm may become a hinderance to continued growth and profitability. The business planning process will greatly improve your ability to identify competitive opportunities and to position your business to effectively take advantage of them. The process will also improve your own professional management skills.

It was a real pleasure to meet and work with you and your father. I look forward to our future sessions and working with you as your business grows and prospers.

Sincerely,

Timothy M. Baye

> **Your business plan will help you understand your business better.**

You Need a Much Sharper Focus
David H. "Andy" Bangs

Author of Business Planning Guide, Market Planning Guide, Cash Flow Control Guide *and several other books, Mr. Bangs is the founder of Upstart Publishing Company. He has also been a commercial loan officer.*

Dear Jack:

You've done a remarkable job of building a profitable, growing business from such a slender base. It's a tribute to your acumen and hard work. I'm impressed with how much you've accomplished.

I'm not overly concerned about your cash crunch. You'll get through it. It's normal and expected for slimly capitalized businesses that are enjoying growth. I'm more concerned that you take advantage of this scare to set your business up for even more growth in the future. I also hope that the cash crunch doesn't become a recurrent theme.

What you now need to do is step back, work out a careful business plan with detailed financial projections covering a variety of scenarios, and set down clear, consistent goals to help you consolidate and build on your achievements. While you can get a lot of help in writing a business plan from advisors, the guts of the plan—the goals and objectives and scope of the business—have to come from you. Your business plan will help you understand your business better, highlight areas of possible growth and potential danger, and minimize the chances of running out of cash before you reach your goals.

Should you take the two or three days it takes to write a plan?

It depends on what you hope to achieve. If your aim is to owe a million dollars, I'd suggest that you keep on as you are doing without a plan, but I'm not sure why you would adopt owing a million dollars as a goal. Plenty of people managed to go broke playing that game in the 1980s. It's easy to do: find gullible bankers and speculate in commercial real estate. You've managed to do well at that so far, with over $300,000 in outstanding mortgages. Add in another $350,000 or so in business liabilities and that puts you two thirds of the way towards the dubious goal of owing a million dollars.

But I know you better than that. As I understand it, your long-term goal is to build a strong and prosperous tire business and become a real millionaire, with clear assets worth $1,000,000 or more. A solid business plan will help you reach that goal.

I have four specific pieces of advice for you. If you want to call me up and get more details, or argue with me, please do so. Your growing pains are good problems to have—they are eminently solvable. That doesn't mean they're easy, but you've shown that challenges don't overwhelm your excellent business instincts. I'd bet that at this time next year you'll have the cash flow problem licked. Your debt load is not dangerous and your prospects remain excellent.

You need a much sharper focus. It is not clear to me what your plans are. In the past, you have been opportunistic, which is fine when you have little at stake. It's less desirable when you are running a business with sales pushing $1.5 million. The bigger your operation becomes, the less acceptable a "bet the company" or "growth at any cost" strategy will be.

As an investor, my first questions are:

- What is this business all about?
- What's special about it?
- Why will it be a good investment?

Any confusion on these questions means I don't invest. I'd urge you to ask yourself these same questions, and then answer them clearly enough to satisfy the most cautious banker.

What business and markets are you in? You began with a tiny niche: selling used tires for semis that would be trundled about on railroad cars. But now you've added retreads, new tires, a sizable service effort and are thinking about buying a tire dealership somewhere outside of Chicago and ultimately manufacturing retreads. That's a pretty broad agenda.

The best way to develop and maintain a consistent focus is to write a business plan *and then follow it.* Get as much input as you can from your employees; this gives them ownership in the plan and gives you the benefit of their practical experience and close contact with your markets. Ask your board to review the plan. Involve your bankers; they have a stake in your success. Have your accountant develop the financial projections with you, expressing your ideas and goals in standard financial formats to make the job of comparing and evaluating your financial performance easier.

The hardest part of your planning effort will be to determine what business you're in and what you want your business to become over the next several years. What's your "mission"? What do you want Eastern Tire to be known for? Who are your best markets and how can you best meet their demands? What are your best products? These aren't easy questions to answer, and they are just the beginning.

It helps immensely to regularly discuss your business with an advisory board or a board of directors who have a different way of looking at your business than you do. Get a banker or professional investor to help on the financial side. Get someone with administrative experience—perhaps in an unrelated field—and get someone with a marketing background. You'd benefit by getting more points of view than that of my old pal Bill. He's a salesman first and foremost. Salesmen are optimists (otherwise they'd go mad) who are more concerned with driving the top line than making sure that the rest of the picture is well-balanced. He does have a lot of experience in the tire industry, to be sure, but remember that he hasn't been an administrator or financial officer. You need more balanced advice than he alone can give.

The purpose of your plan is to set a realistic, measurable long-term goal for Eastern Tire and figure out a strategy to reach that goal. The simpler the strategy the better. If the retread manufacturing fits in with your current business and markets as well as I think it does, it would be an excellent goal. It sets financial parameters: $300,000-500,000 for equipment. It sets a time line: five to ten years. It will sharpen your focus and make your decisions about what to do clearer. For example, it would help you make this tough decision: *Don't buy the dealership outside of Chicago.* It's tough enough to have fast-growth cash flow problems without adding the complexities of multiple locations and entering a new business to the mix. The dealership won't help you raise money (it will eat capital); it will distract you from your long-term goal; it will diffuse your efforts.

A written business plan will keep your business on track. An "it's in my head" plan won't.

You need at least another $65,000 in invested capital. You probably need more. Under-capitalization shows up in your Debt to Equity, Return on Equity, Return on Total Capital, and Return on Assets ratios. These are important warning signs. Although the trends over the last three years are moving in the right direction (toward normal ranges) you still have a long way to go.

You could slow down and accumulate some capital from earnings but that will take a long time at your current pace. You will probably have to invest more cash yourself or find new investors. To do so, you will have to be clearer about what business and markets you are really

Get as much input as you can from your employees.

in, and also develop more detailed financial statements than those you sent me.

Investors, whether bankers or otherwise, need information to make their decisions. The better the information you provide, the better their decisions will be.

You need a cash flow pro forma. Push it out for at least three—preferably five years—with monthly detail for the next 12 months. For years two through five, quarterly figures will be sufficient. Why do this? For the discipline (it becomes a cash budget), for the insights it will give you into the workings of your business or businesses, and for the ability to work with different scenarios that might play out over the near future. I'd also like to see you with balance sheet and P&L projections for the same periods for the same reasons.

Make sure to annotate these projections. The assumptions that you make today are easily forgotten tomorrow. To get the greatest benefit from your projections, review them monthly, change them only when conditions have obviously changed (or some of your assumptions are clearly wrong), and use them as a guideline. Volumes have been written about how to do financial projections, and plenty of help is available if you aren't comfortable with financial matters. You have better things to do than to become an accountant. However, you have to know enough about management accounting to run a $1.5 million business. Take a course, read books, or simply sit down with your accountant and go over all the statements carefully.

Pay special heed to your management personnel needs as your business grows. If I were you, I'd immediately seek out and hire a part-time financial officer, perhaps a retired financial executive or controller from a larger company, to keep your business on its proper financial feet until you can afford a full-time CFO.

I'd also consider adding a management development consultant to your list of advisors. A once-or-twice-a-year consultation can avoid major woes in this highly tricky area. Since Eastern Tire is a family business (inverted, with your father effectively your employee instead of the more usual child working for parent) you might want to address family business issues as well. But that can wait for another day.

That should be enough free advice for one letter! You're doing a terrific job. Give my best to Carol and Bill.

Sincerely,

Andy Bangs

David H. "Andy" Bangs

> *If I were you, I'd immediately seek out and hire a part-time financial officer.*

Build Flexibility into Your Long Range Plans

William A. Delaney

Author of Micromanagement: How to solve the problems of growing companies *and other books, Mr. Delaney is the founder of two small businesses. In 1982, he won the SBA's national award for Prime Small Business Contractor of the United States.*

Dear Jack:

Thank you for sending me your company history and the detailed financial statements for the years 1993, 1994 and 1995.

I note that you started your company in 1989, so permit me to congratulate you for surviving the first five critical years. The fact that you are still in business augurs well for your future.

As you may know, the SBA statistics indicate that 75 to 80 percent of new businesses do not last five years, and only about five percent last more than ten years. The main reasons for failure are lack of planning, lack of capital, or both.

In surviving these crucial five years, you have passed through the danger zone, wherein most fail to survive, and into the open country in which you may now expand rapidly since you need not concern yourself about daily survival any longer. You can now make long range plans, and you should as soon as possible.

There are many pitfalls that await you as you grow and try to prosper, but your letter indicates that you and your Dad are well aware of most of them by now. You survived two robberies and a client who did not want to pay his bills to you, so you have some staying power already.

When I started my company in 1964, I visited the SBA office in Boston and a man, Mr. Boltz, told me the following: "Most small businesses fail, but not because the entrepreneurs do not know the answers. It's worse than that. It's because they don't even know the questions to address and answer."

I asked for his advice and I followed it and it worked for me, so I now pass it on to you. He said to plan every step in as detailed a manner as possible, starting with sales projections—which are by far the most important thing to get right. If you have the sales projections right, you can make all kinds of other mistakes and still survive.

When you finish your plans, have someone else go over them for you and let him/her throw stones at them and play "what if" with you and make you respond to unexpected questions. You can find this service free of charge at the SBA offices from SCORE (Service Corps of Retired Executives). The members of SCORE volunteer their services to small-business entrepreneurs who come in for assistance. They will review your plans and give you some good information and advice based on their own long and successful careers in finance, marketing, corporate planning, and even special technical fields. You well might find someone with a background in your own field of tires. It is worth at least one visit to the SBA to find out how they can assist you. That's their job and they are good at it.

Now let's get on to your planning. First, make a monthly sales plan for five years, from year one through year five.

In reviewing the detailed financial statements that you sent for the years 1993, 1994 and 1995, I note that your sales were the same for all three years, around $1.3 million. Now you should choose your sales goals for the next five years and everything else will be based upon these sales figures.

I noted that your percent of sales rates for all costs and profits were stable for the past three years. It is likely that these percentages will not be too far off the mark for planning purposes, so use them in making your projections and *pro forma* P&L and balance sheets. You can run them out monthly for the next five years with projected sales as the independent variable and everything else as dependent variables (upon sales). This first set of projections is what you honestly expect to happen in your business—not wishful thinking, but your best-educated guess.

In addition to your best guess, you should also make a sales plan for the best that you think can happen, and the worst, as well. The three sales curves will look something like Chart 1.

Now the highest probability is your actual sales will fall somewhere between the best and worse case. You are not tied to just one plan.

From all of the reports that you generate from these sales projections, you can see what will change and how. You can estimate your growing cash requirements well in advance of the actual time so you can go to the banks or lending institutions and make your case and show them your computations and estimates well before you need the money.

Go to more than one institution and get as many lines of credit as you can. Having just one can be dangerous if they suddenly stop lending to you for reasons not of your making, and you

have no other source. Sometimes, when banks merge or change their leaders, they suddenly change their loan policies.

If you approach any lender with a good, reasonable set of *pro forma* figures, and the lending officers believe them, you will probably get the line of credit. This is how the big boys and girls get millions from lending institutions with good, reasonable and believable numbers and profits from which the lender gets his/her interest. As you may well know, the best way to get a loan from a bank is to prove to the bank that you do not need the loan.

When I started my company in 1964, I needed monthly loans until I got paid by my clients so that I could pay my employees, rent, insurance, utilities, etc. I had to pledge my home each month as collateral for these loans. One day, in the bank, the loan officer told me that the interest on my 30 day loans was going up and I asked why. He said it was due to Charles De Gaulle, who was then the president of France. The bank officer tried to explain to me that De Gaulle had done something to the international price of gold and by some convoluted reasoning, which I did not understand, this caused the prime lending rate to go up, which caused the interest rate for my loans to also go up. Things like this will happen to you, so don't get too upset when they do.

Years later, when my company was on solid financial ground, this same bank officer called me to ask why I stopped borrowing from his bank. I told him we did not need to borrow any more due to our retained earnings and cash-rich position. Now, Jack, are you ready for this? He said I now had a $300,000 line of credit with that bank whenever I chose to use it on my signature alone. I never used it. About six months later, he called again to ask why I was not using the open line of credit, and I told him the same thing that I did six months earlier.

The best way to get a loan from a bank is to prove to the bank that you do not need the loan.

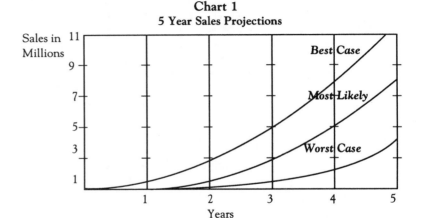

Chart 1
5 Year Sales Projections

Make three sets of plans: the most likely, the best and the worst.

Now you can guess what he did, can't you? He raised the unused line of credit to $500,000 and I never used that either. This is all true, Jack.

I relate this vignette only to emphasize that you should get your lines of credit well in advance of the need, and I repeat, get as many as you can, so you can select from whom to borrow and when. Shop around while you have the time to do so.

Show your intended banker your *pro forma* P&L and Balance sheets at the start. As the months roll along, and your actuals are close to your projections, show these too to the bank officers well before you ever approach them for a business loan, so they can feel comfortable with you and your company and believe in your numbers and projections.

Again, Jack, you have a lot going for you because you have survived the dangerous first five years.

Now let's discuss growing too fast. This can kill off any company—big, small, or in between. Today we read in the financial pages the horror stories of some very big companies who went quickly down the tubes from expansion to meet market demands that never came. With a small company, over-expansion can kill even quicker because the small firm does not have the cash reserves to survive even one big mistake.

Expand in an orderly and controlled way. Economics 101 teaches us to never put all of our business eggs in one basket. Great, but that is exactly what many of the now bankrupt and very big banks and S&Ls did by overinvesting in the construction business alone. The profits on the *pro forma* financial statements looked too good to be true, and they were.

Now, Jack, let's end this with a discussion of serendipity, or unforeseen and unsought good fortune (sort of like winning a lottery with a number that someone else picked out for you). Serendipity is beautiful, generous, and rewarding to those who respond. However, it is fickle. It comes by just once in a great while, and, if you do not immediately recognize and respond to it, then it goes on to someone else.

Always keep an eye out for serendipity. Be prepared to receive it. One good definition of success is the intersection of two straight lines; one is opportunity and the other is preparation.

When serendipity strikes, all bets are off. It's time to redo your plan and shift gears to an entirely new game in many cases, or you re-deal the cards for a new game. You must first recognize that it has happened and then decide what to do about it.

Serendipity visited me twice and fortunately for us we were able to take advantage of the unexpected situations. They were the two biggest and most profitable jobs we ever had and we still have one that has been going since 1970. The other one lasted 20 years. Both were unsolicited and came to my door by chance, not by design. When I realized what was before me, I jumped straight up and never stopped until the jobs were safely in our company. Watch out for these, Jack.

In the military they are called "targets of opportunity." During World War II, a British fighter plane group was on a mission over France. The first attack destroyed the primary target, so the flight leader told the pilots—who still had unused weapons—to go for targets of opportunity on the way home. Pilots love this because it releases them from the discipline of the mission's original plans. One of the fighters saw a German staff car on the road and he shot it up. Guess who he got? Rommel. He went to the hospital and later was killed for trying to remove Hitler from power in July, 1944.

Rommel was removed from power at the most critical time in the battle by being a target of opportunity. This target of opportunity was far superior to the planned mission, so be ready to recognize and react when they come your way.

In summary then, Jack, we have discussed:
- Make your long range plans now.
- Make three sets of plans: the most likely, the best and the worst.
- Get a second party review of your plans, as your mother advised you to do. She's right.
- Base the plans on level of sales.
- Seek lines of credit before you need them and get more than one.
- Keep an eye out for serendipity or targets of opportunity.

Consider all of the foregoing to be data for your personal career computer program. Use it or do not use it as you think best, and write your own program to process this information in any way you choose. Good luck!

Sincerely,

William A. Delaney

William A. Delaney

Chapter 2

"Convince Us You Can Solve Your Cash Flow Problems."

Robert Gruber, Ph.D. and Catherine Stover

David McLimans

E llen Whitten had finally made it. Fifteen years after founding Whitten Office Supply and Design, she was on the cover of *Portland Business Magazine*. People she hardly knew congratulated her in restaurants. Her teenage daughter said, "Gee, Mom, I didn't know you were so important." A week after the issue came out, she was invited to join Rotary.

Now, as she walked through the bank lobby, holding a copy of the issue in one hand and her briefcase in the other, the word *empowered* kept floating to the top of her thoughts, the way a song or jingle can surface at odd times. She was on her way to see the banker who had been there from the start, Jane Parker.

The receptionist directed Ellen to the conference room, where Jane was waiting, standing with her back to the door.

As they shook hands, Ellen wondered why Jane looked a little tired. Even her grip was a little less enthusiastic than usual.

"Good morning, Ellen," Jane said. "Thank you for coming."

Robert Gruber is an assistant professor of accounting at the University of Wisconsin-Whitewater.

Catherine Stover is the editor of the Small Business Forum.

What! After fifteen years, you want a plan?

"Good morning! I was surprised that you called. And now I'm surprised that we're meeting in the conference room," Ellen said as they sat down. "Not that I mind the view," she added, feeling almost pleased that the whole city stretched before her. Awash in the sunlight, Portland seemed to glisten with self-assurance.

"We're meeting here because they're putting new carpeting in my office this morning. I'm finally getting rid of that green rug you've always hated," Jane said, then, she added, smiling, "Someday I'm going to talk them into letting me hire you to refurbish the whole office. I really enjoyed seeing the before and after pictures in *Portland Business Magazine*."

"Ah! So you've seen it!"

"Yes. It was great publicity for you. It's really something to be called the hottest office design firm in the city. I bet the phone is ringing off the hook."

Ellen laughed. "We've had some inquiries about our prices."

Jane Parker looked down at her navy blue suit for a moment before speaking. "I am sure you are wondering why I asked you to meet with me today."

Ellen smiled.

"I've been looking at your financials," Jane said slowly. "Two years ago, you had a net profit of $43,200. Now, for the first time in your history, you are facing a potential net loss. Your inventory turnover has decreased and your receivables are up."

"What are you saying?" Ellen asked, sitting up straight in her chair.

"Last time we met, we decided to monitor your cash flow more closely. Now, it appears that we are going to have to take some steps to improve the situation."

"Jane, I have to tell you, I don't know what to say. In the fifteen years we've worked together, you've never talked to me like this. What is going on?"

Jane paused for a moment. "I'm doing a lot of things I've never done before. We have a new board of directors, and they are more aggressive than our past boards have been. The savings and loan crisis has made everyone quite a bit more careful." Jane looked out the window, then turned back to Ellen.

"Your note is due in six months. Before we can extend it, we need to see how you plan to improve your cash flow."

"What! After fifteen years, you want a plan? What kind of plan are you talking about?"

"Ellen," Jane said, "it's precisely because we've worked together for fifteen years and

because you have a good payment record that I want to help you succeed. Times have changed. Right here, right now, money is tight and credit is tighter. I have seen the board turn down requests from businesses that are even older and bigger than yours."

"But what about this piece in *Portland Business*? I'm finally getting the breaks that I've worked all my life to get. Look, I know I've been preoccupied with the design side of the business lately, and I know that my cash flow isn't where I'd like it to be. But it's just a temporary slump."

"Ellen," Jane said, standing up to pour them each a cup of coffee. "You take it black, don't you?" At Ellen's nod, Jane returned to the conference table with the coffee. "I don't mean to scare you. I am on your side. It may be unprofessional of me to admit to having favorite clients, but the fact is I have always been in your court. You started your business at about the same time that I was promoted to the office with the ugly green rug. I'm not exactly a blazing feminist, but I do think that you and I have had to take more than our share of knocks to get where we are right now."

Ellen took a long drink of the strong coffee and looked at the smiling reflection of herself on the magazine in front of her.

Jane said, "The main reason I wanted to have this conversation with you today is because I want things to go smoothly six months from now. And I also want you to know that the board is not extending loans the way they used to.

"I'll be straight with you," Jane continued. "Even with my support, you will not be able to extend your note for three years, like we did in '88 and '93. The current policy is to extend for one year—and then only if you put a very convincing plan together that shows exactly how you are going to improve your cash flow."

"This publicity—the new clients—should convince them—"

"No. Numbers will convince them. You will need to show them how, for example, you are going to improve your inventory turnover. How you're going to do a better job of collecting on your receivables. How you know exactly who your customers are and what they want and how much they will pay you. You will have to justify the salary that you pay yourself and your staff. In other words —"

"In other words, everything. They're not assuming that because my business is the oldest and best-established office supply and design business in Portland that it means anything."

Ellen noticed that she was clenching her left fist.

"Times have changed. The way we are doing business has changed. We don't make assumptions the way we used to. Everyone has to prove, to document, to work from a budget . . . Remember when the banks put Donald Trump on a budget a few months ago? His banks didn't make assumptions about him, or take him—the king of big-time business—at his word."

"Is it absurd to say, 'Now I know what Donald Trump must have felt like?'"

Jane smiled. "If I were you, I'd talk to the best advisors or experts or consultants that I could find. I'd do whatever it takes to show how you can and will turn your business around."

"This publicity will t—"

"And I wouldn't count on the publicity. I would sell your management ability and policies, rather than counting on something like that. You know, I think that you may really benefit from having to go through this—"

"This hell—"

"This...whatever." Jane stood up and extended her hand. "Please," she said, looking directly at Ellen. "Call me if you think I can help you."

To prove that I should stay in business, Ellen thought. "Thank you for your candor and for your support, Jane," she said as they left the conference room.

Driving back to Whitten Office Supply and Design, through the clogged streets, facing the ugly glaring sun, Ellen wondered what—or how much—she should tell Jacqueline, her Manager of Design Services. Even though they had worked together for three years, Ellen felt as though she really didn't know Jacqueline Marchey well enough to be able to predict how she would take the news that future funding from the bank was uncertain. Sometimes Jacqueline spoke of returning to California where "offices can be more expressive." At other times, she hinted that she would do things differently if she had her own design studio. But lately, with all the attention from the publicity, she had seemed elated and committed to Whitten Office Supply and Design.

Ellen sometimes wondered if Jacqueline was worth the $30,000 she paid her. On the one hand, Jacqueline was clearly the most creative and bold designer in Portland. People recognized her distinctive work. But, on the other hand, Ellen had seen Jacqueline insult clients without even knowing it, by saying things like "You want to get rid of this boring grey stuff,

don't you? And find something a little less trite?"

When Ellen met Jacqueline in the back office, Jacqueline said, "Oh, Ellen! I have had such a wonderful idea while you were out! Let's use the article to launch a new advertising campaign—"

Jacqueline stopped speaking. "You look as though you have just had a vision from hell."

"I have." Ellen sat down. Will she tell the whole town about this?, she wondered. "My banker wants me to put some information together..."

"Oh, bankers! If they had any personality they would be dangerous!"

"Jacqueline," Ellen said, shaking her head, smiling. "Have we actually signed up any new clients since the issue came out last week?"

"Is that what they want a report on?"

"Well, that's sort of part of it."

"These things take time. The pictures tell the story so well. We've had so many calls—"

"But how many proposals have you actually made?"

"I have not visited any new places but that's because —"

"Excuse me," Cindy Johnson, the bookkeeper said, as she entered the back room. "Ellen, do you have a minute?"

"Is it urgent?"

Cindy nodded.

Ellen got up and walked with Cindy to a quiet corner of the store.

"I know you have been very busy with the design part of the business lately, and I hate to bother you, but —"

"You're not bothering me. What's up?"

"I need to talk with you about which bills we should pay."

"Which bills? What do you mean, which bills? We always pay our bills right away. We always get discounts for paying early."

Cindy took a step back. "Last month I told you that our checkbook balance is low and that our line of credit is used up. But if this isn't a good time..."

"I'm sorry. I've had a long morning." Ellen watched some customers leave—emptyhanded. "Let's sit down after lunch and look everything over. In the meantime, would you mind double checking the bank statements? Maybe we forgot to write a deposit in."

"Sure. I'll get the adding machine and go through it all again. Let me know when you're ready to meet with me."

As Cindy turned and walked away, Ellen closed her eyes. What was she going to do? She opened her eyes and counted the customers in

Last month I told you that our checkbook balance is low and that our line of credit is used up.

her store. Eleven. Eleven people with money, she told herself. As she went toward the back office, she heard Jacqueline laugh, and wondered why that sound didn't cheer her up.

She went in the office, got her purse, and left for lunch without asking Jacqueline to join her. She had some serious thinking to do.

What should Ellen Whitten do? *Experts in the fields of turnaround management, banking, finance and marketing provide a range of perspectives on Ellen's predicament in the letters that follow. The experts were asked, "If Ellen had consulted you, what advice would you offer after your second meeting?"*

Whitten Office Supply and Design
Income Statements
For the years ending June 30, 1991 - 1995
(in 000's)

	1995	1994	1993	1992	1991
SALES:					
Retail	$510.8	$498.6	$474.9	$413.0	$350.0
Wholesale	278.9	275.5	239.5	184.2	125.3
Total	789.7	774.1	714.4	597.2	475.3
COST OF SALES:					
Retail	348.7	331.9	306.3	264.3	220.5
Wholesale	170.1	165.3	137.7	101.3	75.2
Total	518.8	497.2	444.0	365.6	295.7
GROSS PROFIT:	270.9	276.9	270.4	231.6	179.6
OPERATING EXPENSES:					
Salaries & Wages	92.6	89.5	87.1	55.5	40.0
Payroll Taxes	6.9	6.7	6.5	4.9	4.2
Postage	3.8	3.4	3.1	3.0	2.0
Advertising	6.1	5.0	5.0	13.4	9.2
Dues & Subscriptions	1.2	1.1	1.1	1.0	1.0
Professional Fees	3.6	3.0	3.0	2.4	2.4
Depreciation	11.2	14.4	13.8	8.6	6.4
Utilities	6.4	5.7	5.1	5.4	4.5
Rent	33.0	33.0	30.0	30.0	25.0
Insurance	14.1	10.6	9.4	8.5	8.0
Repairs & Maint.	9.3	8.6	8.0	7.8	3.9
Travel	8.8	7.0	6.3	6.6	6.0
Telephone	7.2	6.6	6.0	5.4	4.8
Office Expenses	12.0	12.8	12.8	10.7	8.5
Miscellaneous	7.7	6.6	7.1	6.0	4.8
Total	223.9	214.0	204.3	169.2	130.7
Net income before other items	47.0	62.9	66.1	62.4	48.9
OTHER ITEMS:					
Interest expense	18.3	12.1	10.1	10.5	6.2
Income taxes	4.3	7.6	9.2	8.5	6.4
Total	22.6	19.7	19.3	19.0	12.6
NET INCOME	**$24.4**	**$43.2**	**$46.8**	**$43.4**	**$36.3**

Whitten Office Supply and Design
Statements of Financial Position
June 30, 1991 - 1995
(in 000's)

ASSETS	1995	1994	1993	1992	1991
Current assets:					
Cash	$6.9	$12.0	$16.6	$27.5	$34.7
Trade receivables	133.4	116.6	94.2	67.7	51.4
Inventories	202.7	168.8	157.2	125.9	71.1
Prepaids	5.7	6.6	4.2	4.9	2.5
Total	348.7	304.0	272.2	226.0	159.7
Long-term assets:					
Equipment	101.6	81.1	58.4	41.6	25.5
Furniture & Fixtures	94.5	94.5	79.3	54.2	51.0
Accum. depr.	(78.6)	(67.4)	(53.0)	(39.2)	(30.6)
Total	117.5	108.2	84.7	56.6	45.9
Other long-term assets	7.7	2.0	3.9	1.8	1.9
Total Assets	**$473.9**	**$414.2**	**$360.8**	**$284.4**	**$207.5**

LIABILITIES AND EQUITIES

	1995	1994	1993	1992	1991
Current liabilities:					
Trade payables	$117.5	$91.1	$75.6	$52.3	$31.1
Notes payables	68.8	53.3	30.7	24.6	25.4
Taxes payables	4.3	7.6	9.2	8.5	6.4
Total	190.6	152.0	115.5	85.4	62.9
Long-term liabilities:					
Notes payable	57.3	48.0	49.3	46.8	37.4
Other liabilities	7.4	8.3	8.3	6.8	5.2
Total	64.7	56.3	57.6	53.6	42.6
TOTAL LIABILITIES	255.3	208.3	173.1	139.0	105.5
Owner's equity:					
Common stock	56.0	50.0	50.0	50.0	50.0
Retained earnings	162.6	155.9	137.7	95.4	52.0
Total	218.6	205.9	187.7	145.4	102.0
TOTAL EQUITIES	**$473.9**	**$414.2**	**$360.8**	**$284.4**	**$207.5**

Whitten Office Supply and Design
Statement of Cash Flows
For the years ending June 30, 1992 - 1995

OPERATING ACTIVITIES	1995	1994	1993	1992
Cash received from customers	$772.9	$751.7	$687.9	$580.9
Cash disbursements for:				
Merchandise purchases	(526.3)	(493.3)	(452.0)	(399.2)
Operating expenses	(211.8)	(202.0)	(189.8)	(163.0)
Income taxes	(7.6)	(9.2)	(8.5)	(6.4)
Cash provided by operations	27.2	47.2	37.6	12.3

INVESTING ACTIVITIES

	1995	1994	1993	1992
Cash was provided by:				
Sales of other L-T assets	—	1.9	—	.1
Cash was used to:				
Purchase equipment	(20.5)	(22.7)	(16.8)	(16.1)
Purchase furniture & fixtures	—	(15.2)	(25.1)	(3.2)
Purchase other L-T assets	(5.7)	—	(2.1)	—
Net cash used for investing activities	(26.2)	(36.0)	(44.0)	(19.2)

FINANCING ACTIVITIES

	1995	1994	1993	1992
Cash was provided by:				
Issuance of notes payable	24.8	21.3	8.6	8.6
Issuance of other L-T liabilities	—	—	1.5	1.6
Sales of common stock	6.0	—	—	—
Cash was used to:				
Retire other L-T liabilities	(.9)	—	—	—
Pay interest expenses	(18.3)	(12.1)	(10.1)	(10.5)
Pay dividends to owner	(17.7)	(25.0)	(4.5)	—
Net cash used for financing activities	(6.1)	(15.8)	(4.5)	(.3)
Net decrease in cash	$ (5.1)	$ (4.6)	$(10.9)	$ (7.2)

Begin a Profit Improvement Planning Program

Herbert E. Kierulff, Ph.D.

Dr. Kierulff currently holds the Snellman Endowed Chair in Entrepreneurship at Seattle Pacific University and teaches courses in finance, new enterprise formation, and smaller business management. He has consulted in the fields of turnaround management and new venture start-up since 1967. A contributor to Harvard Business Review *and other journals, Dr. Kierulff is also the author of* The Economics of Decisions.

Dear Ellen:

I came away from our initial meeting on August 3rd and the working session on August 7th impressed with your company and encouraged about your future. But you need to regain control of the company immediately and begin generating profits and cash.

Jane sincerely wants to help, but red ink is a giant red flag to creditors. The more losses you post, the less willing they can be to act as your financial partners.

You asked for a written summary of our two meetings and an outline of the four-phase profit improvement planning program we talked about. Variations of this program have been used hundreds of times to improve profits and cash flows in smaller firms. This is what your banker has in mind. Here is the summary.

Meetings on August 3 and 7. At our first meeting, we discussed in some detail your personal interests and objectives for the next five years, the role you wanted to play in Whitten Office Supply and Design, and the mission and long-term objectives of the company. At our second meeting, we examined in detail your market, competition, strategies and operations. We discussed the major risks in your business, and the key factors for success in your industry.

We concluded that your market is strong—even though profits are down and sales have been leveling. In almost all cases, a company can be turned around if the market has not collapsed and if capable management is willing to implement the four-phase program described below.

Phase One: Goal Setting. A sound profit improvement program will be structured around four sets of goals: personal, profit, cash flow, and sales. We establish these goals in Phase One.

Personal goals are the most important of the goals owner-managers establish. In my experience, conflict between personal goals and company health is the most frequent cause of "financial" problems in smaller companies.

We were both pleased to see the good fit between you and your company when we discussed personal goals on August 3rd. You don't expect something of yourself as owner-manager that you cannot deliver without seriously compromising your other personal goals. Your work gives you a sense of accomplishment. You are doing what you are good at, and what you really want to do.

Profitability goals should be high enough to give you a reasonable return on your investment in Whitten—in addition to your salary. Otherwise, it makes financial sense to sell the company, invest the proceeds in something that will earn you a reasonable return, and go to work for someone else. Your overall income will be higher that way.

Of course, I understand that you are not in business purely for financial gain. There are other rewards of working for yourself. Still, you deserve a return on invested capital which is sufficient to account for inflation and to justify the risk you take in keeping your funds in the company.

In your case, the best method for determining the value of the investment in Whitten is to subtract total liabilities on the balance sheet from the market value of all company assets. Assuming your 1995 balance sheet really showed what you could get for your assets if you sold them off over the next few months, the company value as of June 30 would be the owner's equity: $473,900 - $255,300 = $218,600.

We multiply owner's equity (at the market value of assets) by a percentage return on equity (ROE) figure. My rule of thumb for the latter is 30 to 40 percent. The result will be a pre-tax profit goal which should account adequately for annual inflation and risk. Naturally, the percentage will vary by industry and by the amount of inflation expected. Using your current balance sheet, the minimum goal would be: $218,600 X .3 = $65,580.

Cash flow goals are necessary because it is possible to earn a profit and still run out of cash to pay the bills. Your cash on hand and in the bank should always be at or above the minimum necessary to do business and keep all loans, payables and trust accounts up to date.

In almost all cases, a company can be turned around if the market has not collapsed and if capable management is willing to implement the four-phase program described below.

Figure 1: Information for Profit Improvement Planning

- Company financial statements for the past three to five years and the most recent four quarters.
- Sales by month by service or product for the last three to four years.
- A list of employees by name, position, and gross wages or salary.
- A 12-month schedule of general ledger costs excluding labor and materials.
- Last-month-end accounts receivable and accounts payable aging schedules.
- Monthly receivables to sales and inventory to sales ratios for the last 12 months (Month-end receivables and inventory should be used).
- A schedule of all loans, including name of lender, current balance, payment amount, annual interest rate, date of monthly/annual payment, collateral, and current status of the loan.
- A list of all preferred and common stockholders, shares owned by type of stock, and annual dividend paid (if any).
- A letter on your letterhead and signed by you authorizing your bank(s) and me to discuss company affairs among us.
- Published product information about your company (brochures, articles, etc.).
- Current written business plans and financial projections (if any).
- Name, address and telephone number of outside accountant, lawyer, board member(s), other consultants.

Cash flow goals are necessary because it is possible to earn a profit and still run out of cash to pay the bills.

Sales goals define how large the business *can* get over some time period (say, three to five years) and/or how large you will *allow* it to become. You already have three-year goals. We now need to construct two annual sales projections on a month-by-month basis.

The first will be one that you have a 50/50 chance of achieving or bettering. This "best estimate" forecast is the one you will use to motivate your sales force and yourself.

The second 12-month projection will be conservative—a less-than-expected sales forecast. You should be 80 percent sure that you can reach this sales level or better it. This forecast should be so conservative that you will be able to go to bed at night and sleep soundly, convinced that you will reach your goal. If you think you might wake up and worry, the forecast should be lower.

As a practical matter, the less-than-expected forecast will probably not exceed, and it may fall below, your Fiscal 1995 sales. We will use this forecast for budgeting purposes.

Phase Two: Analysis and Evaluation. After the goals are set, we will create a pro forma one year income statement and balance sheet by month. We can base it upon the data you have been gathering since our first meeting (see Attachment 1). Cindy said that she would have these data available by our next meeting on August 10.

The pro forma income statement will show what less-than-expected case sales, costs and profits will be over the next twelve months, starting with August. The pro forma balance sheet will display future cash flow: expected liabilities plus expected owner's equity minus expected total assets. Cash flow on the balance sheet is sometimes called financing required.

We will do the financials together, but the numbers must be yours so that you have "ownership" of them. My job will be to:

- Guide you through the technicalities of the process.
- Encourage you to be realistic (but conservative).
- Challenge your assumptions.
- Make suggestions based upon experience.
- Keep notes on our discussions and assumptions. We will call in Cindy, Jacqueline, and others to help as needed.

The pro formas will presume that things go along about as they have in the past. The idea is to create a foundation upon which to build the program—to understand what is likely to happen over the course of the next year if nothing much changes in the way you do business. Inflation should be built into the costs, but we will wait until later to raise prices.

We base the pro formas on the less-than-expected sales forecast for good reasons. If your conservative pro formas show that you will achieve your profit and cash flow goals, you will probably do even better. This means that you will sleep well and your banker will be reassured.

If the pro formas show that you will be unable to meet your goals given the status quo, you will have proven to yourself with your own numbers that changes are necessary. It is vitally important that this conclusion be yours, not mine. If you do not believe the numbers, you will not act on the basis of them.

I should note that throughout this exercise, there will be a strong temptation to reach your goals simply by increasing sales volume. Almost all of my clients have insisted at one time or another that a big order was "right around the corner"; that quick fixes in advertising, personnel, production, etc. would save the day through more sales; or that a new product was ready for introduction and would generate fast cash.

Belief in sales volume salvation is a common trap. The big orders somehow fail to materialize. The quick fixes are never as effective as you expect. The new markets do not open up rapidly. The new products are slow to gain market acceptance.

The owner-manager who relies on increasing sales volume in a dramatic way is usually left with a plan that cannot be achieved, and promises that cannot be kept. We will avoid the trap by sticking with our conservative sales forecast and by increasing sales revenue only through price increases.

Incidentally, it's now easy to explain why goal setting should be done early on. A significant number of my clients, when they find that the goals and the less-than-expected forecasts are far apart, will "fudge" on the goals. They will be willing to settle for less profit than is indicated by the risks in their business, and for less cash. This should not happen if the goals are set first.

Phase Three: Profit Improvement Planning.
The objective of Phase Three is to eliminate the variances between the goals and the pro forma profits and cash flows. Most of the decisions which will make up the plan may be implemented immediately or within a short time period.

I will transcribe your plan on 8½ x 11" lined paper which will be divided into three columns. The first column will be headed "Categories";

the second, "Effect on Profit Goal"; and the third, "Effect on Cash Flow Goal." Just below the second heading, I will show the difference between the pre-tax profit goal and the pre-tax profit total in the less-than-expected case pro forma. The number for the cash flow shortfall will be just below the third heading.

You make up the differences between goals and the less-than-expected pro formas in five ways:

- Reduce overhead costs.
- Decrease cost of sales.
- Reduce assets as a percentage of sales.
- Find additional sources of financing (especially equity).
- Raise prices.

We will begin by scrutinizing each item on the less-than-expected pro forma income statement. Why is this cost so high? What can be done to reduce that expense? You may find it necessary to increase a cost. For example, you and I discussed the need for a computer in your business. You may need to increase advertising.

Our preliminary analysis (Figure 2) showed that cost of sales has been increasing rapidly over the last few years, and has seriously eroded profits. Cindy will be responsible for the spreadsheet analysis of materials costs and prices on the products that make up approximately 80 percent of sales. We all agreed that this would be completed by August 14 with the part-time help of your college student intern.

As we move down the line items on the less-than-expected pro forma income statement, I will record each of your decisions to change a cost under the "Category" heading. I also will record the annual dollar implications in the next two columns, keeping track of progress toward our goals in this way.

When we move to the pro forma balance sheet, we will do the same line-item-by-line-item evaluation to increase cash available. Receivables and inventory will require special scrutiny because of their increase as a percent of sales over the past few years. Also, why were common stock and notes payable increased to pay the dividend (which is not tax deductible)?

The exercise sometimes takes several iterations. We stop when the total changes in the pro formas correspond to the totals at the top of the first page of our three-column worksheet. At that point, we will have a profit improvement plan—a list of decisions which, when implemented, will permit you to achieve your profit and cash flow goals. Since the new pro forma balance sheet will demonstrate a positive cash flow, it can be used to formulate a detailed plan to pay overdue bills.

Belief in sales volume salvation is a common trap.

Figure 2: Historical Analysis Whitten Office Supply and Design
Financial Statements as % of Sales June 30, 1991 - 1995

PERIODS	1991	1992	1993	1994	1995
TOTAL SALES	475,300	597,200	714,400	774,100	789,700
BALANCE SHEET					
Cash	7.3%	4.6%	2.3%	1.6%	0.9%
Trade Receivables	10.8%	11.3%	13.2%	15.1%	16.9%
Inventories	15.0%	21.1%	22.0%	21.8%	25.7%
Prepaids	0.5%	0.8%	0.6%	0.9%	0.7%
Total	33.6%	37.8%	38.1%	39.3%	44.2%
Equipment	5.4%	7.1%	8.2%	10.5%	12.9%
Furniture & Fixtures	10.7%	9.1%	11.1%	12.2%	12.0%
Less Accumulated Deprec.	-6.4%	-6.6%	-7.4%	-8.7%	-10.0%
Net Fixed Assets	9.7%	9.5%	11.9%	14.0%	14.9%
Other Long-term Assets	0.4%	0.3%	0.5%	0.3%	1.0%
Total Assets	43.7%	47.6%	50.5%	53.5%	60.0%
Trade Payables	6.5%	8.8%	10.6%	11.8%	14.9%
Notes Payable	5.3%	4.1%	4.3%	6.9%	8.7%
Taxes Payables	1.3%	1.4%	1.3%	1.0%	0.5%
Total	13.2%	14.3%	16.2%	19.6%	24.1%
Notes Payable	7.9%	7.8%	6.9%	6.2%	7.3%
Other Liabilities	1.1%	1.1%	1.2%	1.1%	0.9%
Total	9.0%	9.0%	8.1%	7.3%	8.2%
Common Stock	10.5%	8.4%	7.0%	6.5%	7.1%
Retained Earnings	10.9%	16.0%	19.3%	20.1%	20.6%
Total	21.5%	24.3%	26.3%	26.6%	27.7%
Total Lia. & Equity	43.7%	47.6%	50.5%	53.5%	60.0%
INCOME STATEMENT					
Sales: Retail	73.6%	69.2%	66.5%	64.4%	64.7%
Sales: Wholesale	26.4%	30.8%	33.5%	35.6%	35.3%
Total Sales	100.0%	100.0%	100.0%	100.0%	100.0%
Cost of Sales: Retail*	63.0%	64.0%	64.5%	66.6%	68.3%
Cost of Sales: Wholesale+	34.1%	38.3%	45.0%	49.8%	48.8%
Total Cost of Sales	62.2%	61.2%	62.2%	64.2%	65.7%
Gross Profit	37.8%	38.8%	37.8%	35.8%	34.3%

Figure 2, continued

PERIODS	1991	1992	1993	1994	1995
Operating Exp. & Other	30.1%	31.5%	31.3%	30.2%	31.2%
Net Income	7.7%	7.3%	6.5%	5.6%	3.1%

*Cost of Sales Retail as % of Retail Sales
+Cost of Sales Wholesale as % of Wholesale Sales

RATIO ANALYSIS

	1991	1992	1993	1994	1995
Return On Equity	35.6%	29.8%	24.9%	21.0%	11.2%
Times Interest Earned	7.89	5.94	6.54	5.20	2.57
Total Asset Turnover	2.29	2.09	1.98	1.87	1.67
Average Sales/Day	$1,302	$1,636	$1,957	$2,121	$2,164
A/R Collection Period	39.47	41.38	48.13	54.98	61.66
Inventory Turnover	4.16	3.71	3.14	3.05	2.79
Debt Ratio	0.51	0.49	0.48	0.50	0.54
Current Ratio	2.54	2.65	2.36	2.00	1.83
Quick Ratio	1.41	1.17	1.00	0.89	0.77
Debt Equity	1.03	0.96	0.92	1.01	1.17

When we revise the pro formas to reflect the decisions on our worksheet, we will have the set of financials Jane wants to see. You should review them with her first.

Then, the numbers should be presented in appropriate form to your employees. After all, they are the people who will help you make the plan happen. They need to understand your goals and what must be done to reach them if they are to help you.

Besides, I can guarantee that all of them know about your financial plight now and are worried. They expect you to do something soon. And they will be relieved to know that you have a plan, even if it calls for them to make some sacrifices or change their behavior. Employees understand the need to make a profit in return for risk taking if risk and alternative uses for capital are explained clearly.

You should do as much of the actual presenting as possible, since the plan is yours and you will implement it. Use me as a backup only. This will improve your credibility.

Phase Four: Implementing and Monitoring.
The revised pro formas become the plan against which you monitor monthly progress using variance analysis. The first column of this analysis should show the income statement and balance sheet line items. The next column should display the forecast for the previous month; the third column should contain the actuals for that month.

In the fourth column, the dollar difference between each forecast and actual line item should appear. A column showing percentage differences may be added if it is helpful to you.

When possible, you should look at three months of variance analyses at a time. Three months' data will give you perspective and allow you to note trends. If a line item actual is significantly different from your plan, you should know why. Then, you should determine what, if anything, to do about it.

Cindy should have the analysis to you no later than the 15th of each month. Otherwise, the information will be too old to be of much practical value. Get the analysis even if a few actuals have to be rough estimates.

With Cindy's help, monitoring with variance analysis should not take an inordinate amount of your time. My clients tell me that they feel much more in control and experience much less anxiety when they run their businesses "by the numbers" in this way.

My clients tell me that they feel much more in control and experience much less anxiety when they run their businesses "by the numbers" in this way.

When these controls have been established, I will meet with you each month for a few months to review progress. During those meetings we will discuss uses of your new computer, other simple control and management-by-the-numbers techniques, employee incentives (including profit sharing), marketing strategies, new product lines, product mixes and market segments. We want sales volume to increase after you get your current situation under control.

I am confident that we will be successful. Between us, we have everything necessary. You understand your business, have many years of management experience in your industry, and enjoy a fine reputation with customers and suppliers. I have a methodology for improving profits and cash flow which I have applied successfully in many industries for 15 years.

When we are finished, you will have learned what I know about planning and control, and I will have worked my way out of a job. You should be firmly in command of Whitten and confident of your future.

Sincerely,

Herbert E. Kierulff

Herbert E. Kierulff

Manage the Trends that Undermine Your Business

Dean Treptow

Dean Treptow was president of a bank that has specialized in small business services for 16 years. He is currently chairman of Polaris Group, Inc., a firm engaged in small business investments and financial consulting. Mr. Treptow received the National SBA Banker Advocate of the Year award in 1982, and is the author of Bank On It: A Banker Talks to Small Business Owners, *which will be published next summer.*

Dear Ellen:

We've had two meetings in which you explained your circumstances to me and shared your financial statements. Here is a summary of the message I heard from you.

You're understandably hurt and a little indignant because you believe that your bank and banker have suddenly become disrespectful of your long-term relationship. You're uncertain about your designer. You are perplexed by the irony of the fact that the people whom you have counted on for years have suddenly betrayed you at the very time you are reaching the pinnacle of business success (as evidenced by that great article in *Portland Business Magazine*). You've had 15 years of solid, successful experience in your business, but now your bank is asking you to prove yourself like a stranger with a start-up business.

Your problem is not as severe as you may believe. You're suffering from a malady very common to successful entrepreneurs at a certain point in the life cycle of their businesses. It's a problem of perspective—they become preoccupied with a myriad of decisions and issues in their businesses and fail to see the emerging trends that are undermining their historical strengths. To help you understand, I will try to peel away aspects of the problem that really aren't relevant and will only distract you from focusing on the appropriate issues.

The demands of your bank are not unique in the banking industry, nor are they uniquely addressed to you as a specific customer. Largely as a result of the savings and loan crisis, bank regulators are giving banks little credit for their historical track record and are demanding that the banks defend their loan decisions and prove their viability on a current basis. The banks have responded by making the same demands on their customers. I happen to believe that they are using a shotgun where a surgeon's scalpel would serve better. However, that's irrelevant. Your bank's attitude is a reality and will remain so for many years. Accept it and learn to adapt to it.

Don't reject your loan officer. She really was trying to do you a favor, albeit in a somewhat clumsy and defensive manner. You should have some understanding of the changing environment in which banks operate. But she made it appear that you are the innocent victim of S & L failures and changing bank boards of directors. The fact is that banks want the same things the owner wants—liquidity and profitability. Serving your own interest will also serve the bank.

Despite that failure, it appears that your banker remains your advocate and is at a level in the bank where she carries some influence. That's more than many business owners are getting from their bank officers today. Nurture that relationship.

You seem to have ambivalent feelings about your designer, Jacqueline. You question her loyalty to you and her customer relations skills. You state that you have been spending a lot of your time recently on the design side of the business, yet you refer to Jacqueline as the most creative and bold designer in Portland. Put her out of your mind for now. I'm neither a marketing nor a design consultant, but I believe you may find answers to your dilemma with Jacqueline after I take you through my financial analysis.

With those things off of your agenda, let's address that self-interest of yours in a way that will also satisfy the bank. Your financial statements portray the net result of the interaction of numerous interdependent variables at specific points in time. You, the business owner, control those variables more than anyone else, whether you realize it or not. As a financial consultant, I can point out the issues to you, but only you can make the decisions. The bank wants you to increase cash flow. There are only three ways to do that: 1) Borrow more money; 2) Reduce assets; and 3) Make more profit. Let's take those one at a time.

I think it's reasonable to conclude that the bank doesn't plan to give you more long-term debt to solve your cash needs. Collectively, your trade suppliers have been lending you increasing amounts every year. Five years ago your trade suppliers were funding 15 percent of your assets. Today, trade payables are 25 percent of your assets. On the basis of average days outstanding, your trade payables have gone from 38 days to 83 days over the five-year period. You seem to be under the impression that you have always paid bills on time and taken discounts. This obviously isn't true. If you were to bring your trade payables down to 30 days, you would require an additional $74,900 cash. Okay, no solutions there. I'm making the problem worse.

How about reducing assets? Here we have something to work with. Over the last five years, the average period that your receivables remained uncollected has increased from 40 days to 62 days. If you could collect those in 30 days, you would create $68,600 of new cash. What about that inventory? Back in 1991 you carried enough inventory for 88 days of sales. In 1995, you had enough for 143 days. Just suppose you could reduce that inventory to 100 days of sales. That would reduce your inventory from $203,000 to $142,000 and generate $61,000 in cash. In my experience, your equipment, furniture and fixtures investment is pretty

reasonable. There's no significant savings to be made there.

So far we've used up $75,000 on getting those trade payables in line but we've recovered $130,000 by reducing assets. This gives us a net gain of $55,000 in cash. Your trade suppliers are probably happier and you may be getting better prices and service. There may even be the first hint of a smile on your banker's face. We haven't even touched profitability issues yet. Profitability is primarily a function of the volume of sales, pricing and expense control. Your operating expenses have consistently stayed around 28 percent for the entire five years. Components of your operating expenses all seem to be very reasonable. I have no suggestions for improvement in expense control. This directs our attention to sales, volume and gross profit margins.

Your sales have grown nicely without interruption. A mix of wholesale versus retail remains virtually constant over the last three years, but gross profit margins on both wholesale and retail declined significantly during that period. The gross margin that a business can generate has a direct correlation with the perceived value-added component from one company relative to competitive alternatives.

A business with low value-added content has little to differentiate itself from its customers other than price. Such a business, to attain growth in sales volume, must do so by offering lower prices than its competition. The ability to attain relatively higher gross profit margins is going to be dependent upon building that perception of added value. Here's where the management of gross profit margin gets all tangled up with how fast you're going to collect your receivables and the level of inventory that you're going to manage. Your customers may know that they can take longer to pay you than your competitors would permit. In effect you're making a free loan to them, and that's value.

Another piece of value you provide is prompt delivery on orders or in-house availability of merchandise. If all of your customers can get immediate delivery from you, you've obviously provided some increment of value. Your management of accounts receivable policy and inventory levels is going to depend upon your judgement of how much people are willing to pay for any given level of service. Those methods of differentiating value are most important to businesses that are dealing strictly with commodity-type items. You're selling a number of those kinds of items but your design services are unique and cannot be exactly replicated by any competitor. The values are

The demands of your bank are not unique in the banking industry, nor are they uniquely addressed to you as a specific customer.

subjective and will be valued differently by every individual customer.

The indications are that the market is placing a high degree of value on your design services. The magazine article is strong evidence of that market support.

This leads me to a puzzling question. There's every reason to believe that the market's perception of your value added has increased over the last three years, but your rate of sales growth has slowed materially. 1992 had a 26 percent growth over 1991. That percentage declined steadily to a two percent annual growth rate for 1995. During this time, your gross profit margin declined from 39 percent to 34 percent. You made almost twice as much money in 1993 on $714,000 in sales than you did in 1995 on $790,000 of sales.

Has competition increased during this time period? Has the total market for your goods and services declined in the last three years? Are you reluctant to charge a price that the market will bear? Is it possible that you are acknowledged for doing quality work and providing quality products, but somehow you alienate customers? The slowing of growth and the declining gross profit margin all started three years ago. Isn't that about the time Jacqueline came to work for you? Is there a connection? Or, maybe you're the source of the problem. Did you start behaving differently three years ago?

The financial solutions in your business are quite easy. Get your accounts receivable and inventory under control and increase gross profit margins. I'm convinced that to a large degree, your receivable and inventory problems are really due to a lack of management attention. Some orderly procedures in collecting your accounts receivables in a timely manner and communicating your expectations to your customers should accomplish a lot.

Inventory management is just a better control over purchasing relative to sales. Inventory levels and accounts receivable policies really are marketing issues. Of course, generating more gross profit margin is also a marketing issue. We've expressed the beliefs or made the assumptions that you're providing high quality service all wrapped in an aura of credibility. Something is wrong in our beliefs or assumptions. If we're correct in all the areas we've assessed, I do not believe that your sales would be declining right along with your gross profit margin. Here are my recommendations to you:

Before you do anything else, ask your bookkeeper for an aging of your accounts receivable and do your own personal audit of your inventory. My experience tells me that

your accounts receivable and inventory just might not be what they appear to be. I hope that you do not find that while most of your customers are paying you in 30 days, your average is being driven up by a few very large accounts that are well over 90 days. This would tell me that you have some uncollectible receivables and you're going to have to write them off and reduce the assets on your balance sheet and recognize the loss on your income statement.

A similar concern exists with your inventory. It is not uncommon in firms like yours for obsolete, unsalable inventory over a period of many years to be discarded or put aside in a storeroom but never written off on the financial statements. Look for things like expensive material that was purchased for draperies or upholstery in one particular design project. For whatever reasons, a substantial portion of it became scrap and would never be used for another project. Is that scrap still carried in your inventory? Think in terms of little things like all those 1993 datebooks that you carried in your retail store that were left over in 1994. You threw them out with the garbage, but did you reduce your inventory and increase your expenses accordingly? If you find a problem in either one of those areas, call me immediately.

At our last meeting, I gave you a brochure that described how to produce a business plan. You should follow this guide in putting together a plan for your bank, projecting your operations over the next three years, supported by all the assumptions you are making about market needs, size of the market, pricing policies, inventory and accounts receivable policies, as well as all the other issues identified in that guide book.

I strongly encourage you to engage a marketing consultant to assist you with the marketing assumptions to be employed in your business plan. I have experience with three specific consultants who are knowledgeable in your type of business. If you will call me, I will be happy to discuss their individual characteristics with you and make introductions as you desire. As I've said throughout this letter, I think your fundamental problem is a marketing problem, and you really could use some professional help as well as someone with an external perspective to your business.

Make a decision about that designer you have on your staff. In producing the business plan, you'll probably determine how important design talent really is to your business. After making that decision, you can better

---

Are you reluctant to charge a price that the market will bear?

decide whether your current designer is really providing value.

If you conclude that design is important to the future of your business, you'd better make sure that your present designer is doing the job, or find one who will.

Make a permanent commitment to maintaining a proper degree of perspective on all of the issues that will impact your business in the future. The best way to do that is by creating an advisory board comprised of people with individual experience in each of the critical areas of your business management. They will not only supplement your knowledge and expertise, but they'll give you someone to talk to when you really need to share ideas as well as problems. I would suggest that the advisory board include at least four individuals. One should have financial expertise, the second should have marketing skills, the third should be another successful business owner who understands the kind of problems that you encounter as an entrepreneur. The fourth should be a highly respected customer or vendor of yours. Be sure you get people who are going to be the best kind of friends. Those are the people who think so highly of you that they will tell you what you need to hear even if it hurts.

I could offer a proposal for doing much of the work that I've suggested at my usual fees. I'm a firm believer, however, in teaching someone how to fish rather than selling them the fish.

I think it's going to be a very important exercise in your evolution as the owner of a successful, growing business. I stand ready to help you, but I encourage you to do that investigation yourself on your accounts receivable and inventory and make that first effort at committing your business plan to paper. After you've started to work on that business plan, I think you will realize that it raises many questions that you never thought to ask yourself. Once you have personally committed yourself to finding the answers to those questions and issues, I can be a much more productive resource to you. Please feel free to give me a call and I'll be happy to discuss this letter and its content with you in whatever detail you deem appropriate.

Sincerely,

Dean Treptow

Don't Panic: Plan

Aaron Caillouet

Dr. Aaron Caillouet is director of the Small Business Development Center at Nicholls State University in Thibodaux, Louisiana and has taught management and accounting there for 17 years. He is the author of numerous articles dealing with the management of small business.

Dear Ellen:

Our recent discussions about your present situation were very informational. As we agreed, I called your banker, Jane Parker, to get a full understanding of their position. As a result of our meetings and my conversation with Ms. Parker, I have attempted to identify the major issues. Without identification of these issues, a plan of action at this point would not be possible.

I also reviewed the financial statements for the past five years. Financial statement analyses can provide very important keys to potential problems. Not only did I compute several important ratios, but I also recast the statements in a common-size format and performed some trend analyses. This review substantiated some facts that were previously brought out by your bank, and also caused other important points to surface.

There is no reason to panic at this point. Your problems are not unique. Dwindling profits and cash flow reductions are normal for growing firms that have experienced success in the past. Every business needs to periodically review where it's been, where it is and where it's going. Because of your past relationship with the bank, you haven't been forced to do this. Consequently, the liberal lending policy of your bank lulled you into a false sense of security.

You should remember two things at this point. First, the presence or absence of cash is not in itself an indication of the financial condition of a business. Business owners should act *before* cash flow problems arise.

Secondly, most responsible lenders today want to see a plan. After all, they want to be repaid, just like you want to be paid for your products and services. So look at this as an opportunity to do something good for your

Table 1 Solvency Indicators

YEAR	1995	1994	1993	1992	1991
Working Capital $ (Thousands)	158.10	152.00	156.70	140.60	96.80
Current Ratio	1.83	2.00	2.36	2.65	2.54
Quick Ratio	0.76	0.89	1.00	1.18	1.41
Avg. Collection Period (Days)	60.80	54.20	47.40	40.80	38.90
Inventory Turnover (Per Yr.)	2.79	3.05	3.14	3.71	4.16
Current Debt to Assets (%)	40.20	36.70	32.00	30.00	30.30
Long-term Debt to Assets (%)	13.70	13.60	16.00	18.80	20.50

Table 2 Profitability Factors

YEAR	1995	1994	1993	1992	1991
Net Profit (%)	3.1	5.6	6.6	7.3	7.6
Return on Assets (%)	5.1	10.4	12.9	15.2	17.5
Return on Equity (%)	11.2	20.9	24.9	29.8	35.6
Gross Profit (%) - Retail	32.0	33.0	36.0	36.0	37.0
Gross Profit (%) - Wholesale	39.0	40.0	43.0	45.0	40.0
Gross Profit (%) - Total	34.0	36.0	38.0	39.0	38.0
Total Expense to Sales (%)	28.4	27.7	28.6	28.3	27.5
Adver. Exp. to Total Exp. (%)	2.7	2.3	2.4	7.9	7.0

business by plotting your course for the future. I don't think you've really done that in the past fifteen years. So let's start now.

I would recommend that you continue working with your present bank. They are still showing a willingness to work with you. Besides, Jane Parker is solidly in your corner. That's extremely important in getting the needed funds.

The major issues facing Whitten Office Supply and Design are both immediate and long-term. The immediate issues involve solving a cash crunch in the next six months. Jane Parker pointed out the glaring problems of inventory turnover and increasing accounts receivable balances. There are others that are obvious when we look at the financial statements in depth.

Long-term issues have resulted in decreasing profits over the past several years. They include such things as employee performance, pricing strategy, target markets, sales and the effective allocation of expenses.

Inventories and accounts receivable. We have all agreed that inventories and accounts receivable are a major contributing factor to immediate cash flow. As you can see in Table 1, your average collection period of receivables increased from 38.9 days to 60.8 days during the last five years. Your inventory turnover is also causing problems. It went from approximately 4.16 times per year to only 2.79 times per year during this same period. These indicate substantial drains on your cash.

Working capital. The gain in working capital from $96,000 to $158,000 is misleading. You have some expansion simply because of the overall increase in the size of your business. True indicators are the current ratio and the quick ratio. Both show significant declines. This is a result of the inventory and the receivable problems. You're having to use cash to keep that extra inventory and finance your customers at zero interest.

Debts. Your debt trend shows a definite pattern. You are using current debt to finance long-term assets. Current debt goes up from 30.3 percent to 40.2 percent of assets, while long-term debt goes down from 20.5 percent to 13.7 percent of assets. Your debt should be structured so that capital assets, which can be used as collateral, are fin-anced with long-term loans and not lines of credit.

Profitability factors. The factors in Table 2 are designed to establish trends in profitability. The income statement you furnished did show net income falling from $43,000 to $24,000 during the past full year and is expected to show a loss for this year. Your statement shows a steady decline since 1991 from a percentage stand-point, going from 7.5 percent down to 3.1 percent in 1995. Your returns on assets and equity reflect this condition.

Since expenses are constant when compared to sales, your problem is somewhere above the gross profit line. The gross profit ratio declines at the same rate as the net income ratio. Profit margin on the wholesale operations is also constant. So the income statement culprit is the margin on your retail sales. This offers several solutions that are going to be discussed later.

Please also note that advertising expenditures are down dramatically as sales increase. From a profit standpoint at a given period in time, this is good. But for continued growth, you need to take a close look at your commitment to the advertising and promotion of your business.

Employee evaluation. A decision needs to be made about Jacqueline Marchey. She seems to be very creative but she is not very tactful with clients. She doesn't seem to be very good at selling and is not enthusiastic even now, after all the recent favorable publicity. She did not visit any new places since the magazine article. This situation is critical to your survival.

Conclusions and recommendations. Begin now to improve your cash flow to show your commitment to success. This will be a plus when the bank reviews your plan in six months. It can be achieved by concentrating on your receivable, payable, inventory and dividend policies.

Send out past due notices, make phone calls and visit customers if you have to. But get those receivables in now. Tactful letters to good customers explaining your current cash dilemma will get results, even with accounts that aren't past due. You'll be surprised.

There's also room for cash flow in payables. Your trade payables are averaging about 57 days. Contact your large suppliers and ask for more time. They want your future business and are appreciative of your past patronage over the years.

In order to sell excess inventory, reduce your slow-moving items. Items that have been in stock for several months should be reduced substantially, even below cost. Remember that your immediate goal is to increase your liquidity. Even reduce items that sell fairly well, as long as you can restock quickly if needed. Keep in mind that this is a short-term solution, and is not recommended as a long-term policy. In the long run, you can't make a profit unless you sell above cost.

If you can reduce receivables from 60 to 45 days, increase your trade payables from 57 to 65 days and reduce your inventory by 10 percent, you will generate additional cash of about $60,000. The collection increase in your receivables by 25 percent will generate about $30,000 in cash, while the postponement of 15 percent of your payables will net another $12,000. Selling your slow inventory could bring in another $18,000.

These are not impossible goals for the next six months. But they are actions that will make your bank board very happy. A continuous effort to accomplish the above will also result in lower future loan requests and higher profits because of lower interest costs.

After you put the immediate cash generation goals in place, start thinking about how you can improve your business in the long-run.

I suggest you address some of the following recommendations.

Hire a salesperson. Jacqueline Marchey is not sales material. She will be happier doing design work. A salesperson can work better with clients. Her disposition should change. If it doesn't change right away, work with her to change it. Try to keep her, if possible. She's good at what she does.

Concentrate on your wholesale business. Your profit margin on wholesale business is much larger than on retail, and it has held steady at about 40 percent past five years. Utilize your new sales person to increase your sales in this area. The result will be more dollars on the bottom line. Your wholesale business is now about 35 percent of total. Any increase in that area will increase your profits.

Advertise more. In 1991 and 1992 you were spending two percent of sales on advertising, but then you reduced it to less than 1 percent by 1995. In 1992 your sales increased by 26 percent and by 20 percent in 1993. After the reduction in advertising, your sales increase fell to two percent by 1995. This indicates to me that your advertising may have a positive impact on sales. After you carefully review your ad policy and

Your profit margin on wholesale business is much larger than on retail, and it has held steady at about 40 percent past five years.

calculate your return on ad dollars, you may see a benefit in increasing your advertising.

Dividend policy. For some reason your dividends increased substantially during the past two years. When you were making money, you were taking little or no dividends. Try to tie your dividends to a percentage of profits. It will be an incentive for you to make profits, and the bank will be much more receptive to that type of policy.

I haven't prepared any pro forma statements for you because you need to decide if my recommendations are feasible and can be implemented. You also need to make some realistic sales projections based on your final plan of action. I believe that if you incorporate my changes into your plans, your cash flow will be very acceptable to the bank. If I can be of further service, please write or call. Your business has the potential for a very successful future.

Sincerely,

Aaron Caillouet

Aaron Caillouet

Consider These Marketing Concepts

Alvin J. Williams
Steven K. Lacy

Alvin J. Williams is chairman and professor of marketing at the University of Southern Mississippi, Hattiesburg. He is an active writer and seminar leader in marketing and purchasing.

Steven K. Lacy is a visiting instructor at the University of Southern Mississippi. He has most recently served as the corporate marketing administrator for Sanyo Fisher (USA) Corporation and an analyst for the Northrop Corporation.

Dear Ellen:

As we stated at our last meeting, we are very impressed by your company and its accomplishments. You have worked exceptionally hard to build a reputable interior design firm, and you have a competent staff and loyal clientele.

However, there are some key marketing concepts that can help you continue to compete effectively in the dynamic Portland market.

In today's complex and ever-changing environment, it is important to plan to maximize efficiency and minimize risk. A successful business plan will describe your place in the market, your strengths and weaknesses, your product and services offering, and how your business will keep pace with the changing needs of your target market.

In this letter, we will discuss: the role of marketing in a small design firm, segmenting markets, and your marketing mix.

The role of marketing. First, you must know who you are and what you are trying to do.

The obvious statement would be, "I provide professional interior design services to commercial enterprises in the Portland area. I also sell offices supplies."

But let's look at your business in a broader sense. Your decorating services increase aesthetic satisfaction and enhance the capacity of the business to meet the needs of the customers. Your office supplies improve the efficiency of the work place. This broader definition will allow you to view other aspects of your company from a fresh vantage point.

You are probably wondering why this is important. By understanding the nature and range of the market, you will be able to serve the needs of your primary target market better. You will also discover a wider array of activities that are directly and indirectly related to your new business definition. This will make the firm more attractive to more people.

In addition, profit margins on some of the new activities may be more lucrative than your current ones. They will contribute to the overall financial health of your company.

A final note about the role of marketing: You must remember that marketing, finance, human assets, design and production all must work together to achieve profits. In the past, you have not always made this connection.

Market segmentation. When we talk about market segmentation, we are talking about dividing your market into pieces. In your case, we may start by dividing your clients into groups (called segments) based upon the size of their company. By doing this, we may discover, for example, that 75 percent of your design services are commissioned by businesses that have annual sales in the five to ten million dollar range.

Or, we may decide to segment your market on the basis of geography, SIC codes, buying characteristics, or volume of business. By knowing *who*

Little Efforts Earn Large Savings

John Cunniff, *Associated Press*

This article appeared in many newspapers nationwide during July of 1990.

NEW YORK — The Miller brothers, Jack, Harvey and Arnold, thought they ran their office supplies company with unusual efficiency until they came up against the biggest challenge of their lives.

In just a few years, the multibillion dollar industry's historical arrangement of wholesalers and retailers was upset by the development of big-volume, low-price retail superstores.

Quill Corporation, which the Millers had developed in 34 years to sales of $275 million, making it perhaps the biggest business-to-business supplier of office supplies, had to cut prices while improving service and efficiency.

It was an enormous and unexpected challenge to an industry accustomed to traditional ways of doing things.

"We discovered unbelievable efficiencies," said Jack, the president, from his office in Lincolnshire, Ill. "We thought we were rough and tough, but we were just pussycats."

Miller believes his is a message for independently owned businesses everywhere. Yes, he says, you too can raise sales and improve efficiency and service without resorting to large-scale layoffs. Maybe even raise morale, too.

The first step was to lower prices 18 percent, and that "forced us to say we had to be sharper than in the past," he said. "It was a kick in the pants to profit margins. We had to find savings from the smallest to largest."

Here are a few of the smaller ones:

• Negotiating a new, long-term contract with the primary long-distance telephone carrier, a savings of about $32,400 annually. (Quill is a direct mail supplier; most of its business is done by mail, fax and phone.)

• Recycling scrap cardboard at an annual savings of about $7,200.

• Conserving energy by replacing two 15-watt incandescent bulbs in emergency signs with one 12-watt fluorescent bulb. Savings: $1,800 in the first year, $3,000 for the second year.

• Microfiching documents closer together. Annual savings: $12,000.

• Saving on benefits without reducing them. Because many medical-care providers issue duplicate copies of bills, Quill's benefits department stopped making copies for employees. Savings: $10,000 a year in materials and labor.

Encouraged by messages in the company newsletter, in a special weekly bulletin and on a display outside the lunchroom—to say nothing of their stake in the profit-sharing plan—employees cooperated.

The philosophy of efficiency spread. Workers asked themselves, "What is it I am doing?" Nothing was too minor to recommend. Now that you think about it, you too can turn old file folders inside out and relabel them.

"You don't have to bribe workers," says Miller. "People want to do a good job."

Major strategic ideas were implemented.

Everyday low pricing was instituted, sharply cutting the expense of frequent catalog changes. Whereas orders used to be shipped within eight to 32 hours, a goal of no more than 24 hours was established.

While that immediately improved service on most orders, it had additional beneficial consequences. There was, for example, a quick dropoff in people calling to ask about their orders, thus saving time and labor.

Whereas orders had been spot-checked for accuracy before shipment, workers were added and the company went to 100 percent checking. The savings were immediate, in customer service, freight and returned merchandise.

Such efficiencies never would have been discovered or implemented had not the industry been turned upside down by the super stores, or large-volume retail outlets that completely redefined pricing.

With profit margins permanently cut, Quill now must continue its policy of everyday efficiencies. "It's fantastic to see the kind of efficiencies competitive pressures can generate," says Jack Miller.

we're marketing to, we can figure out *how* to market to them.

Before you can do anything else with your marketing plan, you must know the answer to these questions:

- Who are your customers?
- What are their needs and wants?
- What are their buying patterns and expectations?
- Are you providing the caliber and types of service they desire?

This information is critical. When you are ready, we will show you how to go about gathering it.

Marketing Mix. All businesses have five basic marketing tools: their product/service, their price, their promotions, their distribution, and their people. Your strategy for bringing all of these tools together is your marketing mix. Your goal is to get the right combination of these tools so that you can achieve your overall marketing objective. Let's take a brief look at each of these five:

Product/service: Earlier, we talked about your product definition. We have also described why your products and services should match the needs and wants of your target markets.

Price: Your pricing strategy should be consistent with customers' perceptions of quality and value. Your decision to price below, above, or at market prices should be determined in part by how your products and services compare to your competitors. Are you, for example, the only one in Portland who offers free deliveries of office supplies? Or, are you known for carrying a full-line of upscale products? Keep in mind that items like manilla folders will probably be more sensitive to pricing issues than your design services will be. Why? A folder is a folder, but quality of design is more intangible and harder to compare.

Pricing is also influenced by: inventory management and control, sales and cost analysis, efficient purchasing, and logistical matters.

Promotions: The article in *Portland Business Magazine* contributed to the positive awareness of your company. However, it did not necessarily generate increased sales or profitability—at least yet. That tells us that we have more work to do.

Your income statements show a lot of fluctuation in your advertising expenditures. Are you uncertain about the value of advertising? How do you decide how to spend your advertising dollars? Are you getting the most for your money? These are all important questions that we need to explore.

We should talk more about how advertising, personal selling, sales promotion and publicity can help you achieve your goals. We should also explore the option of telemarketing. We may conclude that with the right training, your sales personnel could utilize this low-cost approach.

Distribution: Are you providing your products and services *where* they are wanted and *when* they are wanted? We should talk about how convenient and accessible your business is, and how getting the goods and services to your customers can affect their perception of quality. We may conclude that the distribution portion of your strategy is functioning well as it is now.

People: Especially in service businesses, the quality and reputation of the people involved is critical. That's why you need to determine whether Jacqueline is an asset. You must ask yourself this: Is Jacqueline's bold decorating style right for your market? And is her communication style right for your market?

These five marketing tools must be combined so that the marketing strategy as a whole is capable of satisfying customer needs and wants. Slight changes in one of the five variables can greatly influence the end result of your marketing plan. It's critical to recognize this relationship.

Your strategy will certainly be shaped by external forces such as competition and social, political, economic and technological factors. Of course, these factors will not weigh equally in their influence. However, as an astute and perceptive business owner, you should definitely be aware of the potential impact each factor could have.

Questions that you will need to answer include: Who are your competitors? How are you different? How is your industry influenced by fluctuations in the economy? (Our guess is that the design part of the business is more sensitive to the economy than the office supply part is.) What new technology will have an impact on your industry?

We have covered a lot of ground in this letter. Gathering the type of information we have described is the first step in your marketing plan process. There is a lot to do, and it will take a lot of time. We hope that we have been able to convince you that you will benefit from the information you will collect. We are looking forward to working with you on this project.

Sincerely,

Alvin J. Williams

Steven K. Lacy

You Need to Return to Managing and Marketing

Susan G. Macy

Susan G. Macy is the lead center director for the University of Houston Small Business Development Center. Her staff helps over 1,200 small-business owners each year to identify their problem areas and develop strategies to correct them.

Dear Ellen:

I enjoyed meeting with you last Friday. You are to be commended for establishing a growing business in a very competitive industry. I know you are distraught right now over the possibility of seeing everything you've accomplished fail. However, keep in mind how much you accomplished when you started your business with minimum resources. Let that inspire you to focus on overcoming your current problems.

As the lead center director for the University of Houston Small Business Development Center, I have seen many small businesses fall into similar cash flow problems. Luckily, you have not actually had a net loss yet. Your banker, Jane, is projecting a "potential net loss" if things continue as they are. Thus, you still have time to avoid this and to get back on the right path. At my staff meeting this week, I presented your information to our counselors. What follows is a plan of action that evolved from their analysis of your situation.

Renew your commitment. The first step to recovery is to renew your commitment to your business. It is *your* decision to do what it takes to turn Whitten Office Supply and Design around. The recovery will not be easy and will take some difficult actions on your part. Your commitment to making it successful again is needed to get you there.

Stop the cash drain. The second step is the hardest and most crucial. You must stop the drain of cash from the business. Stop the bleeding immediately. Some options available to you are:

Retain all earnings in the firm by stopping all payments of dividends. During the last three years, your cash flow statement indicates dividends paid. Dividends should only be paid when excess cash is available. You can resume paying dividends when your company is financially healthy again.

Increase operating profits by reducing expenses. Over the last five years, salaries increased 131.5 percent while revenues increased by only 66 percent. Reducing salaries, and eliminating non-vital expenses must be seriously considered. This can be very difficult and lead to the resignation of some of your staff. You need to be prepared for this possibility. Keep in mind, however, that these steps could be temporary. When you reduce salaries, discuss with your staff that if you succeed in saving the business by increasing revenues and increasing cash flow, current salary levels could be re-established. Explain to them that the alternative to reducing salaries could be the failure of the business.

Explaining to your staff the need for the cutbacks, keeping them informed, and setting yourself as an example for immediate cutbacks will elicit their support and loyalty during this difficult period. Their willingness to continue high quality performances with reduced resources is your most critical and difficult task.

Involve them in the decisions about lowering expenses. Listen to their suggestions and implement those that will enhance the cash flow without eliminating vital expenses. For example, miscellaneous expenses have increased 62 percent over the last five years. How vital are these miscellaneous expenses to the operations?

Reduce total assets by implementing a plan to collect account receivables and by selling off excess inventory and equipment. Your account receivables have increased by 159.5 percent and your inventories by 185 percent since 1991. This is not in line with the 66 percent increase in revenues. These assets are significantly contributing to your cash flow problems. They need to be used to generate cash now.

Start by developing and implementing steps for collecting your account receivables. Call each account, and follow up with a reminder letter and another phone call. Be friendly and polite, but firm. Remember, you have provided a quality product and they are responsible for paying. For those accounts over 60 days, you might ask your lawyer to write a letter or utilize a collection agency.

Sort your inventory. Identify those items that for various reasons are no longer marketable or will be difficult to sell. Have a fire sale with them. Holding on to them is expensive, while getting rid of them will bring in some cash and provide some write offs on your taxes.

Reduce debt using the proceeds from the sale of assets and the collection of receivables. This

Your account receivables have increased by 159.5 percent and your inventories by 185 percent since 1991. This is not in line with the 66 percent increase in revenues.

will allow you to improve your cash flow situation on a continuous basis so that you can take advantage of discounts for early payment to your suppliers. This will also improve your business's attractiveness to the bank. The most important criteria to a banker when deciding to make a loan is the ability of the business to repay the loan. Your ability to repay a loan is, of course tied to your cash flow.

Increase sales without increasing assets or debt. Don't just watch a client in the store—help them make a buying decision. If your service is as outstanding as your quality, word-of-mouth advertising will spread and bring in more clients.

You must tell Jacqueline that she has, on occasion, insulted clients unintentionally. Use the examples you provided and hold her accountable if a client is lost because of her lack of sensitivity. This step will either force her to change or force her to leave. You must be prepared to handle both situations.

Your advertising budget has decreased 33.7 percent since 1991. While you cannot afford to implement a massive advertising campaign, perhaps some money in miscellaneous and office expenses could be diverted for additional promotions. It is important to get the word out about your success and enhance Whitten's image in order to generate more clients.

These are difficult measures to implement, but they will stabilize the financial health of Whitten Office Supply and Design.

Establish management controls. Once you have stopped the cash drain, you can take the time to determine what led you to this predicament and establish some systems to prevent it from occurring again. You mentioned to me that you have been very busy with the design part of the business lately. Yet, you are paying Jacqueline to be a manager of design. And no one is managing the cash. You stated several times how wonderful Jacqueline's design abilities are. Consider letting Jacqueline manage design within the parameters of a budget you establish for her, so that you can get back into managing and marketing the business. You've had fifteen years of solid experience. Now you need to return to managing and marketing.

Your current lack of financial controls and inventory controls significantly contributed to your current problems. If you would like, I can coordinate a meeting for you with one of the SBDC counselors who will teach you more about bookkeeping systems that can provide the information you need in order to make sound financial decisions. You can also learn how to tie your inventory data to your financial information to make better purchasing decisions.

Develop a business plan. As part of establishing sound management principles, I strongly recommend that you develop a business plan to help you keep focused on the issues over the next year. Also, you'll need to present a good business plan to the bank in six months to convince them to make your loan. Jane very clearly told you that she needs information and data to back up her recommendation. That information must come from you.

Your business plan should start with an analysis of the office supply and design industry, and information about how this industry functions in your area. Include a competitive analysis of all the other office design and/or supply businesses that you directly compete with. Look at them objectively and compare their strengths and weaknesses to Whitten.

Next, research the office design and supply market in your area. What is the potential size of it, both in terms of potential clients and the dollar value? Develop a client profile—a picture of what your typical client looks like. How many potential clients are there? Who are these clients—by name? What is the potential for making a sale to each of these typical clients that you target? What is your strategy to sell to them? Your success and recognition could be effectively used for this.

Your strategy for reaching these clients should develop from your analysis of the market data you collected. The market strategy can be used to develop the sales figures for the financial projections in your business plan.

I imagine that you must be exhausted by now from reading my advice. However, I cannot stop yet because your business plan would be incomplete. You must include your management plans as well. Start by defining your key management roles and who is responsible for what. An organizational chart can clear up much confusion and instill confidence in your ability to manage. Include also a brief resume of your accomplishments.

Let me summarize now the four steps you need to implement in order to turn Whitten Office Supply and Design around.

- Recommit yourself to the success of Whitten Office Supply and Design.

- Stop the drain of cash from your business.

- Establish management controls to prevent a repeat of these problems.

- Develop and implement a business plan for Whitten Office Supply and Design.

This summary seems so simple, yet each step has several complex components. We'll take it step by step. Let me know when you would like to meet again. We are ready to help you succeed.

Sincerely,

Susan G. Macy

Susan G. Macy

You are in Business to Earn Cash—not Profit

Donald T. Nicolaisen

Mr. Nicolaisen has been with Price Waterhouse since graduation in 1967 from the University of Wisconsin - Whitewater. He is a partner and the firm's national director of accounting services in its national office in New York City. Mr. Nicolaisen has served a variety of businesses from large multinationals to small concerns in a broad range of industries including manufacturing, insurance and retail.

Dear Ellen:

I enjoyed meeting with you last Thursday to discuss some of the problems and challenges facing your company. Your company's record of achievement certainly has been impressive and I believe it can have a bright future.

The operating issues you must deal with are not uncommon in business today. Weakness in the economy and pressure from banking regulators resulting from the savings and loan crisis have led to a tendency to establish closer control over large and small loan relationships. Bank directors and management are demanding far more information and support from their customers prior to accepting new credits or approving continued credit to long-term customers like yourself.

It is vital to your business that you respond in a prompt and thoughtful manner to your bank's requests. You must continue to maintain a positive relationship with your loan officer as she controls the flow of information between your business and your bank's credit decision-makers. Based on our discussions I am convinced that Jane is on your side, that her early warning was thoughtful and she has provided you with time to respond to your business problems in a positive way.

Many times entrepreneurs react in a defensive "why me" manner. This serves no purpose and results in wasting time and effort. It is critical that you avoid this and channel your energy into taking steps to improve the performance of the business. You can begin by reviewing the Cash Flow Control Guide I gave you at our last meeting. You should follow this guide in preparing the sales and expense forecasts, cash flow projections and cash flow budgets that your bank requested. It is important that you and Cindy begin working on these forecasts immediately so that over the next few months you can fine tune these reports before meeting with the bank.

Well then, let us begin to deal with the major business issues. Your bank's immediate concern is the company's cash flow; the longer term concern is restoring the level of profitability. In this letter I would like to deal with cash flow management and planning issues first, and later we can focus on other profit improvement programs. It is also important to note that good cash management results in reduced costs and therefore improved profits. An analysis of the historical financial information we discussed last Thursday indicates a significant deterioration in cash flow over the past few years.

Before we discuss the specific problems, let me first summarize the objectives of good cash management we discussed at our last meeting.

Many small companies like yours have a significant hidden asset beneath the surface of their cash handling system and do not realize the benefits it conceals. This asset is the ability to manage their cash position to enhance earnings by reducing costs. The following are the three principal objectives of good cash management we discussed:

Enough cash to meet business needs. When most individuals are asked "Why does someone operate a business?", they respond "to make a profit." This response seems quite reasonable. However, the real reason most of us are in business is to earn *cash*. The point is that you can have a very profitable business and tie up all the profit in receivables, inventory and nonproductive assets. What you ideally want to do is minimize your investment in these assets and produce cash.

Business is conducted with cash; without enough cash the business stops. Therefore our primary objective is to have cash available when we need it and in sufficient quantities to meet

Your current lack of financial controls and inventory controls significantly contributed to your current problems

our needs. This does not occur by chance, it takes hard work and discipline.

Accurate cash reporting and accurate cash forecasting are essential to planning and managing the remainder of the business. Good business strategy, inventory management, capital management, etc. are not possible without accurately identifying and predicting cash flows since decisions relating to these areas are all contingent on the availability of the limited resource, cash to finance them.

Minimize the cost of cash. After we achieve the first objective, cash available to meet our business needs, our cash management responsibility has not ended. Our first objective can be satisfied at a wide range of cost and this is where our second objective comes in. The cost of meeting our first objective should be minimized through the use of efficient cash management techniques and efforts. Proper cash management ensures that cash is available when needed while keeping interest expense to a minimum.

Use cash to its full potential. Good financial management requires the assessment of the costs and benefits of various investment opportunities. Proper cash management policies discipline managers to consider the costs and benefits of incremental business opportunities. Much like you consider various investment opportunities for the amount of personal savings you have available, you must also consider the costs and benefits of each business opportunity you pursue. For example, has your increased investment in equipment, furniture and fixtures really enhanced your ability to earn cash?

Now that we have considered the principal objectives of good cash management, let's consider your specific circumstances. Recent financial trends in your business indicate that two areas of the financial management of the business require immediate attention from a cash management standpoint; your company's increased investment in trade receivables and inventories.

Trade receivables. The company's investment in trade receivables has increased at an alarming rate. To put it simply, the time it takes to collect each dollar of sales has increased from less than 40 days in 1991 to more than 60 days in 1995. This means that cash flow from sales is now not available for an additional 20 days. Ask yourself, is there a good reason you should finance customers for this extended period? I think not. In order to finance this additional investment in receivables (almost $50,000), trade payables have been extended and addi-

> *It is also important to note that good cash management results in reduced costs and therefore improved profits.*

tional borrowings have been made. The cost to maintain available cash to meet the needs of the business can be seen in the increase in interest expense, which has tripled since 1991. In addition there may be an intangible cost here as well, damaged relationships with vendors, because the time it takes vendors to collect from you has more than doubled since 1991. Enough about the problem. Let's talk about how to fix it!

It was very easy to allow that additional 20 days to creep into the collection cycle. It will take some hard work and discipline to reduce it to an acceptable level. This is referred to as managing the cash inflow cycle and it can be broken down into three periods, each of which can be influenced by good cash management:

Invoicing period—How long does it take your company to process an invoice and get it to the customer?

Customer holding period—How long do your customers hold your invoices before they remit a payment?

Collection period—How much time passes from the time customers mail their payments to the time you receive and record the payment?

How can I reduce these time periods, you ask? Well, let's review what you might do to influence cash flow during each of these time periods.

Invoicing period. The first step should be to change your invoicing practices for retail customers. Many of your retail customers would pay for purchases at the time of sale, if you simply requested it. One way to painlessly convert customers is to begin accepting credit cards. This will allow your customers to continue to buy on credit and get the cash to the company quickly. I can help you with a cost/benefit analysis to consider this change.

Timely invoicing—Are your customers invoiced promptly for products delivered? Seldom will a customer remit a payment before receiving an invoice, therefore any delay in the time it takes to generate and mail a bill may delay ultimate cash collection. Take a look at your billing procedures to ensure that bills are being prepared and going out on a timely basis. Personnel shortages or absences, system deficiencies or large volumes of small dollar invoices often result in bottlenecks in the invoicing process. The company must ensure that the ultimate cash inflow is not delayed because of internal invoicing inefficiencies.

Progress billing—What are the billing arrangements for orders which take a long time to complete? A significant amount of resources can be tied up in major customer design orders requiring long lead times. You should consider routinely negotiating deposits and progress payments on these orders to pay for your investment in the work which is in process.

Identify the proper addressee—Many times delays can result from mailing an invoice to an improper location or in identifying where an invoice should be mailed. This is particularly common when dealing with multi-location customers, such as subsidiary office location designed by your firm for large companies. Proper billing addresses should be determined at the time products are shipped. Ideally, addresses should be obtained at the time an order is first accepted.

Customer holding period. Once an invoice is received by your customers it is to their advantage to delay payment as long as possible. Do not give your customers an excuse by making simple billing errors which result in delays while the problem is researched, corrected, and a new invoice issued. Second, know your customers' payment habits. If you know a particular customer pays invoices at month end, make sure invoices are delivered in time for payment where possible, or if a customer is consistently a late payer, consider adjusting your prices or other means to influence the timing of his payments.

The first step to knowing these customers is to carefully study your company's latest trade receivables aging and ask Cindy why those that are past due are late and whether they are consistently slow paying. Third, certain inducements and/or pressures can be applied to encourage prompt payment and reduce the holding period. These can be of a "positive" or "negative" nature:

Use of positive inducements—You should consider offering cash discounts for early payment. The discount offered, however, needs to be measured against the benefits realized. It may be possible to build such discounts into the selling price of your product. Another positive inducement might be having your accounting manager inquire politely when payment may be expected prior to the actual due date for large orders.

Use of negative inducements—Commonly used inducements for late payers are charging late payment fees, suspension of credit or pressure from collection agencies. Although these inducements are often times effective, they may result in deteriorating customer relations. Therefore the use of negative inducements should in most cases be used as a last resort.

Collection period. Collection float is the time period between the customer mailing his check and deposit of the funds by your company. Collection float can be reduced by expediting in-house processing of cash receipts. At a minimum, checks should be deposited daily. It is surprising how checks are sometimes held in someone's drawer for days or even weeks before being deposited. Not only does this result in poor cash management, but it also demonstrates poor internal control. As we discussed, you should also discuss the availability and cost of a lock box system.

Inventory. The company is carrying significantly higher amounts of inventory for each dollar of sales. In 1991, the company carried the equivalent of less than three months of sales in inventory. The results for 1995 indicate that the company is carrying the equivalent of almost five months of inventory. An improvement in the usage of inventory to the company's 1991 levels would reduce the investment in inventory by approximately $75,000. A reduction can save the company by reducing interest and insurance costs. Current inventory management takes hard work and discipline also, but it is simply the linkage of purchasing and sales. After there has been a buildup of excess inventory, the process becomes more difficult.

The first step in dealing with a buildup of excess inventory is to attack the source of new inventory by controlling new purchases. You should immediately begin by reviewing open purchase orders and recent sales activity to ensure that open purchase orders are properly linked (both in quantity and expected timing) to historical sales trends and future sales expectations. Orders that are not linked to your sales expectations should be reduced, delayed or canceled if possible. Any new purchase orders should also be "tested" before release. You can set goals for various products, balancing the need to maintain the lowest possible quantity on hand, considering lead times, with the effect of shortages.

In cases where quantity discounts are available, make sure you consider the cost to carry that extra quantity for the period you expect to hold it in inventory. This can sometimes be a trap that leads to excess inventory. Just as you need to know your customer, it is equally important to know your vendors, so that you can take advantage of any flexibility they allow. For example, some vendors allow smaller delivery quantities to better match the flow of purchases with sales. Some may allow you to

You should consider routinely negotiating deposits and progress payments on these orders to pay for your investment in the work which is in progress.

negotiate monthly or annual quantity discounts rather than those measured based on each order.

The second step is to audit the inventory on hand. This may appear to be an overwhelming task because of the number of different items in inventory. However, if you have Cindy prepare an inventory listing in descending dollar value with historical sales activity, you can knock off a large balance of the inventory in quick fashion. I expect that you can reduce the level of inventory quickly by concentrating on the large dollar balances.

After you have completed your review of the large dollar balances, the remaining inventory will take a longer period to review with less bang for the buck. It may well be that you will have a significant amount of product from "that job that got away," "that job we measured wrong" and "that job the owner changed his mind on" which you have been telling yourself you will use someday.

Well, someday has come. You must consider the cost of holding this inventory and make some discounting decisions to get rid of it. One method I have seen used effectively is to make a list of the material that you want to dispose of on a discounted basis and provide the list to your salesman with an additional commission incentive for a sale. You may also be able to dispose of these products by negotiating discounted returns to vendors or discounted sales through your wholesale channels. Finally, maybe increased advertising could help sell excess inventory and improve cash flow!

Just as you need to know your customer, it is equally important to know your vendors.

The third step is to continue to maintain the same level of control over purchasing and to audit your inventory periodically (at least on a limited basis) with a full review in connection with your year end physical count.

I am convinced that the solutions to the company's cash flow problems are outlined above. I also believe that significant progress can be made toward improving your company's cash flow before your loan relationship is up for renewal. Remember, banks are interested in results, not plans. After you have had time to review this letter we can meet again to discuss a more detailed work plan for meeting your goals and your progress on the cash flow plan. I will call you next week to discuss the contents of this letter and any other questions you may have.

Sincerely,

Donald T. Nicolaisen

Donald T. Nicolaisen

Editor's Note: *The editor would like to thank Robert Sullivan of Price Waterhouse and Dan Scott of the National Office Products Association for their contributions to the case study.*

Chapter 3

"I Know I'm Relying Too Heavily on Two Key Customers. But What Can I Do?"

Catherine Stover

David McLimans

J an Staple, the owner/operator of Quality Honey Distributors, Inc., had known her banker, Tim Veering, all her life, which perhaps is why her annual meetings with him were typically informal and cordial. This meeting was no exception. She had been banking with him for the 14 years that she had been running her business, and she usually looked forward to their annual "conversation" in the conference room.

"It looks like 1995 was a pretty good year," Tim said, looking up briefly from her financial statements. "Sales went up from a million eighty-six to

a million one-seventy. Net income is up. Margins seem to be steady. Looks good to me."

"Well, yes, but 1996 might be difficult."

"How come?"

"The federal government is bowing out. Even though I haven't sold honey to the government in years, the fact that they are discontinuing their price support programs is going to have a big impact on our industry."

"Really? How?"

"No one knows. In the early '80s their guaranteed price was much higher than the market price. However, in the last ten years

Catherine Stover is the editor of the Small Business Forum.

51

I know it's tough when you have to choose between taking care of your customers and taking care of your sales.

or so, their price supports have been lower than market prices—but at least they were there to provide a safety net in case the market suddenly collapsed. Now the price support program is gone—so we are all a little nervous.

"Now everyone is scrambling. And pricing drives everything. We're all selling the same product—so we all have to be competitive."

"If you're all selling the same thing, what sets you apart?"

"It seems like our customers want three things: price, volume and consistency. If you can't provide the first two—price and volume—consistency doesn't count. But if you've got the price and volume they're looking for, you can talk about consistency."

"And what do you say?"

"It's an art. Consistency is an art."

"How do you do quality control?"

"It's a pretty unexplored area in our industry. There are some things that we can measure and some things—like taste—that we just can't quantify."

"So how do you control consistency?"

"Well, we've been buying more imports from China and Argentina through brokers..."

"I remember we talked about this last year. As I recall, the advantage is that it comes already blended, which saves labor on your part."

"That's right. It makes a big difference. I'm down to three employees at this point. When I buy domestic honey, I have to heat it, filter it, blend it and then package it. The imported stuff is already blended. And it's more consistent."

"Very good. Last year, I noted that you were hoping to expand your customer base in 1995. How did that go?"

"It didn't. I turned down one big opportunity because the margins were too low. But I didn't get any new customers. Now that we are a four-person operation, I've got a lot of hats to wear. It seems like I have too much to do to pursue new customers."

"Well, let's take a look here. Last year, you said that 65 percent of your sales were going to your two key customers. Is that still true?"

"No. It's closer to 70 percent now. One of my smaller accounts is shrinking."

"Does having only two key customers concern you? Does it make you feel vulnerable?"

"Of course it does. I know I'm relying too heavily on those two accounts. And it scares me. If one of them gets a lower bid, I'm sunk. But how do I find the time to pursue this? If I

don't spend all of my time making sure that my current customers are getting exactly what they want, I'll lose them."

"Who do you sell to now?"

"The big ones are a bakery and a manufacturer."

"Tell me about them."

"The bakery is actually a chain. They have two confectionery products that require a very high quality honey. It needs to be a light amber clover or apple blossom honey. Sometimes it's hard to keep up with their demand.

"My other big customer is a bread manufacturer. They have two different bread products that require honey. I'm not their main supplier—I supplement their supplier. I've never been able to get their big account, which is probably good because the volume might be greater than I can handle. But I have been selling to them for five years. It hasn't been consistent, but it has been growing."

"Have you tried selling to grocery stores?"

"I tried that, but I can't make any money with them. They call all the shots. And I have to compete with local beekeepers who bring in honey and sell it at a price that doesn't take into account any of their time. My other accounts are with general food distributors."

"Well, Jan, I don't know what to tell you. I can see why you feel frustrated. Maybe this is a good time to get some outside advice. Have you ever talked with someone about writing a marketing plan?"

"My marketing plan is shoe leather, at this point. I know I need to sit down and examine some broad marketing issues—but I don't know where to begin. And I don't have time to invest in something that might lead nowhere. I would be happy to get some advice—as long as it will get results."

Tim Veering finished writing notes in Jan's file. He closed the folder and looked across the table. "Jan, I know what you mean. But I hope you will consider taking steps to increase your customer base. I know it's tough when you have to choose between taking care of your customers and taking care of your sales. If you would like some suggestions on people to contact, please let me know."

"I just might. I know it's time to take this seriously. I need to find a strategy that will work." •

What advice would you give to Jan Staple? *We asked five experts in the field to offer advice and suggestions.*

Grow by Thinking Small: Not Everyone is a Prospect

Kenneth J. Cook

Author of The AMA Complete Guide to Small Business Marketing *and* The AMA Complete Guide to Small Business Strategic Planning, Mr. *Cook is president of General Business Consultants, Inc., Greenville, South Carolina.*

Dear Jan:

Thanks so much for the jar of honey you sent. It was nice to hear from you, and to know that—despite the problem you mentioned—things are going well.

You are right to observe that having only two customers contribute 70 percent of your sales volume puts you in a vulnerable position. I commend your foresight in recognizing that you need to expand your customer base. If you do not, you may be, as you said, "sunk." To address this issue, I am going to give you one primary piece of advice that on the surface may seem a little strange. That advice is: think small in order to grow.

Let's recap your current situation:

- Seventy percent of your sales volume comes from two customers.
- Customer #1 is a bakery that requires a very high quality honey.
- Customer #2 is a manufacturer who uses you to supplement their primary supplier.
- Your company is doing $1.7 million in sales with only four employees.
- Your arrangements with suppliers allow you to deliver a consistent, high quality product while keeping labor costs down.
- You and your competitors are extremely price sensitive and vulnerable since the discontinuation of government price support programs.
- This volatility reduces customers' buying decisions to one primary factor—price. To gain a competitive advantage, you are forced to search for some other factor upon which to differentiate your product and service.

I conclude from these factors that your position with your two key customers is good, not great (because you are vulnerable to competitors' price cuts). Your sales levels are solid and increasing. You and your competitors are searching for ways to differentiate yourselves (which also means opportunities abound). Your product meets customer requirements, and offers you some potential competitive advantages. Time and resources are scant, yet you need to leverage what you have in order to grow.

So back to thinking small to grow. Let's take advantage of the opportunities in your current situation, and create some focus for your efforts. Rather than attempting to go after all types of new customers (such as grocery stores), focus your efforts on the type of client you've already had success with. The fact that you are succeeding means that you already have competitive advantages. Identify what those advantages are, and find prospects who will understand and appreciate them.

Specifically, I would like to see you do the following:

Determine why your two key customers do business with you. Visit them and spend some time with them. Ask them what it is about you, your company, your products, your services, etc. that motivates them to continue to give you orders. Here are some key questions to ask:

- What is critical for me to do in order for us to continue to work together?
- If I am able to meet or exceed all of your expectations, how do you and your company benefit?
- If you could change anything about our relationship, what would it be?

Remember, you are looking for the "why" behind your business relationship. If you can find out why it works, you can turn that "why" into competitive advantages with other customers.

Identify key factors that differentiate you from competitors. Look for some aspect of your company and/or offerings that uniquely satisfies the customer's needs. That uniqueness motivates the client to select you over a competitor. Consider your bakery chain. Your differentiation with them might be the consistency of your honey. Your supplier relationships allow you to deliver that and overcome an apparent industry-wide problem. Because your honey is of a high quality and is consistent, you provide a unique solution that delivers value to the bakery chain.

If you can identify differentiators, some very powerful tools fall into place for you. First, you have a competitive advantage to which the client assigns value. Second, that unique value allows you to shift the focus in the customer's mind from strictly price to some other important factor. You extricate yourself from your industry's price war, and reduce your vulnerability to price cuts because customers perceive a value in the relationship other than just price.

Focus your efforts on the type of client you've already had success with.

Jan, if I remember correctly, you are a very visual person. To help explain what I am talking about, please look at this diagram.

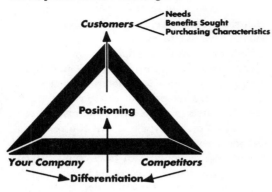

Three variables will impact your marketing and sales success: the customer, your company, and the competition. Your goal is to satisfy customers' needs profitably. Your marketing goal is to identify something you offer that satisfies those needs in a unique manner, and differentiates you from the competition.

Leverage your knowledge. You leverage it by looking for other companies where you could meet similar sets of needs. You will find those sets of needs in similar type companies. In marketing terms, I am suggesting you identify some target markets to pursue. On the surface, I would say you have two target markets—bakery chains and manufacturers of bakery items.

With those target markets in mind, go to the library and spend 15 minutes with the reference librarian. Tell him or her that you are trying to research names of companies that are in these two markets. The number of sources available for uncovering prospects will surprise you. I won't bore you with a long list, but some examples are: the *Yellow Pages*, *Chamber of Commerce Directories*, *Gale Research Co.'s Business Rankings*, *Ward's Business Directory of U.S. Companies*, and *Dun's Directories*.

Go make some sales calls. Now that you know the target markets and the prospects you want to go after, and you know what you want to emphasize with them (your success factors and point of differentiation), you have one more thing to do: sell your product.

I don't want to review Sales 101 with you. However, I do want to say this: don't go in selling. Go in asking. Find out about the prospect's business. Confirm that the needs you believe exist actually *do* exist. Confirm that the prospect is willing to consider you and is in a position to buy. After you think you know enough, then sell your solutions. And that is what your differentiation

You must focus your efforts and think on a smaller scale. Not everyone is a prospect.

factor is, a *solution*. It is a satisfaction of a need that only you can uniquely provide to the customer.

To help with your selling efforts (e.g., to make sure you put your selling hat on), schedule a half-day appointment with yourself once a week. Treat that half-day as if it is your best customer, one who requires your undivided attention. Avoid interruptions and sell. If you do, you will improve the likelihood of finding a new best customer to supplement your bakery chain or bread manufacturer.

Jan, if you follow these four steps, I am sure you will reduce your marketplace vulnerability and increase your customer base. This approach is sometimes difficult because you must focus your efforts and think on a smaller scale. Not everyone is a prospect. If you act as if they are, you will end up wasting your time and resources, with limited results.

But by thinking smaller—in terms of one or two target markets to pursue—you will get a greater return on your efforts. All you want at this point is one or two target markets where you can establish a leadership position. That leadership will be determined by the strength of your differentiation. If you can do this, your reputation in that target market grows. Market share grows, revenues grow, and profits grow. Vulnerability decreases. Relying on a small number of key customers disappears.

I hope these suggestions help. Don't forget that you have a lot of things working in your favor. You just need to find a way to take all of those positives and share them with some carefully-selected new customers. I wish you well, and look forward to our next conversation.

Sincerely,

Kenneth J. Cook

Kenneth J. Cook

Learn More About Personal Selling Techniques

Mark Stover, MBA

Mr. Stover is the director of the Small Business Development Center at the University of Wisconsin-Stevens Point, where he works with many small-business owners in a variety of industries.

Dear Jan:

It was a pleasure meeting you the other day and learning about your honey distribution business. I was impressed with the efficiency of your operation. Thanks also for the honey samples. They were delicious. I can *taste* how you have earned your reputation for quality.

And like the lay art critic who "knows what he likes when he sees it" I know what I like when I *taste* it. Your honey has outstanding flavor and color ... the best I've ever had. In this environment of market shifts, I strongly recommend that you play to your strengths. Yours is a very high, perhaps *uniquely high-quality* product. Your current customers recognize that.

Basically, you have two jobs: learn how to emphasize your strengths, and learn more about personal selling techniques.

Take this opportunity to educate other potential customers about why your product has this exceptional quality. Talk about your experience in the industry, provide some insights into how you put this exceptional blend together, and have the university help you with some chemical analysis of the constituent plant sources. (I gave you the number of the Food Science Department on campus in our meeting.) In other words, talk to your customers and potential customers about quality. Be prepared to answer their technical questions. And make sure you have samples along for them to taste.

Gathering the technical data is something on which I know you already have a good handle. However, if you should find you need additional assistance with locating sources of information, our SBDC will be happy to help. It should be easy for you to talk with people about how wonderful your product is. After all, you went into business not because you wanted to manage a business, but because you wanted to sell honey. Most small-business people start a business because they believe in the product, not because they want to practice marketing or accounting.

Starting a business simply because you believe in a product—even an outstanding product like your honey—is not enough, though. If you want the business to survive you are going to have to acquire the ability to successfully and aggressively take the message of your high quality product to the market.

It is possible for you to hire someone (a marketing manager, perhaps) to do this for you. However, you strike me as the kind of person who is going to want to do things for herself. So I encourage you to learn as much about marketing a product as you possibly can. Take the time

to do this. Look at your time as an investment in the growth of the business that makes your exceptional honey available to others.

Please note, by the way, that marketing is not just sales and promotions. Marketing is the art of knowing what your customers value better than your competition does. Marketing with a capital "M" involves investigation into the way customers think and behave in the buying process. It involves knowing who your competitors are and what opportunities or threats their offerings present to you. Marketing does include sales and promotions, but those considerations are just part of a larger management outlook of focussing first on customers.

In general, I think most small-business owners could stand more rigor in the way that they approach the market. Most small businesses operate without any marketing plan except for the gut instincts of a hopefully savvy owner. While a reactive approach to marketing may be fine in the short run, it is almost always a recipe for disaster in the long run. It is clear to me from our conversation that you recognize the need and value for a marketing plan in your business, especially under the conditions of growth and change you are currently experiencing in your market.

Our SBDC has an excellent series of courses on marketing management scheduled to begin at the end of this month. I have enclosed a brochure on that series for your convenience. Please call our office to register for the series, or give me a call if you have any questions on the courses described. Attending this series of courses will give you that introduction to the broad marketing principles you asked about.

While these courses will address your need for some basic marketing information, I think you may still feel you haven't gotten the results you're after unless you do something else. That is, you need to assess your personal selling skills. Be honest in this assessment, too. Do you enjoy the negotiation and give-and-take in a sales presentation? Do you enjoy getting someone else to say yes? If you answer no to these questions, that is probably normal. As I noted before, most small-business owners don't start a business as an excuse to get to practice sales techniques. Nonetheless, I think learning more about the power of personal selling is going to be critical for you and the future of your business.

The reason I think this is because it was also clear to me in our meeting that you can find a hundred other things to do before you would bring yourself to put your product (which obviously means so much to you) on the line for

Marketing is the art of knowing what your customers value.

Learning more about the power of personal selling is going to be critical for you and the future of your business.

rejection. You mentioned that you felt you need to spend all your time keeping your current customers satisfied. But let's face it, with only two major customers you must have *some* time available to spend on finding new customers. So it's not time; it's fear.

Sales is a tough job because you have to be able to deal with rejection regularly. I suspect that it may be difficult for you to get up the nerve to put your product out there because you are afraid of the rejection. Jan, that is perfectly normal. Deal with the fear by recognizing that you have something of exceptional value to offer your customers and their customers. Those people won't get to experience the ambrosia you bottle unless you make the effort to sell it.

Successful personal selling begins by qualifying potential customers. In other words, you want to find people who appear to be interested in buying your product before you go to see them. You will discover some of these kinds of people as a result of the general market research you do. Others may be discovered by word-of-mouth referrals. That is another reason why it would be a good idea for you to visit your current, satisfied customers as part of your market research effort.

When you talk with the potential buyers, go to them with questions rather than with a "buy or be damned" attitude. Ask them what they are currently getting from their suppliers. Ask if they are completely satisfied. Ask what they would *like* to have from a supplier if they could have anything they wanted. Be prepared to address their questions and objections about your product. Are you going to be able to do this flawlessly the first time? Probably not. Like anything else, sales skills take practice to hone.

Don't worry too much about making mistakes. You have an ace-in-the-hole in that you're the owner and not a professional salesperson. That gives you a built-in credibility that no salesperson you might hire is *ever* going to duplicate. Again, you could hire someone to do this for you, but I don't think you're that kind of owner. Besides, there will always be plenty of room for another person on the payroll after you build the customer base.

Remember one other very important thing as you practice your personal selling techniques. Remember to ask your potential customer for the sale. It is very easy to leave that out of your presentation. After all, you may reason, you've answered all the objections, you've explained the benefits of the product to the buyer, they've even sampled the product and fallen in love. Surely they will ask where to sign. But that is not how most people operate. You need to ask

them. And you can ask in a direct but inoffensive way, like: "How many cases per week shall we schedule?" That would work nicely. Ask them to say yes.

Jan, I recognize that this is probably a lot to digest at once. Consider what I have suggested. Review the enclosed bibliography of books on personal selling and pick up a book or two at your library. I'll call you in about a week to see what you think and schedule another meeting with you. Learning to manage a business may not feel like as much fun as learning to blend honey, but it is likely to make a big difference in your ability to keep making this marvelous concoction. I look forward to playing a small role in making that happen.

Sincerely,

Mark Stover

Mark Stover

Take Four Steps to Develop a Marketing Strategy
Paul Dunn, Ph.D.

Co-author of Market Analysis: Assessing Your Business Opportunities, *Dr. Dunn is dean of the College of Business Administration and Distinguished Professor of Small Business and Entrepreneurship at Northeast Louisiana University, Monroe and director of the Small Business Development Center.*

Dear Jan:

It was nice to talk with you by phone the other day. It had been some time since we last talked. Your honey distributing company seems to be doing reasonably well, but you do have two sets of key issues to attend to as soon as possible.

The first set consists of short-term, tactical issues related to expanding your current customer base. The second consists of longer-term, strategic issues related to what markets your firm will be serving in three to five years.

Before I get into these, however, let me restate the information you provided in a slightly different way, and add some. Your industry seems to be doing well. You indicated in your fax that you were concerned about the discontinuation of government support prices. Your fax also states that the market price was above the support price and that you are importing Chinese honey. This information indicates that the market for honey is reasonably strong. Also, you are presently selling in only one part of the honey market.

Another good indication, from your point of view, is that the market for both bread and bakery goods has been rising. *The U.S. Industrial Outlook '93* shows that the demand for bakery goods and bread products has increased four or five percent per year since 1989. You may be underestimating the total demand for honey. You should look into the total market for honey in your industry's publications to get a thorough understanding of the current markets and the trends in each market segment.

My first concern is your heavy dependence on two major customers. As a small-business owner, you do have a lot of hats to wear, but sales and marketing are essential in a business such as yours. According to Dun and Bradstreet figures, approximately half of all business failures are due to inadequate sales.

You must either attend to sales and marketing yourself, or get someone to do it for you. Insuring that current customers are satisfied is important, but that would not seem to be a big task since there are so few customers. You may be using this as an excuse to avoid the sales and marketing aspects of your business. Many small-business owners enjoy one aspect of their business more than another, but neglecting other critical areas can lead to failure.

Your first task is to decide what your short-run program will be and who will do the job. Since you are familiar with your current customers, developing a sales plan for yourself should not be too difficult. You just have to be willing to invest the time and effort required to do it.

You are right in being concerned about losing one bid, but you say that you missed an opportunity to increase your customer base because the margin was too low. Did you negotiate—or just bow out—when the customer indicated what he or she wanted to pay? You should be aggressive in your sales efforts and in negotiations. That additional customer would have provided more stability in your current market.

Additional sales in existing markets often do not add to overhead. Consequently, they add more to profits per unit of sale. Did you calculate your total profits with this potential new customer's sales and cost of sales included before you made your decision? You might want to go back and reconsider that decision. Here is a general rule I use in making decisions of this sort: If a particular sale will cover its costs and contribute to overhead and I have no other opportunities for my time, effort, and resources, I make the sale.

It is usually less expensive to expand in existing markets (market penetration) than to pursue different types of markets (market development). Market penetration means you should attempt to sell to other bakeries and bread manufacturers. This is basically a sales job. Have you developed a sales strategy for your firm? For example, how do you identify prospects?

In industrial marketing of the type you are doing, you can develop a prospect list from your state's directory of manufacturers. Every state that I know of has a manufacturers' directory. In the current *Louisiana Directory of Manufacturers*, 29 bakeries are listed. In addition, many business directories are published for each state. You can use these to find prospects for your business. Do not ignore customers in nearby states. Most university, business school, or Small Business Development Center libraries have one or more of these directories. Check these possibilities out.

Once you have compiled your list, begin calling these prospects to determine their needs for honey. A quick telephone survey of these potential customers will help you assign priorities to them. Most colleges and universities have Small Business Institute programs that can take on this marketing research project in a class for you. Once you have the information, assign priorities on a profitability basis, not a sales basis, to each potential customer. Do not pass up a small bakery close by just to call on a larger distant bakery based on sales volume alone.

Once you have established your priorities, begin calling on these prospects. You seem hesitant to pursue sales aggressively. If you cannot or will not do the job, you need to seriously consider investing in a sales person. Good sales people often work on a commission and can be depended on to pay their own way.

The second, longer-term, set of issues will need your immediate attention too. A strategic plan will give stability and profits for your honey distributorship over the long run. You need to develop a marketing strategy for your business now.

Your first task is to decide what your short-run program will be and who will do the job.

Marketing strategy development involves four steps: (1) Determine long-term objectives, (2) Do a SWOT (strengths, weaknesses, opportunities, and threats) analysis, (3) Identify potential target markets, and (4) Develop marketing mixes to meet the needs of each of the markets identified.

1. Determine long-term objectives. You should consider whether you want to grow or get to some profitable level and remain stable there. Do you want to focus on one or a few activities, or become more diversified, i.e., branch into other syrups or flavors? What do you want the firm to become and provide for you and your family?

2. Do a SWOT analysis. A SWOT analysis involves a hard look at yourself and your operation. You know a great deal about honey and are learning (and can learn more) about the honey business. Other questions you need to address are: Are you committed to what you are doing? Are you willing to do the work required to become better informed about your potential markets? Are you willing to sacrifice short-term satisfaction for long-term satisfaction? Are the people around you as committed as you are? Are you using them to their full potential and allowing them to be a part of the firm? Is your family committed to what you are doing? Look at all your firm's strengths.

Weaknesses are sometimes harder to assess in a small firm because you have to be critical of yourself. For example, you do not seem to be as aggressive as you will need to be if your firm is to survive. You seem unwilling to do the quantitative analysis on information available or to seek the additional information you need to make a reasonable decision. You took the initiative to begin importing honey from China—I believe you have what it takes to develop a marketing strategy for your business.

Opportunities are unknown at the present, except that you missed a customer last year and that the market for honey seems at least stable and may be growing. A thorough analysis of potential markets will reveal opportunities. In developing your plan, you need to think about how big you want to get. The old saying, "If you do not grow, you fail," has killed off many otherwise smart small-business owners. You do not have to do that to yourself.

Current threats are limited to your dependence on too few customers and your hesitance to step out and pursue other business opportunities. If you begin to market your business effectively, I think the other threat will be neutralized as well.

3. Identify target markets. There are many target markets for your honey, including other customers in your current industrial market, the resellers market (wholesale and retail), government markets (local, state, and federal entities), and institutional markets (universities, hospitals and other nonprofit entities outside government).

When you do a target market analysis, you must avoid ruling out possibilities based on your current operation. Remember, you are searching for business which may require you to adjust current operations.

Since you are already in the industrial market, it would make sense for you to pursue other quantity purchasers first. That includes other companies that use honey in large quantities. Cereal companies come to mind immediately. Other food processing companies probably use honey as a sweetening and flavoring agent. Look through the *Thomas Food Industry Register*—there are probably many possibilities you have not even considered. For example, barbecue sauce manufacturers often use syrup in their sauces.

4. Develop market mixes. Marketing outside your traditional market will require you to rethink your current operation and re-orient your thinking to these new opportunities. Purveying your honey products to government agencies, institutions, retailers, and wholesalers offers many opportunities for market development. You will need to develop marketing mixes (the combination of product, location, promotion, and pricing to meet each market) to suit each market.

These new markets will require that you sell in smaller quantities, but the technology is well-known and can be acquired over time. You need to look at the profit potential of each market possibility. In retailing, for example, you could start by developing private labels for retailers and wholesalers without having to spend the money to market your products directly to the final consumer. Once you have established those channels, movement into your own brands becomes much easier because retailers and wholesalers know your product. These markets require increased effort to develop outlets, and new and different approaches to promotion. But they offer you the opportunity to develop a customer franchise that allows for higher prices and profits over the long haul.

Government and institutions are likely to purchase honey in much the same way. They will want portion control packaging and large quantities—and you will sell on a bid basis. This is often a good market in which to expand sales

Since you are already in the industrial market, it would make sense for you to pursue other quantity purchasers first.

and profits once you have reached break-even in the retail and wholesale markets.

As you can see, Jan, there are many opportunities available, if you want to pursue them. I encourage you to think about what you want to do, put your thoughts on paper, and give me a call when you want to talk more.

Good luck on both your short-term and long-term efforts to develop your business.

Sincerely,

Paul Dunn

Paul Dunn

Understand What Customers are Looking For

Alfred L. Whiteman

Mr. Whiteman is a partner in the accounting and consulting firm Walpert, Smullian & Blumenthal, P.A. based in Towson, Maryland. He is a recognized expert in wholesale distribution, a specialty of WS&B.

Dear Jan:

I have given a great deal of thought about our conversation yesterday. Tim Veering's advice to you was correct; unless you develop a strategy to respond to changing market conditions, you will not be able to preserve, much less grow, the business you have nurtured for the last 14 years. His suggestion that I help you increase your customer base is a result of our long-term working relationship. Over the last several years, Tim has referred me to similar clients and we have worked together to help them strengthen their business operations and re-evaluate their marketing strategies.

My firm specializes in working with distributors. I know that your industry is in a very difficult period right now. It may be helpful to put the current situation in historical context.

After World War II, wholesale distribution began to thrive as an industry in the United States. While American manufacturers were leading producers, there needed to be a vehicle to get products to market efficiently—to group representation of complementary product lines manufactured by different companies to retail outlets and commercial users.

The wholesaler-distributor industry experienced continuous growth from the 1950s to the 1980s as demand exceeded supply and the right distribution franchise generated handsome profits.

In the late 1980s, three factors reduced the need for the growing distribution industry. Demographic changes reduced the expanding "demand pie." The demands of an international economy forced manufacturers to take their products to market through the most efficient distribution channels. An increasingly more powerful customer base forced prices to fall as distributors (and powerful distributor/retailers) competed for fewer customers.

The net effect on the wholesale distribution industry was a 15 to 20 percent consolidation/reduction of companies. The current survivors are faced with shrinking profit margins and customer demands for more services. The future survivors will have to be successful at meeting changing customer needs, emulating the industry's best practices, enhancing operational efficiency, acquiring new technology and implementing total quality distribution.

I appreciated your candor in describing your current position. The following comments should help you focus your thoughts for our planning meeting next week. Philosophically, you need to view the glass as "half full." You've been running a business successfully and profitably for several years. We'll be able to draw on your knowledge of the industry and its product lines from two vantage points: expanding the list of potential customers for your products and exploring additional and complementary product lines that will add value to customer relationships.

You have a close personal and professional working relationship with your banker, Tim Veering. His bank is a strong source of potential capital for the future. Your frank discussion about your concerns for the coming year was an important first step in keeping him informed about improvements you will make in company operations and any remedial actions you take to solve your current problems. This information will be the key to Tim's bank's ability to continue to invest in your company.

Although you fear price competition, you believe your customer base is currently loyal. We'll need to look closely at your current

I know that your industry is in a very difficult period right now.

customer relationships and assess your strengths and weaknesses from their perspectives.

Over the years, I have found that executives sit in their offices and develop programs/services for their customers without ever checking with them to see if the programs/services are valuable to them. How do they know what their customers want unless they ask them? Often, these programs/services developed in a vacuum are costly and ineffective.

Distributors must talk continually to their customers to understand the changing needs from the customers' perspective. The feedback process can be formal or informal.

For example: I work with a very successful flooring distributor who makes a point of formally surveying customers and tailoring programs specifically to customer needs. The distributor looks at various factors:

- Are product lines broad enough to meet customers' needs?
- Are sales reps helpful and knowledgeable?
- Are displays maintained to customer standards?
- Are any delivery schedules disruptive to the customers' business?

They treat every customer as a "niche of one" and ask two very powerful questions: How can we help you? and How are we doing?

You face the challenges of finding new customers and competing with price-cutters. You also face the threat of losing a major customer. In essence, you will continue to be at risk if you remain a non-value added supplier of a commodity product.

I'd like to take a moment to discuss the terms "value added" and "non-value added." They refer to the important advantages that you may have over your competitors.

All businesses try to develop a strategy to gain a competitive advantage and differentiate themselves from their competitors. The basic service a wholesaler-distributor provides is credit, product and delivery. This basic level of service does not create a competitive advantage.

Value added services structured around customer needs are a competitive advantage. Examples of value added services are: computer-to-computer ordering, product training, automatic re-ordering, delivery frequency/speed and technical support.

We need to develop a business plan that first assures that you have competent people focused on measuring and increasing customer satisfaction levels of your current products and services. Then, depending on the level of change your

organization can successfully handle, you need to expand your current customer mix to reduce your business's dependence on your two largest customers.

I know you believe this is not the time to hire a high-level employee. But, from my experience, this is *just* the time to invest in a management level individual who can free up your time at this critical stage.

You must determine where your time is best spent. If you have the rare skills to develop new customers, you must find the best individual to run your internal operations, making sure your current customers are serviced well. If internal operations is your best and highest time use, you must hire a sales and marketing expert who can both help you promote your product and expand your market. A strong sales and marketing professional won't be cheap, but you can put together a base and incentive program that will limit your risk and be highly attractive to a good salesperson.

At our first strategic meeting, we'll spend the time exploring the following issues:

- Where is the company now?
- Where does the company want to be in the future?
- How are you going to get there?
- What resources are required to get there?
- What are the risks?

Your business plan should contain the elements listed on the enclosure.

Your suppliers will be critical in the success of your new business plan. They must be made aware that you are considering an aggressive growth campaign and that, with their support in the early stages, they can expect that your purchases will increase substantially. This negotiation must be handled carefully and should include discussion of:

- Volume discounts,
- Special dating terms,
- On-time delivery,
- Consistency in the quality of their products,
- Promotional materials, and
- Marketing assistance dollars.

Understanding the level of supplier support will better help us when we determine your point of entry into the market.

We will conduct a customer survey to determine why your customers are presently using your company, why potential customers are not, and what your customers and potential customers think of your competition. We'll ask what they perceive as your strengths and

> *Distributors must talk continually to their customers to understand the changing needs from the customers' perspective.*

weaknesses and what services they would like to receive that they are not currently receiving. Combining this information with supplier support, we will be in a position to develop a focused plan to strengthen the company.

Your marketing strategy will be a two-pronged approach: solidifying your relationship with your two large customers and expanding your customer base. If your current customers are happy with your pricing, the quality of your products and the level of service they receive, they may want to form a strategic partnering relationship with you where they will guarantee a certain volume of business if you maintain specific price, quality and timeliness factors. Most large companies are looking to work with a few suppliers they can depend on in order to lower their operating costs. Adding complementary high quality products to your company may provide an opportunity to broaden your distribution base and enhance your relationship with these high-end users.

The second prong of the marketing attack will be to first identify prospective customers who meet as closely as possible the profile of your existing customers. Ideally, you want to make the least modification to your present operating format and increase profits by either charging a premium for additional value added services or by eliminating services that add no value.

Our overall purpose should be to develop a strategy to link your suppliers, your company and your customers into a highly efficient/high quality/cost competitive distribution channel. Ultimately, you will have to increase your ability to handle larger orders from existing and future customers. Without the ability to handle higher volumes, you may be squeezed out during a supplier consolidation.

Finally, we will explore the possibilities that might elevate your product from commodity status. These include value added processing, repackaging of products that use honey as their primary ingredient, and developing a "honey-rich" product. While you don't want to compete on price with local beekeepers, grocery stores or gourmet specialty shops may be interested in a value added product targeted to high-end customers.

In summary, the plan will call for:

- Meeting with your banker and reviewing your plan in detail. The purpose is to get a financial commitment to help fund manageable growth.
- Considering a strategic hire.
- Having sales people call on existing and prospective customers.
- Meeting with your suppliers on a regular basis to cement your role as a strategic partner.

- Meeting with your large customers on a regular basis to cement your role as a strategic partner.
- Negotiating new product lines to sell to your existing customers.
- Assessing the quality of your services in terms of meeting your customers' needs.
- Monitoring your actual performance against your plan.
- And, writing yourself a big bonus check!

We have a lot of planning to do if you are to achieve the results you want. I believe today's economy will not tolerate the faint-hearted. You must take bold and decisive steps to ensure your company a secure place in the future. Our meeting next week is a good first step. I look forward to a long and productive relationship.

Sincerely,

Alfred Whiteman

Alfred L. Whiteman

We will conduct a customer survey to determine why your customers are presently using your company.

Consider Developing a Network of Regional Food Distributors

Rachel Sager, MBA

Ms. Sager is a honey packer/distributor in the southeast. She is the daughter of a beekeeper.

Dear Jan:

What a surprise to find out at our 20th class reunion that we are both packaging and selling honey! It was wonderful to share stories and experiences with another who has faced the same pressures and difficulties of the honey business.

I share your concerns about the future. The changes in the government honey program have heightened the uncertainty our industry is facing. In 1994, beekeepers were no longer able to receive a government subsidy of several cents per pound. Honey may still be placed under government loan for nine months, but the loan rate is now 50¢ per pound, as opposed to 53.7¢ per pound in 1994. I fear that many beekeepers will not be able to continue their operations.

Your Business Plan

1. A Mission Statement — Who are you? What does your company do?

2. An External Market Analysis:
   A. Customers
   • Who are your customers? What are their needs and wants?
   • How and where will you serve them?
   B. Competition
   • Who is your competition?
   • What are their strengths and weaknesses?
   • How does your company size up?

3. An Internal Analysis: the company's strengths and weaknesses and competitive position.

4. Objectives: determining the customers and market segment you will operate within.

5. The strategy: achieving your objectives.

6. A road map: implementing the strategy.

7. The Financial Plan.

8. Monitoring the Plan.

Buyers talk about the importance of product quality, record keeping, a clean plant, but the bottom line is truly price.

Since I buy honey from some of these beekeepers, I am worried about maintaining a high quality supply of honey. It is possible to replace this with either honey from other areas of the country or imported honey, but the flavor profile of the honey will not be the same. Just as you do, I market my products on consistency of color and flavor. I need these beekeepers to stay solvent so my supply does not fluctuate!

Another industry concern that is very much in your thoughts these days as you concentrate on maintaining your two key accounts, is the impetus in the food industry to drive costs down. I believe the poor economy of the early 1990s has had a negative impact on their profit margins. They see one way to improve these margins is to lower the costs of their incoming materials, such as our honey. Buyers talk about the importance of product quality, record keeping, a clean plant, operating under Good Manufacturing Practices and HACCP (Hazard Analysis of Critical Control Points), but the bottom line is truly *price*.

I share your concern that a competitor could come to one of your longstanding customers with a price a few cents below your price. The competitor's price might be so low it barely covers their fixed costs and you know there is no profit margin. What do you do? Match the price and lose money just to keep the customer, or do you walk from the business? Not any easy decision, but it's one we will be facing more often, I believe.

Usually when I attend regional beekeeping or honey packers' meetings, everyone is afraid to be too friendly with advice because in a sense we are all competitors. But since you and I are living more than 1,000 miles apart, and will never be trying to steal each other's customers, I thought I would give you a few ideas to think about regarding your current problem of over-reliance on two customers. One idea is from personal experience. The second is one I would love to implement if I had the necessary equipment (you have that equipment!).

Since my father started our honey packing business nearly 50 years ago, we have been through many challenges and several periods of "growing pains." They are similar in a sense to the dilemma in which you find yourself. We were faced with a situation nearly 25 years ago that drastically changed our method of selling honey, but has certainly strengthened our company and increased our sales over the years. I think this story might be helpful to you and offer a suggestion as to how you might be able to increase the size of your customer base and boost your sales volume.

Dad made this change when he realized the demands of running the business were having a negative impact on his ability to maintain regular contact with our customers and generate new business. At this time, some of our old customers were beginning to buy from other honey packers. Arranging deliveries, blending honey, and filling drums or pails monopolized all our time. We just took the purchase orders and filled them. No time was spent improving relationships with customers, initiating new honey product ideas, or looking for new business. We did not have the time for these activities.

What changed Dad's way of conducting business was a phone call from our largest customer, who politely explained that if we did not have the time to find someone to call on him on a regular basis, help his R&D department with new product formulations and keep him updated on the happenings in the honey industry, he had representatives from three other honey packers knocking on his door every week and would gladly give one of them a shot at the business. As you can imagine, Dad sat up and listened.

Dad had the same type of financial constraints you have, thus hiring a salesperson was out of the question. In addition, his love was running the plant. He did not want to leave the day-to-day operations to anyone else so that he could attend to sales. Fortunately, our largest customer had an excellent suggestion: Find a large bulk ingredient broker or food distributor to represent us to buyers such as himself. He explained that buyers meet with brokers and distributors every day. They are the sales force for many companies and they provide a valuable service to their principals. He even suggested four companies he found to be superior in their performance.

The more Dad thought about it, he realized that considering a broker and/or distributor was a good decision for his company. Within an hour, he had set up meetings with these companies to discuss future opportunities.

I suggest that you consider this type of sales management. I'll explain the differences between brokers and food distributors. Depending on your current accounts and your growth needs, one might be more suited for your business than the other. But please realize you can have both and they can work cooperatively.

Brokers typically work on a percentage of dollar sale basis. This percent varies, depending on the type of product being sold and is somewhat negotiable. Brokers typically represent a line of related products. For example, since you are supplying bakeries, you would be interested in a broker who represents the manufacturers of flour, yeast, wheat, high fructose corn syrup, raisins, and other baking related commodities. Large food manufacturing companies work with brokers on items they buy in large quantities. I would imagine the large bread manufacturer you supply deals with brokers. Contracts are typically written between buyer and seller to cover extended time periods. Brokers act as your intermediary during the negotiations. Remember, brokers do not purchase the product from you, they act as your selling agents, but do not take title of your product at any time.

Full service food distributors are also a cost-effective way to increase your number of customers and sales. A large distributor carries thousands of food items, and honey should be one of the items available for their many customers. A food distributor purchases your products (this is one of the differences between brokers and distributors) to be delivered to one of their warehouse facilities. Food distributors

tend to specialize on various market segments, such as bakery, restaurant food service, or ice cream vendors. Usually, distributors call on accounts that would not be able to meet the minimum deliveries required from the food manufacturer. Food distributors have a substantial number of sales persons calling directly on thousands of buyers, some of whom are probably buying honey from other sources. These salespersons can introduce your company and encourage the buyer to give your honey a try, plus they can focus attention on honey and encourage new honey products.

The reason I suggest considering brokers and/or distributors is they have their own sales force that is already calling on the honey customer. You do not need to be bothered with sales calls, for which you stated you do not have the time. They have established a relationship with your potential customers, plus they know where to find the honey customers. The distributors handle the deliveries to each account; you only need to deliver to their main warehouse. Plus, there are no upfront costs associated with this means of selling.

It is essential that you carefully choose the company(ies) that will be representing you to the customer. Your business's reputation will become synonymous with theirs in the customer's mind. Once you have interviewed the potential candidates, toured their facilities, met their sales force, and reviewed their credit ratings, the decision is yours to make. It might be possible to find a broker and a distributor that do not have overlapping customers, thus you will be able to widen your distribution.

Once you have chosen your representatives, training is imperative for all persons who will be selling or handling your product. You must take the time to educate the sales force about honey—its functional characteristics, its shelf life, the differences in flavors, why bakers should use this value added ingredient in their products, and how to convey the consumer's image of honey as a wholesome product to the baker or restaurant owner. Become a resource for the sales force and your potential customers. Provide formulations and technical information to their bakers and cooks. New ideas and applications are always welcome. Very few products sell themselves anymore. You have to become honey's greatest promoter.

My second suggestion is to encourage business in the more profitable retail sector, but not via the large grocery store chains that demand slotting fees, free goods and heavy promotion schedules. Look to different markets, the farm stands, the roadside markets and the small

Full service food distributors are also a cost-effective way to increase your number of customers and sales.

privately owned grocery stores. This is an avenue that I am interested in, but lack the bottling equipment to make an effort at the present time.

The margins are much healthier in the retail segment of the market than the industrial segment. Bottling and labeling honey is more labor intensive than bulk sales, but I believe that you can make a reasonable profit by targeting locations that would value your quality product and pay a premium for it. Customers rarely stop at a farmer's stand for the cheapest corn or watermelon. They buy at a particular location because they believe the products are fresher, more tasty and locally grown. The same can hold true for your honey.

Design an attractive label that boasts local appeal. Use local honey and proudly make mention of this on your label. Does the state's Department of Agriculture offer special stickers to apply to in-state products? If so, these would add to your product's local appeal.

Investigate the honey offerings at farm stands and roadside markets prior to designing your labels or setting prices. Note the types of honey offered, the quality of these products and their prices. Price your products accordingly—you do *not* have to be the cheapest. If your product looks like quality, people will pay for quality.

I hope these suggestions are helpful, Jan. I agree with you that expanding your business by adding several new customers would certainly ease your feelings of over-reliance on two major customers. Please do not hesitate to call if you would like to discuss an idea. If you ever vacation in the vicinity of my operation, please call. I would love to give you a tour. Best wishes as you decide how to overcome this situation.

Yours truly,

Rachel Sager

Rachel Sager

The margins are much healthier in the retail segment of the market than the industrial segment.

Chapter 4

"How Ethical Can I Afford to Be?"

Catherine Stover

David McLimans

I t was a disappointingly damp spring afternoon. Instead of lifting, the fog was getting heavier. It was beginning to look like the kind of fog that Hollywood uses in scenes when bad news is at hand.

And bad news was at hand—but this was the outskirts of Des Moines, Iowa, not Hollywood—and it was happening to Steve Johnson, founder and owner of Johnson Utility Trailer, Inc. Here he was, on a Sunday afternoon, at his son's fifteenth birthday party, sitting in his avocado kitchen with his parents, his wife and his son. And he was looking at his worn-out corduroys, his wife's grey sweat suit, the cake

and melting ice cream, wondering how he should break the news.

After his son opened the last present—a pair of tennis shoes that cost *how* much?—and left to join his friends, Steve knew that if he were a character in a B-movie, he would be able to hear the drum roll in the background. He said, "This is a bad time to talk shop, but there probably isn't going to be a better time to tell you about what happened last week."

Martha, his wife, stiffened and sat up perfectly straight. "I'm glad you're going to tell us. You've been pretty grouchy lately, and I knew there was something wrong."

Catherine Stover is the editor of the Small Business Forum.

65

What if it breaks while it's being pulled uphill? It could slam into the next car and kill someone.

Steve looked down at his coffee cup. "Last Wednesday, one of the trailers that we made in '90 came in for maintenance. One of the guys told me that the joint between the tongue and the trailer looked weak. He was right. It *was* weak."

The word *weak* settled into the quiet of the kitchen for several moments. Then Lars, Steve's father, asked, "But didn't you start using bigger bolts there a few years ago?"

"In '91, we started using three-eighths-inch bolts instead of quarter-inch bolts. We should have put them in from the start. It was stupid not to. I can't even remember why we didn't. They cost almost nothing more."

"But those first bolts met all the specs, didn't they?" Lars asked.

"Of course they did. Don't you remember the week I spent reading six volumes of SAE standards? I almost went blind. Before I hired anybody, I made sure everything met every standard."

Steve's mother, Barbara, said, "Let me see if I understand what you men are talking about. The joint between the trailer and the tongue is wearing out in one of your older models and you could have prevented it by using a bigger bolt, but you didn't. But everything wears out. What's the big deal? You have always been such a worrier, Stevie."

"What if it breaks while it's being pulled uphill? It could slam into the next car and kill someone. That's a big deal."

"But honey, don't you have safety chains?"

"The safety chains go in *front* of the joint, Mom. They keep the coupler from breaking off the hitch, but they don't keep the tongue from breaking off the trailer."

Steve stood up, walked over to the kitchen window and looked toward his shop. It was a big grey building that always shimmered in Steve's dreams. "How could I live with that?" He turned back toward the table. "One law suit could shut this place down."

"Would it be our fault?" Martha asked.

"We say in three different places that the trailer's limit is 1,000 pounds. I'm sure the joint would be okay if everyone did that. The reason we started using bigger bolts in '91 was because we saw that people were rough with the trailers or were overloading like idiots. You wouldn't believe what people would put in trailers. And they drive like they're in the Indy 500."

Martha asked, "The trailer that you saw last Wednesday—had it been overloaded or something?"

"I told the owner that I thought his trailer looked heavily used. He said that he drives over railroad tracks twice every day on his route. He looks like the kind of guy who wouldn't slow down. This trailer wasn't designed to hit railroad tracks at 60 miles per hour twice every day."

"So is it ready to fall apart?" Martha asked. Martha always spoke quickly, and today it annoyed Steve.

"He has a good maintenance record. But when anyone brings a trailer in, we always check the components."

"Components?" Barbara asked.

"The chain, the coupler, and the joint between the tongue and the trailer. All high stress points."

"Are the other two components okay?" Martha asked.

"They're fine. The chains are tested to break at three times their rating. The coupler is at two times. Now the joint is at two, but it wasn't before."

Barbara said, "So the joint wasn't as strong as the rest. It was the weakest part."

"Right. And it didn't have to be stronger to meet the standards. It just made sense to upgrade it after I saw that people didn't take the 1,000 pound limit seriously. It never said anywhere in the standards that all the components have to be equally upgraded. It just made sense to me to strengthen the weakest one."

"You have insurance, don't you?" Lars asked.

"Of course I do. But I never told the insurance company that in 1991 I decided to improve the joint. What if they say, 'You used to make inferior trailers so we won't cover those.' What if they say, 'Your old trailers are not safe and it's your own damn fault'?"

Steve's father cleared his throat. "Everyone makes mistakes. In the 30 years that I ran my business, I learned a lot along the way by making my fair share of mistakes. Lay all your cards on the table and we'll look at your options. First of all, has anyone ever filed a complaint?"

"No."

"Anyone ever bring the joint in for repairs?"

"No. We spotted this one by ourselves."

"You don't think this will happen to the trailers you made since you started using the bigger bolt in '91?"

"I'm confident it won't."

"You opened in '90, right? How many trailers did you make before you improved the joint?"

"I looked it up. We made the change on November 13th, and we had manufactured 916 trailers before that."

"Do you have all those addresses?"

Johnson Utility Trailer, Inc.[1] Comparative Profit and Loss Statements
For the years ended December 31

	1990[2]	1991	1992	1993	1994
NET BILLINGS	$116,230	$289,097	$458,903	$609,733	$681,283
COST OF GOODS					
Beg. finished goods inventory	-0-	$101,050	$133,710	$65,507	$29,597
Cost of goods mfg.	184,198	220,955	249,222	396,758	481,989
Goods available	$184,198	$322,005	$382,932	$462,265	$511,586
End. finished goods inventory	101,050	133,710	65,507	29,597	18,539
COST OF GOODS SOLD	$83,148	$188,295	$317,425	$432,668	$493,047
GROSS PROFIT	$33,082	$100,802	$141,478	$177,065	$188,236
OPERATING EXPENSES					
Selling	$16,871	$44,107	$60,178	$77,470	$98,844
Administrative	14,632	32,244	51,548	72,162	81,240
EBIT	$1,579	$24,451	$29,752	$27,433	$8,152
PROVISION FOR INC. TAX	$505	$7,717	$9,666	$9,362	$2,420
NET INCOME	$1,074	$16,734	$20,086	$18,071	$5,732

[1] A Sub-chapter S Corporation having filed articles of incorporation with the State of Iowa 1 March 1990.

[2] 1990 Figures are for 10 months.

"Yeah. But probably a third or a fourth of the trailers have been resold. And some of the people have moved. It won't be easy to track them down."

"Tracking them down probably won't be the worst part or the most expensive part," Lars said. "The worst part will be disrupting your business so you can make the repairs. And you have to decide if you will cover the owner's cost of bringing the trailer in."

"We can't afford to do that," Martha said quickly. "Remember, we have twelve people on our payroll. Cash is tight. And if the recession hits Iowa the way they say it's hitting the coasts, our cash flow is going to only get tighter."

Barbara said, "Martha, honey, I know this business means a lot to you too. Men tend to think their wives —"

"Let me tell you exactly what my position on this is," Martha said. "We have worked 12 hours a day, six days a week for five years so that we could have a profitable business to pass along to Zachary. We can't put all that in jeopardy just because some idiot *might* overload his trailer or *might* go 60 miles per hour over railroad tracks every day, and then *might* sue us because the tongue comes off! It would be his own fault! Besides, it would be just as likely to break in his own driveway as it would going up a hill in front of a station wagon full of kids."

You want to do the right thing? Then make sure you can stay in business and pay your employees and have something besides debt to pass along to your son.

Johnson Utility Trailer, Inc. Comparative Balance Sheets
As of December 31

	1990	1991	1992	1993	1994
ASSETS					
Current Assets					
Cash	$381	$4,261	$5,009	$3,617	$984
A/R, Net	$9,685	$24,091	$47,802	$58,432	$64,722
Inventories					
Finished goods	$101,050	$133,710	$65,507	$29,597	$18,539
Work in progress	8,328	14,228	14,786	13,253	14,709
Raw materials	10,631	7,609	8,885	12,601	15,761
Total Current	$130,075	$183,899	$141,989	$117,500	$114,715
Total Long Term/Fixed	$78,088	$85,941	$129,971	$160,638	$126,874
Total Assets	$208,163	$269,840	$271,960	$278,138	$293,486
LIABILITIES					
Current	$133,132	$183,172	$149,838	$115,735	$138,267
Long Term	63,957	58,860	74,228	96,438	83,522
Total Liabilities	$197,089	$242,032	$224,066	$212,173	$221,789
EQUITY					
Capital Stock	$10,000	$10,000	$10,000	$10,000	$10,000
Retained Earnings	1,074	17,808	37,894	55,965	61,697
Total Equity	$11,074	$27,808	$47,894	$65,965	$71,697
Total Liability & Equity	$208,163	$269,840	$271,960	$278,138	$293,486

You have no choice but to face this problem squarely and immediately.

"Honey, you might be absolutely right. It may be that nothing would ever go wrong. It also may be that if we send out letters that say 'Guess what? Your trailer might break' that we might be *increasing* our chances of getting sued. But we have to do the right thing."

"The right thing? You want to do the right thing?" Martha lowered her voice to a whisper. "Then make sure you can stay in business and pay your employees and have something besides debt to pass along to your son."

When she left the room, there was silence.

Finally, Lars said, "Steve, I'm sorry if I upset Mar—"

"Don't worry about it. She'll cool off. She's mad that I didn't go to her right away and talk with her alone about it first."

"Of course she is," Barbara said. "But she's also worried about Zack. She told me yesterday that she has a hard time justifying all the hours she has spent doing the books instead of keeping an eye on Zack. Sometimes teenagers— well, we can talk about that later."

Steve sat down and looked at his father. "Dad, what should I do?"

"If I were you, I'd have a very frank discussion with the best product liability attorney I could find. And I would meet with your insurance man and find out what your coverage is exactly. And I would also be prepared to make some tough management decisions. If you are having cash flow problems now, you better get your house in order. The only thing we know for sure is that tough times are ahead."

Barbara started cleaning the kitchen table. She stopped long enough to stand behind her son and rub his shoulders. Steve listened to her bracelets hit each other. "This always helps your father," she said. "It seems like the end of the world now, but I'm sure you'll do the right thing, Stevie. Life goes on. The important thing is to be able to live with yourself."

Steve looked at the empty Nike box next to Zack's plate. Why did Martha spend all that money on a pair of tennis shoes for Zack when she knew that things were tight? But this mess is not *her* fault, he told himself. *I'm* the one who has to decide if we can afford to solve this problem.

Or, if we can afford not to.

When his mother started clearing the table again, Steve stood up. He saw the lights on in the shop, and he went to talk with Martha.

What should Steve Johnson do? *A consumer advocate, an industry expert, an ethicist, a small-business owner, and an attorney provide a range of perspectives on Steve's predicament in the letters that follow. The experts were asked, "If Steve had consulted you, what advice would you offer?"*

Offer a Product the Customers Can Believe In

William Taylor

William Taylor wrote *The Big Boys: Power and Position in American Business* (Panthenon Books, 1986) with consumer advocate Ralph Nader. Currently, he is associate editor of *Harvard Business Review*.

Dear Steve:

Last week, I listened to you talk through all the thorny problems created by a quarter-inch-bolt: how to track down more than 900 customers (many of whom may have resold their trailers), whether disclosing the problem creates more legal liability than not disclosing it, and

how the company can afford to address the issue in the current economic climate. I felt like your situation was hopelessly complex.

And yet, the more I've considered things, the simpler the problem has become. This is not a case about product liability, insurance, or cash flow. It's not even a case about a mistake made four years ago. It is a case about *values*. What kind of company do you want Johnson Utility Trailer to be? What kind of business person do *you* want to be?

Let me change perspectives for a moment. I know how much you and Martha and Zack love water skiing. What if we weren't talking about a bolt on a trailer but a part in your outboard motor—a part that wasn't *likely* to break, especially if you treated the motor with the care and attention that the owner's manual spells out very clearly, but that *might* break if you continued to indulge in your daredevil tendencies? And if the bolt did break, it might make you lose control of the boat and create real danger for whomever was skiing.

Would you be very sympathetic to the outboard motor manufacturer as it debated how likely it was for a motor to break, as it complained about the daredevils who used their motors under less-than-ideal circumstances, and whose answer to tough economic times is to decide the problem is too expensive to fix? Would you find it possible to believe in that company again? Would you ever consider buying another motor from them?

You have no choice but to face this problem squarely and immediately. You must do whatever it takes to replace the small bolts with bigger bolts. You may run some financial risk as a result. But consider the risk if just one bolt breaks—even if you are legally insulated. Do you think future sales, no matter how sturdy the trailer, will be unaffected by a tragedy? More to the point, is this the kind of company you've worked 12 hours a day, six days a week, to build? Is this the kind of company you want to pass on to your son? Rather than agonize over whether to act, it's time to focus creative energies on how to solve this problem most effectively—and how to turn it into a plus for the organization.

Let's be straight about another point. Great products today—robust products is the term I prefer—aren't products that perform as promised when used under ideal conditions. Robust products perform as promised under *even the most abusive and difficult conditions*. If we've learned anything from the rise of Japan over the past decade, it's the awesome competitive power of reliability, durability, and quality. In your business, that means building and selling trailers

Did GE wait for lawsuits or blame the problem on customer misuse? No they voluntarily replaced more than a million compressor units.

that perform not just when driven 40 miles per hour over well-paved roads, but when driven 65 miles per hour over railroad tracks. That's what customers expect, that's what the market demands—and it's what you expect as well. Why else did you build in such excess strength in the chains and the coupler?

So what to do? I'm not an expert in insurance or product liability, and given the state of affairs in these things, it certainly makes sense to consult with an attorney or insurance expert for technical details. But those are background briefings. A company with values focuses on the substance of the issue and how best to serve its customers.

I propose two concrete steps:

Invite your employees to help solve the problem. Call a meeting of the entire company and announce that you have discovered this potential problem. Announce the creation of "Campaign Retrofit" and ask a small number of employees—one from sales, one from maintenance, one from manufacturing—to join you on a task force to develop creative solutions to the problem of locating the 916 trailers quickly and effectively. A small group of people can develop great ideas. And think about the effect on employee morale and commitment when everyone sees how seriously you take this issue.

Turn the retrofit process into a marketing opportunity. Your relationship with these customers is likely to become stronger rather than weaker. Let me cite a recent precedent from a much larger company. In 1992, General Electric discovered that it had committed a massive blunder in its new line of refrigerators. The compressor unit—the guts of the appliance— had a design flaw that meant the refrigerator might leak or stop working in certain situations. Did GE wait for lawsuits or blame the problem on customer misuse? No. It *voluntarily* replaced more than a million compressor units, sending repair technicians into homes across the country for service visits that could last up to 90 minutes or two hours—a program that required a charge-off of $450 million! Is GE worse off for fixing a problem before most customers knew it existed? Hardly. Not one lawsuit has been filed and GE's market share in refrigerators has increased over arch-rival Whirlpool.

As competition grows more intense in industry after industry, and as the companies that survive get closer and closer to each other in terms of price, service, and quality, it becomes more and more difficult to differentiate among competitors. One of the few remaining sources of differentiation is values, which means offering a product that customers not only buy, but believe in. This problem—unfortunate as it is—gives your company the opportunity to define its values.

Sincerely,

William Taylor [signature]

William Taylor

You Are Worried About the Wrong Things

G. Medford Smith

G. Medford Smith is the manager of certification services for the National Marine Manufacturers Association in Chicago. He inspects boats and trailers for compliance to federal regulations and voluntary standards for member manufacturers and has been an expert witness in product liability cases as a representative for his former employers.

Dear Steve:

You asked me for advice because you know that I testify at product liability trials. I'll advise you on how to talk with your insurance company and how to do a recall, but I don't think that those are your biggest problems. Your biggest challenge is to run a profitable business. That's hard to do when you overbuild your trailers and incur greater expenses than your competitors.

You seemed surprised when I told you over the phone that your biggest mistake was increasing the size of the bolt. Let me make this clear: overbuilding your products doesn't solve problems—it creates problems. If you manufacture the frame, axle, spindles, hubs, tires, coupler and safety chains in one class greater than standard, you manufacture a product that costs more than the competitions'. That is not good business practice. You will not stay in business long if your costs are higher than they have to be.

Look at your materials costs last year. It appears that the cost of materials increased at a greater rate than the sales volume. What does

Let me make this clear: overbuilding your products doesn't solve problems—it creates problems.

that tell you? Watch your profit margins closely if you want to stay in business.

Now that I've given you advice that you didn't ask for, I'll give you the advice that you did ask for. Here's how I would approach your insurance company.

The first thing I think you should do is notify your insurance carrier. Notice that I said carrier—not agent. If I were you, I wouldn't rely on your local agent for guidance on important probable liability exposures. Contact an officer of the home office and get responses in writing. You need your insurance company on your side, and you cannot afford to have a verbal okay when it comes to product liability.

Don't presume that your insurance company will not stand behind you. Insurance companies know that manufacturers improve and change their products to utilize better materials or improved manufacturing equipment and techniques.

When you write to your carrier, make sure that you keep copies of everything in a safe file and that you are able to show proof of delivery.

Your first letter should include written notification of the date of discovery of the possible weakened attaching point on the trailer, the number of units manufactured with the smaller bolts, and the date that the engineering change to the larger bolts was started in the manufacturing process.

Check to be sure that your insurance carrier is experienced in product liability for manufacturing. (Many companies will sell insurance, but they don't necessarily know how to defend their clients in court.) In the event that you are named as a defendant in a liability suit, you will not have to stand alone in court and pay all the legal fees associated with your company's defense. That is what your insurance company is for. The costs to defend your company are written into your insurance policy.

But in my opinion, you should not worry about product liability. You manufacture trailers that are in compliance with all known standards. You use the normal safety tolerances for the components and their attachments. No matter how strong or overbuilt the product is, misuse and overloading still occurs. But overloading of a truck, a hoist, a boat, or any product is beyond the manufacturer's control. That is why load calculations, stresses and safety margins are built into standards.

If you see a trailer that belongs to a customer who overloads or misuses it, you should have a repair checklist that shows the results of such conditions. Prior to servicing, advise the customer that overhaul is beyond any normal

warranty or service. Give the customer a written estimate of the charges before you begin the service. Consider including a statement on the estimate that indicates that such repairs are to correct the results of misuse and/or overloading beyond the trailers' rated and posted capacity. Then, have your customers sign an Overhaul Work Order that authorizes the repairs.

Of course, you should discuss all of these matters with your insurance carrier.

You asked me how I would handle the recall process if I were you. Briefly, I would consult with the insurance company on the wording they suggest for the reason for the replacement of the bolts. They might even advise you to do nothing. If so, get it in writing.

But if they do suggest a bolt replacement, I would send the replacement bolts, a cover letter explaining what the bolts are for and a complete set of instructions telling exactly how to replace the bolts. Send all such packets by Certified Mail Return Receipt Requested. Keep an accurate record of date of mailing and date received by the customer. Keep your insurance company posted periodically as to the percent of completion of the mailing.

Steve, I hope you make it through this. As I told you on the phone, I think that you're worrying about the wrong things. Anyway, if something comes up, give me a call. I'll be happy to tell you what I think.

Sincerely,

G. Medford Smith

Watch your profit margins closely if you want to stay in business.

Do the Right Thing, But Don't be Naive

Denis Collins

Denis Collins teaches business ethics at the University of Wisconsin-Madison, where he is an assistant professor at the graduate School of Business. He has published numerous articles in the areas of business ethics, participatory management, and social philosophy.

Dear Steve:

I'm sorry to hear about the problems that may be on your business horizon. Based on your letter to me, it appears that you are quite concerned about the potential harms that may be caused if one of the bolts on your 1990 trailer model should malfunction. You considered putting the larger three-eighths-inch bolts on the 1990 model but opted for smaller quarter-inch bolts instead, a size that met allowable standards. Let's not dwell on second guessing the original decision. It's fortunate that your heart was in the right place and you changed over to the larger bolts in 1991. Now you only have to worry about the 916 trailers from the 1990-model year instead of every trailer you have ever sold.

Your business dilemma sounds similar to a play Miss Mezzadri made us read back in high school English. Do you remember when our class read Arthur Miller's *All My Sons*? It's the play about a small-business owner who made a decision to sell a potentially malfunctioning product. Unfortunately, the use of the product caused the accidental death of his son. Neither he nor the other family members could forgive him. Your own situation need not end so tragically, yet it seems as though the possibility of the death of an innocent bystander keeps you up at night.

The way I see it, you have four options: (1) Do nothing and pray that nothing happens, (2) Make sure you are appropriately covered for product liability and then forget about the problem, (3) Bring in all the 1990 trailers and replace the quarter-inch bolt with the three-eighths inch bolt, or (4) Figure out a way to get the repair work done at minimal cost to you. Let's explore each option.

Option one. Do nothing and pray that nothing happens. (After all, there have been no complaints.) However, you do know that people are using the trailers recklessly and against specifications, thus a tragic accident is likely to happen at some point in the future. You realized this when you changed the size of the bolts in 1991. As you said in your letter, you'd consider yourself very lucky if nothing tragic happened. If something tragic does happen you may end up fiscally, emotionally and morally bankrupt.

Option two. Make sure you are appropriately covered for product liability and then forget about the problem. This may fiscally protect your business in case there are any tragic accidents, but one never knows what a judge or jury might decide in cases like these. No matter what the legal system decides, if there is an accident, your conscience will bother you for the rest of your life. Personally, I think attempt-

ing to fortify yourself with liability insurance is a major gamble and you may lose everything, particularly your dignity.

Option three. Bring in all the 1990 trailers and replace the quarter-inch bolt with the three-eighths inch bolt. You noted that you may not be able to trace the owners of all 916 trailers. I think this problem is manageable. You have the list of the original 916 customers. You say that most likely 25 to 33 percent of the trailers have been resold. From an optimistic perspective, this means that between 614 and 687 trailers can be easily traced; that's not a bad start. If the remaining trailers are still legitimately being used for business purposes (the high risk group), I would think you could trace the remaining 229 to 302 trailers from the original owners. The trailers you can't trace may simply be abandoned. Your product liability lawyer should be able to protect you from any claims due to their misuse.

But, even if you can trace the trailers, the cost to bring the trailers in for repair would be excessive and could bankrupt the business. Twelve people do depend upon you for a job, but you can't put these 12 people ahead of the lives of innocent bystanders. Don't use these 12 employees as rationalization for not taking constructive action. They may hate you for it if something tragic does happen. I think your real concern is that you fear this option may force you to go bankrupt. We certainly don't want that to happen. This leads me to a fourth option.

Option four. Figure out a way to get the repair work done at minimal cost to you. This will take some creative thinking on your part, but I have confidence that you can do it. One way might be to send the three-eighths inch bolt to each owner via registered mail and ask that the bolt be installed by their local mechanic at your expense. Find out how much the installation would cost and then guarantee to pay for the installation within a reasonable price range. The owner could send you the bill for the installation cost. You'll have to bite the bullet on this cost. Doing the moral thing in business sometimes entails a short-term expenditure for long-term benefits. You've told me several times that you want to involve your employees in some company decisions. Why don't you ask them how you could minimize the repair expenditure?

As you requested, I looked into your financial situation with my own financial advisor, and we tried to determine what you could afford. Cash is tight right now and you have to be concerned about the cost of

But, even if you can trace the trailers, the cost to bring the trailers in for repair would be excessive and could bankrupt the business.

providing bolts and paying for installation. However, this is not an insurmountable problem even given your current financial position. Let me explain what I mean.

Consider first the cost of the proposed program. Probably the most expensive component will be the cost of registered mailings for 900 letters. I estimate approximately $2,000. Cost of parts will be minimal—less than $300. The cost of your time is more difficult to gauge, but you probably haven't been as productive as you could be during the last few weeks while you wrestled with the problem. So perhaps the direct cost of the program will be $3,000 or $3.28 per one-fourth inch bolt per trailer.

Can you afford to spend $3,000—strictly in economic terms? Do you have any practical ways of raising $3,000? Let me offer three alternatives.

First, your accounts receivable has increased nearly $6,300 in the last year. In fact, the last year's increase is part of a long-term rise in receivables. Some of that is natural as a business expands, but some portion is also controllable. You should investigate the account to see where an increase in cash flow might be available. If you collect only half of the increase in the balance of the account, you will have enough to fund your recall program.

Second, you have a strong equity position in the business. Your debt/equity ratio has steadily declined over the last five years as you have built the business. While your business is not as profitable as it has been, you are not losing money. Bankers would probably be willing to listen to a proposal for a line of credit against which you could borrow in the short-run. Obviously, adding to your debt load may not be a good long-term strategy at this point, but a well-conceived plan for the use of short-term funds is generally acceptable. Besides, what you're really doing is borrowing against future sales growth. Your sales *have* continued to rise.

Third, your gross profit percentage has declined over the last few years, but the story of your decline in net profit is told more forcefully by the rapid increase in operating expenses. You should look very closely at those expenditures. In a cash flow crisis you need to reduce unwarranted expenses. If you check, I'm sure you will find some savings, which when coupled with your enhanced cash flow from collections of receivables, will probably allow you to finance the recall program internally.

In short, even though there are some risks to instituting a recall, you have the financial wherewithal to bring it about. The answer may be in learning to be a better financial manager.

I would also like to say that I think your father has the right idea about checking with the best product liability lawyer around, but don't check with him to see if you can escape responsibility. Instead, check with him to see how you can respond to this problem in a responsible manner. Tell the lawyer that you want to do the right thing rather than shirk your responsibilities. Ask him about sending out the letter, or how to word the letter such that it won't be used against you. Please don't use the lawyer as a means of overlooking irresponsible behavior. But also don't be naive. Some owners might refuse to install the bolt even though you mailed it to them and offered to pay the installation costs. Find out from the lawyer how to protect yourself from owner negligence after you've made them an offer in good faith.

Personally, I think that the fourth option is the best one. It'll prevent any needless tragedies and ease your conscience. Please let me know how things turn out. Don't hesitate to call me if you want to brainstorm other creative solutions, and, of course, give my best to your family.

By the way, I still have a worn out copy of *All My Sons* in case you lost your copy. It's a quick read for a Sunday afternoon. Can you believe that after all these years Miss Mezzadri is still teaching English? It's been almost twenty years since we had her. What perseverance!

With best regards,

Denis Collins

You are Overreacting

Arthur Freeman

Arthur Freeman is co-owner of Spartan Products, Inc., a trailer manufacturer in Minnesota.

Dear Mr. Johnson:

After listening to your problem, Steve, I think that you are overreacting. Let's go over the facts again together.

In 1990 you built a 1,000-pound capacity trailer using a one-fourth inch bolt connecting the tongue to the trailer. You sold 916 of these trailers before making a change in 1991 to three-eighths inch bolt. That means the trailers

Please don't use the lawyer as a means of overlooking irresponsible behavior. But also don't be naive.

with one-fourth inch bolts have been in use for more than four years and you have had no failures.

I understand that a week ago Wednesday a customer brought in one of the 1990 trailers for maintenance work. One of your men inspecting the trailer thought the connection using the one-fourth inch bolt seemed weak. You looked at it and also felt it was weak. You also learned that the owner of this trailer admitted to constantly overloading and driving his loaded trailer at high speeds over railroad tracks. Still the tongue stayed attached to the trailer. Now so far, Steve, do you agree that this is a fair statement of the facts? Okay, so let's go on.

In 1991, you decided to change the one-fourth inch bolt connecting tongue to trailer to a three-eighths inch bolt. You did this because in your mind this would be a safety improvement on your trailer. You determined 916 trailers had been sold with the one-fourth inch bolt.

All 916 of these trailers have been in use for four years. No failures. So where is the problem? I feel it is basically with you.

All 916 of these trailers have been in use for four years. No failures. So where is the problem? I feel it basically is with you.

You doubt that the one-fourth inch bolt connection is strong enough and you fear the tongue and trailer will separate and someone might get seriously hurt. Maybe it would help if you surveyed all the data you compiled in 1990 on standards and strengths before making the trailers. Would you feel better if your review showed one-fourth inch bolts were safe for connection of tongue to trailer? Probably you would still feel some doubt. So let's see how we can ease your mind without taking any drastic action that could endanger the life of your business.

Let's first look at monies available to spend for a solution. That's not very helpful because even at the small sum of $10 per trailer you exceed your last year's profit before taxes. So we must find a way without any immediate out-of-pocket money. Here is a suggestion. Check sales records to see if you can find about 20 or so owners close to your factory. Ask them to bring their trailers in for your inspection. If they will not bring them, you should arrange to pick them up. Carefully inspect these trailers so that you can make a better judgment as to the potential danger of tongue separation from trailer. If after the inspection you are certain that there is no problem, then you can consider this matter closed. If however, you feel there is the slightest danger of separation, something must be done to repair the other trailers.

You should then contact all the owners by Registered Mail Receipt Requested. Inform them about a potential safety problem. Supply a drawing, the right size bolt and nut, and complete instruction on how to remedy the problem. Make sure this is presented as a very serious matter that could be life-threatening. Also, enclose a return postage card for them to send to you when they have completed the repairs. Keep after the owners until you get their cards. Contact them again, and again. Stay after the non-delivered letters to see if you can find the balance of the trailers. If you do this daily, I know you will eventually find all the trailers.

I am certain you agree that if the danger is there, the correction must be made. Even if it takes your profit for the coming season, it is the right thing to do.

Steve, in reviewing the information you sent me, I noticed a disturbing trend. Your gross profit percentage going down, even though your sales have increased. Also, your expenses are going up beyond the extra gross on the increased sales. This results in more sales and less profit. Not a good sign. You should take a careful look at this.

Regards,

Arthur Freeman

Institute a Product Alert and Recall Program Immediately

Richard J. Delacenserie

Richard J. Delacenserie is a partner with the law firm of Boardman, Suhr, Curry & Field in Madison, Wisconsin. A substantial portion of Mr. Delacenserie's practice is devoted to product liability litigation and the counseling of business clients concerning products liability issues.

Dear Mr. Johnson:

You have asked for my advice concerning the potential liability of Johnson Utility Trailer, Inc. for damages or injuries that might result if the tongue joint on one of the trailers manufactured by your company before 1991 fails and causes an accident. Specifically, you have asked me to address two related questions:

- If an accident is caused by failure of the tongue joint on one of he pre-1991 trailers which used the smaller tongue joint bolt, will Johnson Utility Trailer, Inc. be liable for damages or injuries which result from the accident?
- Should Johnson Utility Trailer, Inc. implement a recall of the pre-1991 trailers and, if so, what form should the recall take?

Liability of Johnson Utility Trailer, Inc. A manufacturer of a product has a duty to exercise ordinary care to ensure that the product, when used in an intended or foreseeable manner, will not create an unreasonable risk of injury or damage to the product's user. Failure of the manufacturer to exercise ordinary care constitutes negligence, and the manufacturer can be held liable for injury or damages caused by its negligence. A manufacturer can be negligent by (1) failing to take reasonable steps to incorporate into a product a design which renders the product safe and fit for its intended and foreseeable uses, (2) failing to construct or assemble the product in a workmanlike manner, (3) failing to adequately inspect and test the product before marketing it, or (4) failing to provide adequate instructions concerning the proper use of the product or warnings addressing dangers associated with intended or foreseeable uses of the product.

A manufacturer that exercises ordinary care in the design, manufacture, and sale of a product, and is therefore not negligent, may nevertheless be found liable to an injured party under the doctrine of strict liability. In order to prevail under the doctrine of strict liability, an injured person must show that the product had a defect that rendered the product unreasonably dangerous. It is not necessary to show that the defect resulted from the manufacturer's negligence. A product is considered unreasonably dangerous when it is more dangerous than an ordinary user of such a product would expect. A product is considered defective when it is designed or manufactured in such a way that it is unsafe for normal use. If a product is found to be defective and unreasonably dangerous, the manufacturer of the product may be found liable for injury or damages caused by the product's defect even if the manufacturer exercised reasonable care and took reasonable precautions in the product's design, manufacture, and sale.

If one of your pre-1991 trailers were involved in an accident, the liability of Johnson Utility Trailer, Inc. would depend in large part on the particular facts surrounding the use of the trailer

and the accident itself. It is therefore difficult to predict the outcome of a claim for damages resulting from such an accident. However, based on the information you have provided concerning the design and manufacture of your trailers, I believe that Johnson Utility Trailer, Inc. faces a serious risk of an adverse finding of negligence and/or strict liability if one of its pre-1991 trailers is involved in an accident. Facts which would support a finding of negligence and/or strict liability adverse to Johnson Utility Trailer, Inc. include the following:

- Pre-marketing testing of the tongue joint showed that, with the quarter-inch bolts, the tongue joint was substantially weaker than either the chains or the coupler.
- The danger associated with the weakness in the tongue joint could have been avoided at virtually no additional cost by the use of larger bolts.
- At least since 1991, Johnson Utility Trailer, Inc. has known that the trailers which incorporate the smaller bolts have the potential for failing at the tongue joint under certain operating conditions.
- Johnson Utility Trailer, Inc. has known for quite some time that some users of its trailers overload the trailers and operate the trailers at higher than ideal speeds, which could cause the tongue joint to weaken and fail.
- Johnson Utility Trailer, Inc. knows that failure of the tongue joint could lead to an accident, which under certain circumstances could cause serious injury or death.
- Although Johnson Utility Trailer, Inc. changed the design of the tongue joint in 1991 so as to incorporate larger bolts, it took no steps to correct the potential tongue joint problem in pre-1991 trailers or to warn trailer owners of the danger associated with the tongue joints.
- Based on the fact that the weakness in the tongue joint was discovered by Johnson Utility Trailer, Inc. and has never been the subject of a request for repair by a trailer owner, it could reasonably be concluded that the potential weakness of the tongue joint is a defect which is not apparent to the trailers' users.

If an accident involving one of the pre-1991 trailers results in a claim against Johnson Utility Trailer, Inc., some facts favor your defense. You could show that the trailer as designed and manufactured with the smaller bolts met all applicable industry specifications and standards. In addition, the trailers' owner's manual clearly states the trailers' load limit. You could prove that there would be little risk of failure if the

I believe that Johnson Utility Trailer, Inc. faces a serious risk of an adverse finding of negligence and/or strict liability if one of its pre-1991 trailers is involved in an accident.

Such a program would obviously involve a substantial expense to Johnson Utility Trailer, Inc.

trailers' load limit was not exceeded, and that Johnson Utility Trailer, Inc. has no notice of any previous accident involving a failure of the tongue joint on one of the pre-1991 trailers.

However, despite these facts, I believe that the facts available to be used against Johnson Utility Trailer, Inc. in a product liability action following an accident would more likely than not lead to a finding of negligence, strict liability, or both against Johnson Utility Trailer, Inc.

Product recall. Due to the likelihood that Johnson Utility Trailer, Inc. would be held responsible for injuries or damages caused by an accident involving the tongue joint of one of the pre-1991 trailers, I would recommend that Johnson Utility Trailer, Inc. institute a product alert and recall concerning the pre-1991 trailers.

An alert and recall would serve two purposes. First, and most important, an alert and recall would substantially reduce the risk that one of the pre-1991 trailers would be involved in an accident. Second, implementation of an alert and recall may under some circumstances reduce the chances of a finding of liability against Johnson Utility Trailer, Inc. if, despite the alert and recall, an accident involving one of the pre-1991 trailers does occur.

As discussed above, a manufacturer has an obligation to warn product owners of dangers known to be associated with the use of a product. This obligation extends not only to dangers associated with the intended and proper use of a product, but also to dangers associated with known or reasonably foreseeable misuses of a product. You are confident that the pre-1991 trailers would not fail if used in accordance with the instructions provided in the owner's manuals. However, you know that some trailer owners do not use the trailers in compliance with the instructions and that such misuse of the trailers can lead to failure of the tongue joint.

Accordingly, you must take reasonable steps to warn trailer owners of the danger. The only practical way to fulfill this obligation is to issue a product alert. The product alert could consist of a mailing to all known owners of pre-1991 trailers advising them of the tongue joint problem you have discovered. In developing the language of the product alert, you will experience a natural inclination to downplay the seriousness of the tongue joint problem. I would advise you not to do so. In order for a warning to be legally sufficient, it must be strong enough to fairly advise the product owner of the magnitude of the danger associated with the product's use. Thus, your product alert should

specifically advise that overloading or other misuse of a pre-1991 trailer could cause the tongue joint to fail, which could cause the trailer to separate from the towing vehicle and lead to serious injury to or death of anyone in the runaway trailer's path. You should advise owners to immediately stop using any trailer that shows any sign of weakening at the tongue joint.

There are probably pre-1991 trailers in the field that have already experienced weakening of the tongue joint due to the use of the smaller bolt. Thus, in addition to the product alert, Johnson Utility Trailer, Inc. should institute a product recall or retrofit program with respect to all pre-1991 trailers. You should take steps to replace the smaller bolts on the pre-1991 trailers with the larger bolts you began using in 1991.

You could probably best accomplish this by developing a retrofit kit which would allow for replacement of the bolts by Johnson Utility Trailer, Inc. dealers. For owners not located conveniently near an authorized dealer, Johnson Utility Trailer, Inc. should offer to pay the owner's expense of bringing the trailer to the nearest dealer for the retrofit. For owners who are unwilling to travel to the nearest dealer for the retrofit, Johnson Utility Trailer, Inc. should arrange to have a dealer or factory representative make the retrofit in the field.

Such a program would obviously involve a substantial expense to Johnson Utility Trailer, Inc. However, the cost of a single serious accident involving failure of one of the pre-1991 trailers could greatly exceed the cost of the retrofit program. Thus, institution of the recall program may be an economically sound course of action in the long run.

I believe that implementation of the above product alert and recall procedures would substantially reduce the risk of accidents involving the pre-1991 trailers. I also believe that these procedures would decrease the likelihood that Johnson Utility Trailer, Inc. would be found liable for injuries or damages resulting from an accident. Implementation of the above procedures would, I believe, represent a reasonable attempt to reach trailer owners, warn them of the potential for weakening of the tongue joint in the pre-1991 trailers, and accomplish a cure of the existing problem with the tongue joints.

Implementation of the alert and recall program would not, however, eliminate all risk of future liability for accidents caused by failures of the tongue joints on pre-1991 trailers. Because some of the pre-1991 trailer owners have moved and others have sold their trailers, it cannot be expected that all pre-1991 trailer owners will be reached through the alert and recall program. It is also likely that some owners who are reached through the program will ignore the alert and will decline to participate in the retrofit program. Those who ignore your warnings will clearly have a difficult time prevailing against Johnson Utility Trailer, Inc. in a legal action should they be injured in an accident involving one of the pre-1991 trailers.

An accident involving a pre-1991 trailer whose owner is not reached by the alert and recall program, however, would very likely result in a finding of liability against Johnson Utility Trailer, Inc. Ironically, such claims may be strengthened by your alert and recall efforts. The alert and recall program will likely be admissible as evidence in a case involving failure of one of the pre-1991 trailers, and would probably be considered an admission that the pre-1991 trailers were defective in design. An aggressive attempt on the part of Johnson Utility Trailer, Inc. to locate all pre-1991 trailer owners, however, should limit to a very small percentage the group of owners who are not reached by the program.

Although a product alert and recall program would not totally eliminate Johnson Utility Trailer, Inc.'s risk of liability concerning the pre-1991 trailers, I believe an alert and recall program along the lines outlined above would substantially reduce the risk of loss to Johnson Utility Trailer, Inc. with respect to the pre-1991 trailers. Because a single accident involving failure of one of the pre-1991 trailers could result in serious injury, and could represent a catastrophic financial loss for Johnson Utility Trailer, Inc., I recommend that the alert and recall program be put into effect as soon as possible.

Sincerely,

Richard J. Delacenserie

Richard J. Delacenserie

An accident involving a pre-1991 trailer whose owner is not reached by the alert and recall program, however, would very likely result in a finding of liability.

Chapter 5

"What Should I Do with My Problem Employees?"

Catherine Stover

David McLimans

M r. Shew—and he was Mr. Shew, not Dick or even Richard to anyone in the office—waited until the waiter had taken their lunch menus, and then said to his secretary, "Helen, you—more than anyone else—know that I set up my own accounting firm 23 years ago because I wanted to do what I do best—accounting. Just accounting. Somehow, I lost sight of that when the firm began to grow. Now I've got 30 people thinking that I am their boss, their mediator and their personnel director. I don't know what I'm doing."

Helen, who had been Mr. Shew's first employee, nodded sympathetically.

"I started this business because I'm a good accountant. But I don't do accounting anymore—I'm too busy trying to keep everyone happy. And I'm not very good at that, apparently."

"Are you referring to Jim Morgan?"

"I found out today that he was the one who was spreading the rumor that we're thinking of cutting staff. That son of a —"

"Mr. Shew, may I offer a comment?"

"Yes, Helen."

"When you wait a day before confronting someone, things seem to go more smoothly."

Catherine Stover is the editor of the Small Business Forum.

79

Morgan spits on the floor and Fixby walks on clouds. What should I do?

"I know I should cool off first. But I've had it with that jerk. Why I made him a partner, I'll never know. He was the last one to get in before we wrote our strategic plan, wasn't he? He'd never make it now. He's nothing but a whiner and a complainer. He can't get along with anyone. The secretaries hate him. He berates the younger staff. He doesn't act in the firm's best interests. Marsha Fixby is working circles around him. She's twice as productive—and she's not even a partner."

"Do you think that could be part of the problem?"

"What do you mean?"

"Oh, I don't know. It just seems to me that there are two problems. One is Jim Morgan, who is so negative and mean lately. He even yelled at Sally about the coffee yesterday in front of about five people. The other problem is Marsha Fixby, who is so in demand that she's working 15-hour days. And everyone loves her. But can you afford to take on another partner? Will you lose her if you don't? I know this is beginning to sound like a soap opera, but could it be that Jim Morgan is jealous of Marsha?"

Mr. Shew took his glasses off and rubbed his face. "Helen, you're right. We have two problems. Morgan spits on the floor and Fixby walks on clouds. What should I do?"

"I wish I knew the answer. And I wish I could say, 'Take your time and see. Maybe the situation will resolve itself.' But I can't say that, Mr. Shew. I hate to repeat gossip, but —"

"But nothing! You are the only person in the firm that I have complete trust in. Tell me."

"Yesterday, in the rest room, I overheard two of our new staff talking about Morgan and Fixby. One of them said that on Monday, Morgan told Fixby that if she takes another one of his clients, he'll make sure that she's out of a job."

"Is Marsha taking his clients? She's not supposed to do that."

"Well, I've spoken with two of his former clients myself. Both were women. Both told me that Jim Morgan was patronizing and rude, and that unless I could find someone who was easier for them to work with, they were going to take their business elsewhere. So I facilitated their move to Marsha."

"So that's why he's so bent out of shape. He's been making a lot of unflattering comments about her clothes lately. You know how he does it—he says it just so it's almost out of earshot."

As their food arrived, Mr. Shew said, "Helen, what would you do if you were me?"

"I'd give it my top attention. And I'd ask someone who knows more than I do for advice."

"Remember the good old days? When it was just the two of us? My biggest worry was meeting IRS deadlines. Now look at me. I'm supposed to have all the answers, and I don't. I don't know how to manage these people. Maybe we should just get rid of everyone and move back to our little office on Fourth Street."

"You've built a very highly-regarded accounting firm. There's a lot to be proud of, even if there is a problem at hand that needs to be solved."

"You're right. I have what I've always dreamed of. But it's ready to fall apart. A year ago, you told me that we were having trouble with our other rising star—and about two months later he left. Now he's a partner at Hammerly and Jensen. If I had been the personnel guy, I should have been fired."

"Mr. Shew, you're being very hard on yourself. You've accomplished a lot. The reason your firm is so highly respected is because you have set such high standards for performance—and it has carried through to your whole staff. Everyone respects you. All offices have personnel problems. You just have to find the right person to give you some advice on how to deal with this."

"You're right. And this time I'm not going to wait a couple of months. It's going to be my top priority."

What should Richard Shew do? *We asked seven authors, professors and consultants to offer advice and suggestions.*

You Have Two Problem Employees

Lawrence L. Steinmetz, Ph.D.

Author of Managing the Marginal and Unsatisfactory Performer *and nine other books, Dr. Steinmetz is president of High Yield Management, Inc., in Boulder, Colorado. He is the former management department head at the Graduate School of Business at the University of Colorado.*

Dear Richard:

It was good seeing you at the board of directors meeting the other day. As promised, I'm taking this opportunity to address your concerns with Jim Morgan and Marsha Fixby.

I don't know how helpful I can be with "fix-it" advice until you've had some time to talk to Jim Morgan, but as I told you, there are a few things that distress me about the situation you find yourself in at this time.

Number one has to do with the source of your information. You've indicated to me that most of your feedback comes from Helen, your secretary of 23 years and the first employee of your company. I certainly understand the value of trusted, long-service employees, and they can certainly give you good information. However, a few words of caution in regard to using only one source of information: Don't listen to hearsay—and certainly don't believe it—unless you have verified and/or substantiated that information independently.

It would be a mistake for you to lean on Jim Morgan and accuse him of things that he *may* or *may not* have done. I'm willing to bet—and I'll guarantee it if you should get into a legal ruckus over this—that Morgan's side of the story will be decidedly different from the one you've heard from Helen. You've got to deal with facts, and you absolutely must sit down and address this issue with Morgan, which you've indicated you have not done as yet.

A second thing that concerns me is your complaints about Jim Morgan to Helen—and I assume to other employees. You're letting yourself in for a classic lawsuit on the issue of dehiring if you continue doing this. Dehiring, nicely put, is the fine art and skill of subtly forcing an employee to quit by bringing all forms of pressure to bear on that employee. In its crudest form, it is practiced by employers who berate and complain about the attitude and/or the behavior of an employee to other employees.

Dehiring is like the pecking order in a flock of chickens. When the leader lets it be known to employees that he/she is unhappy about someone's (Morgan's) performance, there is a real tendency for other employees to start "dumping" all kinds of blame and problems on that employee. Often the work situation becomes intolerable for that employee and he or she quits—only subsequently to file charges of discriminatory behavior against the ex-employer.

A third issue I want to raise is that you should deal with *behavior*, not *attitude*. You've stated that Morgan does not act in the firm's best interests—but you've also said that he's a whiner and a complainer, that he can't get along with anyone and that "the secretaries hate him." You're going to have to cope with this as a behavioral problem and you're absolutely not going to be able to say to him that *others* don't like what he's doing and/or that you *hear* that he's doing things to the detriment of the company. You're going to have to deal with hard facts and specific situations.

I'm a bit nervous that Helen has indicated to you that she took it upon herself to switch some of Morgan's clients to Marsha Fixby because two female clients had told her that Morgan was "patronizing and rude, and that unless there was someone who was easier for them to work with, they were going to take their business elsewhere." This type of decision and responsibility does not normally come under the job description of a secretary, unless her duties are really those of a vice president or office manager. While her intentions may be to act as a helpmate, the effects on employee morale and company interests can be disastrous.

The bottom line, Richard, is you've said nothing about having had any personal discussions with Jim Morgan about the problem as you see it, and at this point, you are reacting only to complaints by other employees. A fundamental right for people in the United States is to face their accusers. Another fundamental right is to know the specifics of what one is accused. I think you should start by clarifying with Morgan the fact that he is not *performing* and/or *behaving* in the manner you expect. Again, you must be very specific about your complaints and, I repeat, do not start talking about his attitude. Most managers lapse into scolding employees about attitude when they don't have actual behavior or performance facts with which to deal. I am afraid that will happen to you unless you have *specific, substantial* matters of performance and behavior to discuss with him.

When you do sit down with him, I recommend:

- that you do so with clear-cut standards and expectations in mind,
- that you agree to (or impose) a timetable to specifically review measurable improvements in his performance and/or behavior,
- that you delineate clear-cut measures of rewards and/or penalties depending upon his improvement or failure to improve,
- that you keep this discussion private between yourself and him, and
- that you avoid making any comments concerning his performance to his peers (in contrast to superiors, of which you indicate there are none but you).

It is very important that you have a mentality of trying to *help* Jim Morgan become a satisfactory employee. This means you must have specific, measurable, concrete, realistic, attainable, written, and mutually agreed upon performance/behavior goals and objectives for him. These must be reviewed in the near term after your discussion and you must guard against any backsliding on his part. Clearly delineate the consequences of his behavior with him and review his performance/

Most managers lapse into scolding employees about attitude when they don't have actual behavior or performance facts with which to deal.

behavior against these specific standards. Failure to do so will simply mean that you have given him no chance to measure up. Furthermore, your continued complaining or discussion with other employees about his performance is not only unproductive, but is also detrimental. It may actually trigger the dehiring that I mentioned earlier.

One other thing that I'd like to talk to you about at a future date, Richard, is the concept of the *prima donna*. You didn't really pursue Marsha Fixby's performance or relationship with other employees other than to say, in essence, "Morgan spits on the floor and Fixby walks on clouds." Prima donna employees can be as debilitating to an organization as negative employees. From what you have told me at our board of directors meeting, I see some real storm clouds brewing in that respect. No organization can function effectively with a prima donna. I think you may have one developing.

Richard, prima donnas are the dark side of rising stars. Not all rising stars become prima donnas, but many do. It is really a function of how you handle them. They become prima donnas when they start receiving *unwarranted* special treatment.

How can someone who is really good become a problem? Let me relate a list of things that happen, based on my experiences as a consultant and labor arbitrator:

- "Privileged characters" destroy the morale of others. This is largely a function of the prima donna's personality and how privileged they are.
- Prima donnas often trigger insidious, surreptitious and malicious behavior by those who think there is "unfair" treatment.
- Serious physical damage can occur to property *and* persons, triggered by jealousies on the part of others who feel taken advantage of.
- Work groups become fractionalized and polarized. Cliques develop.
- Serious charges of favoritism/discrimination can be brought (and usually won) when privileges are not shared by all employees.
- Your pay structure may well become a farce. Worse yet, the boss can be made a liar because promises regarding promotions are not fulfilled due to prima donna interference.
- Prima donnas often Peter Principle out. They can be good at lower levels, but find they get promoted too quickly to levels where they are (and often remain) incompetent.
- Prima donnas often end up suffering from the "no other worlds to conquer" syndrome. They get bored, quit, or decide to start competing businesses where they "run the show."

Richard, you may ask, "How should I manage a rising star/potential prima donna?" There are three things you should do now:

- Treat all employees the same, especially if they are at the same level in the organization. No special status or recognition should be given to anyone.
- Rewards must always be: commensurate with the value of the employee's contribution, available to all who perform at the same level, given according to well-established criterion and not changed in an irrational (discriminatory) way just to feed the prima donna's ego.
- Remember always that organizations should not be developed around a person. Anyone can get sick, die, be pirated away or quit to start their own (competing) business. Could Ms. Fixby, for example, quit and take Jim Morgan's ex-accounts with her? This potential problem is ever present with any departing employee, but prima donnas seem to have an especially fine hand in taking accounts with them, largely because they seem to be given more running room in working with accounts.

Richard, I feel so strongly about this that I would like to have lunch with you sometime soon and pursue it a little further. I'd also like to hear how you're progressing with Jim Morgan at that time. I'm gone until the end of this week, but on Monday I'll ask my secretary to give your office a call.

Best personal regards,

Lawrence L. Steinmetz, Ph.D.

Time for a Tough-Minded Interview That Will Get Results

Gareth S. Gardiner, Ph.D.

Author of Tough-Minded Management: A Guide for Managers Who are Too Nice for Their Own Good, *(Fawcett Columbine, 1993), Dr. Gardiner has owned and operated three small businesses. Currently, he is a consultant based in Oakland City, Indiana, and is affiliated with Oakland City College.*

Prima donna employees can be as debilitating to an organization as negative employees.

Dear Richard:

You do indeed have a problem employee situation, and it has all the characteristics of a problem that has been avoided. The problem employee's behavior is getting worse, you are beginning to hate him (but really it's just a projection of your anger toward yourself for doing nothing) and you risk losing productive employees who are demoralized by your inaction.

When you first talked to me about Jim Morgan last year, and went into detail about his nasty and negative behavior, I had a strong sense that you were reluctant to intervene because you didn't know what to do. While these feelings are normal, the time has come for you to sit down with Jim and conduct a tough-minded problem-solving interview about his behavior that will get results, both in the short- and long-run. If you continue to avoid confronting him, you're eventually going to blow your legendary fuse and lash out at him with a classic "tough guy" overreaction.

I am glad that you now recognize that dealing with Jim is going to be your top priority. Like many successful small-business owners, you are energetic, hard-working and highly motivated to build your business. The success of your accounting firm is far and away your strongest interest, and personnel problems represent something of a nuisance to you—something you'd really rather not deal with. I've also noticed that, like most of us, you have a lot of "nice guy" tendencies: you are pleasant and considerate, you want your employees to like you, you dislike interpersonal conflict, and you hope that employee problems will take care of themselves. Alas, nice-guy avoidance almost always makes problems worse because problem persons rapidly take advantage of managers they see as gutless. In addition to the worsening problem you are having with Jim, there is a good chance you will also lose your top performer, Marsha Fixby.

Take heart, Richard. There *is* an effective method for dealing with employee problems that lies between tough-guy and nice-guy extremes, and this is the five-step tough-minded technique that I describe in detail in my book. Almost any manager can learn to use this method, and can regain control over employees who have run amok. This includes you. In taking charge of the problem with Jim, I urge you to follow these five steps.

Step 1. Set up a private face-to-face meeting with him. Nice-guy managers will sometimes send the employee a memorandum advising him or her of the need for a meeting. Tough-guy managers will ask for a meeting, but engage in such authoritarian tactics as setting up a chair for the employee in the middle of the room, or ordering the employee to sit down. In the tough-*minded* approach, ask for a meeting with Jim, and treat him courteously and as an adult. Keep your voice and manner low-key and calm, and engage in a minute or two of work-related small talk with him, if this seems natural. Since he will probably be aware that this is not a social meeting, small talk may ease tension, but it may also easily become an avenue of avoidance, and turn the meeting into a discussion of fishing trips. If you think this might happen, dispense with the small talk.

Step 2. This will be the most critical step in your meeting. It's where you state the problem objectively and factually, as calmly as possible, and with prior rehearsal to keep it objective and matter-of-fact. In this case, you might say something like, "Jim, I want to talk to you about the fact that several of our employees and clients have complained to me about your rude and belligerent behavior. Yesterday, Sally told me that you yelled at her about the coffee in front of several other people. I'd like to talk to you now before the situation gets more serious than it is."

End your problem statement with an open-minded question such as, "Can you tell me about what happened with Sally?" Simply by stating the problem in this tough-minded way, you have taken a major step toward solving it. Here is what you have told him implicitly:

- You are the boss;
- He is responsible for the problem, and must now take action to solve it;
- If he doesn't take action, whatever the cause of the problem, there's going to be trouble down the road;
- Your goal is to get this problem solved, now, not to punish him;
- His behavior is not acceptable in your company; and
- You are willing to talk with him about the problem.

In addition to these vitally important communications, you will also have motivated him (and mightily!) to solve the problem for you. The most powerful motivator may well be his desire to keep the respect of his tough-minded boss who is determined to solve this problem. In the world of gutless nice-guy avoidance, problem employees never hear such a direct and honest statement, and may not even be aware that other employees and clients are complaining about them behind their backs.

There is an effective method for dealing with employee problems that lies between tough-guy and nice-guy extremes.

Step 3. In this step, you will want to give Jim a fair hearing, and clarify the problem. Here you need to use non-judgmental and non-prejudicial listening and counseling skills, such as reflection, clarifying and paraphrasing. In paraphrasing, you simply restate what the employee has said, often in summary form. If Jim tells you that he had a blinding headache when he yelled at Sally, you might paraphrase this by saying, "So you had a bad headache when you yelled at her." In clarifying, you pose a question such as, "Were you in a lot of pain at that time?" Reflection involves feeding back to the employee both the content and feeling of what he has said (e.g., "Your headaches are causing you to be pretty irritable with people"), and is yet another technique designed to encourage him to continue talking.

Your goal is not so much to identify the *cause* of the problem as it is to get the employee to begin thinking of what he needs to do to *solve* the problem. In this step, do a lot of listening, be wary of any attempts to suck you into an argument (since you're human, if this happens, reschedule the interview), or for diversionary tactics, such as blaming others for the problem. It is remarkable that in just five to ten minutes of hearing themselves talk about a problem, employees often make the transition from antagonism and defensiveness to a willingness to cooperate with management in solving it.

Step 4. In this step, tough-minded problem-solving skills come to the fore. In a first sub-step, you hope that Jim will *volunteer* to take action to solve the problem: "I realize, Mr. Shew, that my behavior has been way off base, and I want you to know that I'm going to be a lot more considerate of Sally and our clients in the future. I'm glad you talked to me about this. I didn't realize it had become such a problem." In the real world, of course, this may not happen, so be prepared to *suggest* or *ask* for appropriate action from the employee. If this does not get results, *tell* the employee what needs to be done, and finally, *spell out the consequences* if effective action is not taken. If termination is required (and this is a last resort, not a first one), it can be done on a firm and fair basis if these steps have been followed.

Step 5. This step is the most tedious and mundane in the tough-minded problem-solving process, but perhaps the most necessary: document everything, and follow-up. Learning to document incidents of unsatisfactory performance for all employees must become a basic managerial habit. Each interview with a problem employee should be documented in summary form. If an employee promises to take action, check to see whether or not this has happened. If Jim promises to apologize to Sally for yelling at her, check with her in a day or two to see if he has done so. Documenting and following up gives you the necessary paper trail if you need to take formal disciplinary action later.

So go to it, Richard. I'm not going to try to tell you that you're going to enjoy confronting Jim in this tough-minded way, because dealing with problem persons is almost never fun, but what you *will* experience after you interview him is a big jump in your self-esteem and a wonderful sense of relief that you've finally done something to get rid of this headache. Your other employees will cheer you on, believe me. The last thing your good, loyal employees want to see happen is a problem person getting away with murder because of management's inaction. Word will travel fast that you've taken action to deal with Jim and his abusive behavior. Everyone's morale will go up.

My five-step method is no quick-fix, but it works. I've trained literally thousands of managers, and I have received many letters praising its effectiveness. But it needs to become part of your management style, and part of a philosophy in your organization that problems are going to be dealt with immediately. The more often your employees see you get results, the easier it becomes to continue getting results. Unresolved personnel problems can rapidly destroy even the most successful small business. Nothing is more satisfying than turning a poor performer into a star.

And speaking of stars, Richard, make Marsha Fixby a partner in your firm as soon as you get done talking with Jim. You can't afford to lose her to Hammerly and Jensen the way you did your other rising star. She'll be delighted that you've taken action about Jim and his behavior, and she'll be thrilled that her hard work and positive contributions to your business are being recognized. Your company will become even more highly respected as she continues to excel for you, and as Jim Morgan is given the opportunity to become a satisfactory performer.

Sincerely,

Gareth S. Gardiner

Gareth S. Gardiner

The last thing your good, loyal employees want is a problem person getting away with murder because of management's inaction.

Try Non-Punitive Discipline

David N. Campbell

Co-author of "Discipline Without Punishment—At Last," a Harvard Business Review *classic*, Mr. Campbell is a consultant in Tampa, Florida. Previously, he was a senior human resources executive with TECO Energy Company, Inc.

Dear Richard:

I received your letter today, and I am responding to the sense of urgency that you conveyed to me. I am sending this letter to your home because there will be much in it that only you should see.

Let me first assure you that your problems are shared by most businesses with which I have been associated. They are probably not as serious as you now believe, and they are fixable. But as you suspect, you are the one who will have to do it and do it quickly. In your letter, you expressed the view that you have two problem employees. I believe you have two also, but not the same two that you identified. I also think that these episodes may be symptomatic of some deeper problems resulting from your firm's failure to address some issues that are important to you, your partners and employees.

On the positive side, you have much to be pleased with. You have built a strong practice with many loyal clients, fine partners and committed employees. You have set high standards of professional conduct. You have built a strong sense of pride in your firm through leading by example within your profession. You love accounting and it shows.

Let me start by analyzing each person's situation separately before I deal with their interrelationships. First will be Jim Morgan, because he is causing the most trouble right now. Jim's disruptive, negative behavior is not only causing problems in the office, but also has nearly cost you two clients. Possibly his anger may be directed more toward women in general and younger people within the firm. However, I wouldn't be too quick to jump on that idea without talking to him and others first. I raise it here only because harassment (and particularly sexual harassment) must be taken seriously today.

You also hint that Jim has not embraced your new strategic direction as well as the other partners have. However, you give me no past history of episodes similar to the recent ones. Summing up: you have made Jim a partner, he has performed reasonably well until recently, and now his conduct is getting him in trouble with clients and associates. You have reason to be concerned—even angry with him—but I don't see him as the spherical S.O.B. you described in your letter.

Next is Marsha Fixby. Marsha is a problem I would love to have in my firm. If she is working 15 billable hours a day without complaining about it and has the temperament ascribed to her by Helen, she is an asset you don't want to lose. And did she really cause the problem with Jim? Or, did Helen cause it when she moved the two clients without consulting with you first? Unless there is more to this story than you have told me, I don't consider Marsha Fixby to be a problem employee, in spite of the fact that she may be going a little overboard in trying to impress. She may become one, however, if a clear path to a partnership is not made possible. Right now, I see little reason to confront her with anything. More on this later.

Now you will find out why I mailed this letter to your home. I consider Helen to be the second employee contributing to your problem. Nowhere in your long letter did you tell me that you had delegated to her administrative duties that included moving clients around and particularly from a partner to an associate. Yet, she did this without even telling you that clients were complaining. This situation may not be completely of her making, but she has added considerably to the turmoil your shop is experiencing.

This leads me to you, Richard. It seems to me you have become part of this interrelated problem by becoming too detached from your partners and employees and their working relationships. The relationships have become much more complex than they used to be. But you can't go back to that two-person shop you daydream about. You know it. And your partners and employees are telling you in a variety of ways—some not too pleasant—that they expect you to lead them to your shared future. When they bought into the strategic plan they helped you develop, they expected to be a part of it. Now it's a promise they expect you to keep. Like it or not, you are still the boss, mediator and personnel director.

I must now digress for just a bit before I suggest some solutions.

Several years ago, I became interested in the concept of *non-punitive discipline* when I became convinced that old-style punitive discipline wasn't working any longer in modern organiza-

I became interested in the concept of non-punitive discipline *when I became convinced that old-style punitive discipline wasn't working.*

tions. I felt that punishing employees actually stood in the way of improved teamwork which has become so essential to improving productivity in today's business environment. So a colleague, Jack Fleming, and I initiated a non-punitive discipline program in Tampa Electric, a TECO Energy company, with the help of a consulting firm then headed by Dick Grote. It worked so well that the three of us were invited to share our experiences in a *Harvard Business Review* article titled "Discipline Without Punishment—At Last," (July/August 1985). The three of us have written and lectured on the subject many times since. I have included a reprint of the *HBR* piece, because it gives far more information on how the program works than I can convey in this letter.

Non-punitive discipline is built on the bedrock of modern motivational theory—and it works! Many different types of organizations have now tried it, and it seems to work as well in professional and administrative settings as it does in factories or power plants. I can sum it up this way:

- Adults expect to be treated like adults.
- The best kind of discipline is self-discipline.
- You can't get people to act better and better while you treat them worse and worse.

Now, I'm not saying your firm has been treating people badly, but rather, lately it hasn't been disciplining some of them at all. So why not begin afresh in a positive fashion? A good place to start is with Jim Morgan. I'll walk you through the first step.

The starting point is gathering information. Make notes of all the incidents of Jim's erratic behavior you have observed firsthand. Talk to the two unhappy clients on the pretext of finding out if they are pleased with their current service, but look for opportunities to inquire about why they became dissatisfied in the first place. You can also talk about Helen's role in moving them to Marsha Fixby. Make notes so you don't forget. Interview Helen again to get specific times, dates and other facts. Then organize your material for ease of use.

When you are prepared, arrange to meet Jim somewhere other than the office so it isn't obvious to the whole staff that he has been "called on the carpet." Tell him in general terms that the purpose of the meeting is to discuss some recent episodes that have come to your attention, that he will be given every opportunity to discuss his views, that you have no preconceived thoughts on the meeting's outcome. Tell him your expectations are that the meeting will be positive.

When you meet, Jim will possibly be defensive and even angry. You have no need to be either. As the head of the firm, you have the right and obligation to set reasonable standards of performance and conduct, and to set things right when those standards aren't met.

Start out by telling Jim that you have made him a partner because he impressed you with his abilities and demeanor and, until a short time ago, you had no complaints about either his work or his professional conduct. However, recently you have observed and have been told by others that breaches in conduct have occurred which have hurt client relations and have disrupted the office. Give him specifics. Listen to his response and react accordingly. If he denies, give him more specifics. If he admits, ask him what he plans to do to bring this kind of behavior to an end. Tell him you will help him, but the responsibility to change is his.

Will this approach work with Jim? Who knows? I only can say from experience, it works most of the time. From Jim's standpoint, you didn't threaten his job; you didn't compare his performance to others. But you did discuss an expected standard. You treated him like an adult. You told him the truth in a straightforward way; you appealed to his sense of responsibility as a co-owner of the business; and you laid it on his shoulders to change. You didn't psychoanalyze him. You offered your help.

What's next with Jim? Observe him and give him positive reinforcement to improved behavior. However, don't hesitate to escalate your discussions to the next step if he doesn't respond positively. The *HBR* article spells out what to do in the next step, which concludes with a written agreement with specific outcomes.

It's important to note here that Jim Morgan may not change and you may have to part company. That's okay too, because with non-punitive discipline, you're not looking for a compliant employee or partner. Rather you're seeking a committed one—or a former one. If Jim leaves, you have offered him every opportunity to change. It is he who has chosen not to.

One final caveat before we leave Jim. During the course of your investigation, if anyone tells you of behavior that might be viewed as sexual harassment in today's more acutely sensitive environment, consult a labor lawyer immediately and listen carefully to the advice given. Government guidelines call for quick and definitive action by employers if sexual harassment occurs in situations in which the employer has control.

Now, what about Helen's behavior? In my judgment, you need to have a specific, but

Adults expect to be treated like adults.

informal meeting with your old friend and superb secretary. It, too, should be positive, but she should leave that meeting with the clear direction *not* to move clients without your specific approval. Also, shouldn't clients' complaints be written down and directed to you ASAP?

As you probably have deduced, I see no reason to confront Marsha Fixby with anything right now. Certainly working hard is no sin. If she was not an instigator of the client moves, she hasn't done anything wrong. However, if she was a "behind-the-scenes" participant in that matter, she too, must be dealt with in a similar fashion.

I can't conclude this candid discussion without asking you a pointed question. When are you going to bring someone on board to be the administrative partner to help you with this end of the business? You have told me for years that you don't like this "stuff," as you call it, and it shows. Until you specifically delegate these responsibilities to someone else, you must handle them. Left undone, some overly conscientious—or overly ambitious—person may do it for you, which may result in an outcome you won't like. Sound familiar?

So this letter ends, but hopefully our friendship won't, in spite of my less-than-diplomatic comments. I hope I have helped. By the way, don't forget I'm in the consulting business, and I even like to deal with this "stuff." If you would like me to work with you on this, please give me a call.

Sincerely,

David N. Campbell

The Larger Issue is Improved Communication

Debra A. Hunter, CPA

Ms. Hunter is the firm administrator and a shareholder in the CPA firm of Hunter Hagan & Company, Ltd. in Scottsdale, Arizona, specializing in the areas of tax and closely-held corporations.

Dear Richard:

Since we spoke on the phone last week, I have given your situation a great deal of thought. I am flattered that you have asked me for advice. We have been friends for many years, and you know I will give you my honest opinion about your problem employees. I will also tell you what my accounting firm has done to prevent these sorts of problems.

First, I agree that you have a problem with Jim Morgan and that there may be a potential problem with Marsha Fixby if she isn't given some relief from her incredible workload. However, these behaviors may be the symptoms of a larger problem. If the larger issues can be identified and resolved, perhaps some of the smaller ones will also be taken care of.

I know that it has always been your top priority to have a highly respected, quality accounting firm. After all these years, everyone in the firm still refers to you as Mr. Shew, not Dick or Richard. Your partners and staff respect you. However, because of your position, they do not necessarily give you the benefit of their honest opinion. There appears to be a lack of communication between you and your partners.

Your partners do not appear to have an equal voice in the decisions of the firm. Perhaps because of your seniority and because you founded the firm, you really make all of the administrative decisions. Apparently, decisions that you do not have time to make are made by your secretary, Helen.

We both know that the qualities that make one a good CPA are not necessarily the same qualities that make one best suited for the position of administrative partner. Many firms train their staffs to become technically proficient, but do not teach them the administrative and personnel side of the business. The administrative partner cannot teach what he or she does not know.

You need to increase the communication between you and your partners. This can be done in a variety of ways. You can start by holding monthly partner meetings. I suggest these meetings be held outside of your office to minimize interruptions. At these sessions, you can share your wealth of information and knowledge regarding taxes, accounting and firm administration with your partners. Increasing communication between all partners will help you maintain the highly respected and successful firm you began 23 years ago.

I also suggest that you organize a partners' retreat. Perhaps you could hire a professional facilitator to help you identify the areas that need to be discussed at your retreat. The facilitator

Many firms have staff members review their supervisors, managers and partners annually.

In order for a firm to remain success-ful, staff must be trained and moti-vated so that their strengths can be fully utilized.

should help you identify the strengths and weaknesses of the various partners so the group can help individual partners become more valuable to the firm. The strengths of each partner can be assessed and administrative duties can then be assigned to the person best suited to the task. The facilitator should also teach the partners to communicate better as a group. The goal of the retreat should be to become a more cohesive group, based on mutual respect and abilities.

Consider implementing a review process that is different from your normal annual review of staff and managers. Every year your partners and managers evaluate the people that report to them, assessing technical ability, job performance, etc. Many firms have staff members review their supervisors, managers and partners annually. This process is known as an Upward Appraisal. While these appraisals can be used in a variety of ways, they are intended to enable supervisors, managers and partners to evaluate their own effectiveness as perceived by those who report to them. Results of an Upward Appraisal can help you to determine which managers and partners are the most effective and which managers and partners need additional counseling and/or training in order to increase their effectiveness.

It is imperative that these appraisals be done confidentially. Perhaps Helen could compile the answers and give each person a summary of his or her results. An Upward Appraisal is effective only if everyone is totally honest about those whom they are evaluating and if the partners and managers are honest with themselves about the feedback they receive. The Upward Appraisals should be an enlightening experience.

An Upward Appraisal should be useful in helping to determine the cause of the problems Ms. Fixby and Mr. Morgan are encountering. Jim Morgan may need additional training and counseling on how to get along better with his clients and his peers. You may conclude that you have a partner who has a problem working with women clients and with women professionals in your firm. Thus far, you have been able to reassign the clients he has almost lost, but you may not be so lucky with your staff.

We all try to keep turnover as low as possible and Jim Morgan may be creating unnecessary turnovers. Jim may not be effective as a partner, but right now you have only your gut reaction to go by. Given the results of the Upward Appraisal and the partners' retreat, you can determine whether Jim is willing and able to improve or if he should leave your firm.

You and some of your partners may also want to attend the conference sponsored by the American Institute of Certified Public Accountants

(AICPA) on Marketing and Managing a Success-ful Tax Practice, held annually in Phoenix, Arizona. This is a major conference with nation-ally-recognized speakers. Participants come from all over the United States to find out how to market and manage their accounting practices better. I have attended this conference and it has helped me keep up-to-date on technology and personnel issues.

One of the conference ideas that we have implemented is the sharing of administrative responsibilities. We want to develop our staff to their full potential, both as technicians and as future partners. In order for a firm to remain successful, staff must be trained and motivated so that their strengths can be fully utilized. Our goal is to have strong individuals who can work well together as a cohesive group. We strive to constantly improve both the technical compe-tence and the administrative abilities of each member of the firm.

Let's turn now to the subject of Marsha Fixby. I would suggest that the partners review the firm's strategic plan and partnership criteria to deter-mine if she is eligible to become a partner. As we both know, one does not become a partner just by working 15-hour days. The attributes of a partner and the reasons for adding partners to the firm are complex and far-reaching and cannot be based just on the number of hours worked. Unless Ms. Fixby has most of the attributes that you require in a partner, you cannot promote her, no matter how hard she works. Ms. Fixby either needs additional staff to whom she can delegate work, or she needs training in effective delegation so that she is not working 15-hour days.

If you need help in determining what attributes a partner should have, how to structure a partner-ship document or what questions to ask in an Upward Appraisal, you can get this information by purchasing *Management of an Accounting Practice Handbook* published by the AICPA. This three-volume set has been invaluable to the partners in my firm by helping us to manage our accounting practice. Through our national organization, we have the luxury of obtaining specialized informa-tion that otherwise would take many hours to research and compile.

It is never easy to make changes. However, you and your firm will certainly benefit from the time and attention you are giving these matters.

I look forward to hearing from you soon.

Sincerely,

Debra A. Hunter, CPA

Three Tough Issues Need Your Attention

Edward M. Pickett

Mr. Pickett, professor of small business, directs the Business Outreach programs at the University of Wisconsin-Milwaukee's Small Business Development Center. He also worked for 10 years in personnel and management in the private sector.

Dear Dick:

Thanks for your letter on the personnel situation at Shew and Associates, CPAs, Ltd.

My style is to help you identify issues and options, but you'll have to make your own personnel decisions, which I'm sure you wish to do.

Would you agree that there are three issues which need attention? I think they are: confronting a problem employee, rewarding an outstanding performer, and evaluating your role with your company.

Issue #1 - Confronting a problem employee. It's irrelevant that under your present strategic plan Jim wouldn't make partner today. He is a partner and you take your personnel problems as you find them.

Wouldn't it be great if we could look at Jim's personnel records together? What would they show? Let's see. He's been with you for seven years and was made a partner three years ago. Dick, you need to check out the following:

- When did he become a whiner and complainer?
- Has he always been a rumor monger?
- You say he can't get along with anyone. He berates younger staff and his secretaries hate him. Why?
- You also say Marsha Fixby is working circles around him. She's twice as productive. Is this true?
- Helen states two women clients found him patronizing and rude and she moved them to Marsha. (Helen seems to have a lot of authority for a secretary, but that's another issue.) Is this the extent of the clients he's lost?

Dick, I suggest you establish that the five points listed above are all valid and then try to affix dates to these for when they started. While you're doing your homework, prior to talking to Jim, I recommend you consider:

- Are these five points all the problems Jim has or are there others?
- Check out his billables for the last seven years. I know you have these records. What do they show? A decline, steady performance, or what? Is he a productive partner?
- What prompted you to make him a partner in the first place?
- What do the three other partners think of Jim?
- Can you find out what his present clients think of him without tipping your hand?

This is the homework to do before you talk to him. You will need data to support each of these points when you confront Jim. Yes, I think *you* should be the one to confront Jim because everyone considers you to be the personnel director, mediator and boss. However, I think you should think about your role for the future, and I'll get into that a bit later.

Jim needs a serious discussion about his future with your firm and even his own CPA career. If all of Jim's problems started at approximately the same time, this might indicate a mental or physical problem. If this is true, I am not qualified to help you. You should talk to a counselor and see what he or she says. You should be able to find one in the yellow pages.

If Jim has, as I suspect, been declining in his performance and behavior for years, then your discussion is crucial. It probably won't be pleasant, but don't duck it. You owe it to your firm and Jim Morgan to face up to it.

Block out a couple of hours and start the discussion with his assessment of his CPA work and people skills. Then bring up your bill of particulars and get his side of the story. You should reach a conclusion on this question: Does he just have people problems, or, is he also nonproductive?

Assuming the worst, that Jim is unproductive and has a long-term people problem and he doesn't see it, he must be told four things:

- His billables indicate he is not productive.
- His behavior toward staff and clients is unacceptable for a professional and must improve. He must be able to distinguish between acceptable professional behavior and unacceptable nonprofessional behavior.
- He must agree to a timetable. Show him where he is in billables and set a rising target for him to meet or exceed in a specified time. A timetable to improve his staff-client relationships is also critical. This timetable should not exceed 90 days. You should set up biweekly meetings to discuss progress. These meetings should discuss his problems but should be positive. He should know that if he

If all of Jim's problems started at approximately the same time, this might indicate a mental or physical problem.

doesn't come up to standards, he will be dismissed. It's up to him.

- You must extend an offer to help. Perhaps you can suggest a mentor, or counseling, or training on sensitivity, or training on handling people effectively.

In any event, you and your firm will be winners if you convince Jim that he can once again be a valued and productive partner in your firm. If, in the worst case, you have to let him go, you will be reassured that you did your best to reasonably accommodate him. That will help prevent a claim of wrongful discharge. Jim's problem will not go away by itself.

Issue #2 - Rewarding an outstanding performer. Helen certainly gave you enough personnel situations for a lunch. Good thing you didn't take her to dinner.

While Jim is at one end of the spectrum, Marsha is at the other. This is probably one of the toughest situations all small businesses must face: adequately rewarding an outstanding performer. As you noted, you lost Hank Erlich to Hammerly and Jensen, and now he's a partner there. You don't want it to happen again. By the way, when Hank left, did you talk with him to find out the specific reasons why? This sort of information is very valuable.

You may be wondering where to start. I suggest Marsha's personnel file. What does it show? Did you hire Marsha? Who does she look up to or turn to for advice? How do the other partners feel about Marsha? Does she really work 15-hours a day, five days a week? Why? What are her billables? What does she want out of a career? A partnership? Money? Prestige? More staff?

By the way, is Marsha the only "star" you have? You had better check that out because if you have more than one Marsha, you should take care of both at once. Have you and your partners ever discussed the care and feeding of stars? If you haven't, join the rest of small businesses who don't address this until they have lost one.

Now let's get back to Marsha and let's assume that she is the only star. I think you should lay out a strategy to keep her a productive CPA with your firm. Let me pose questions in five categories:

Money. Does your compensation system directly relate to contribution? Is this based on an individ-ual's performance or on small account-ing teams?

Perks. What do the partners get? How about the non-partners? CPAs? What can you do finan-cially? Is this of any interest to Marsha?

Position. Are you ready to create another partner? Of course, if you fire or demote Morgan, there may be an opening. Does Marsha want to be a partner?

Coach-Mentor. Books have been written on this topic and it would be easy to find one. Could you create a coach-mentor for Marsha? What would this offer her? Who would you pick? Would the relationship click and would it be successful?

Recognition. Does Marsha know that she is appreciated and that her accomplishments are important? How does she get recognition?

Now, if you have answers to these questions, who will talk to Marsha? I suspect it will be you. I recommend that you clear it with the other partners. The purpose of the talk would be to:

- Make sure that Marsha knows that her performance is noted and appreciated.
- Find out what her career plans are and how Shew and Associates can help. But unless you are prepared to grant things at this time, I recommend against making promises.
- Establish a relationship with Marsha that will make her feel open to discussing problems with you.

Dick, Marsha should come out of this talk with the strong conviction that she is appreciated and is perceived to be a great asset to this firm.

Issue #3 - Evaluating your role with your company. I get the impression that you are not happy with the roles of boss, mediator, and personnel director. You love doing accounting work and that's great. You built a highly regarded firm in the last 23 years and you should be proud. Is this the time to take stock of your life and career? You're 55, you have plenty of great years left. How do you want to spend them? The decision is yours. Nowhere is it written that you have to continue to be managing partner, right? I urge you to consider three options: sabbatical, rotation and division.

Think about taking a sabbatical for six months to a year, and picking another partner to be interim manager. If it works out great for both parties, fine. If not, you'll have to reassess.

Or, how about a two-year rotation system among the partners so that all five get to be the manager-director? Life is short; it should be enjoyed. You can go back to the work you love and get rid of the work you don't enjoy. Think about it. Is this the time?

Another option is to divide the management work among the partners. One could be

> *I urge you to consider three options: sabbatical, rotation and division.*

responsible for marketing, another for administration. One could be the personnel person. (This must be common in your profession, because my classes are filled with CPAs who need some personnel education.)

Dick, it's a long letter, but you raise three issues that small business people don't take time to think about. I hope that by doing your homework and by having some timely talks, you will salvage Jim Morgan and keep Marsha Fixby. And I hope that you will consider changing your own role.

Good luck.

Cordially,

Edward M Pickett

Edward M. Pickett

Your Ambivalence Has Created a Leadership Vacuum

Sally Helgesen

Author of The Female Advantage: Women's Ways of Leadership, *(Doubleday/ Currency, 1990),* Ms. Helgesen has another book entitled Building a Web of Inclusion: A New Architecture for Organizations, *(Doubleday/Currency, 1993).*

Dear Dick:

As always, it was good to hear from you, though I could tell from the tone of your letter that you're deeply upset. That's understandable—the dilemma you describe is a tough one, particularly as it's complicated by the subtle yet thorny issue of gender.

But before I offer you my perspective, I have to give it to you straight. You've got to let go of your nostalgia for the days you ran a two-person office. If you really are unhappy and do want to return to full-time accounting, you should seriously consider selling your business and starting a little practice of your own. If you're not willing to do that, you'll simply have to accept the responsibilities thrust upon you by your success, and deal forcefully with the personnel issues that do—and will continue to—occur in a company with 30 employees.

At the risk of being too blunt, the tone of your letter leads me to believe that your reluctance to confront these problems has made matters worse. Jim may well be the insecure bully that you describe, but the leadership vacuum created by your ambivalence about running a large firm has given him the leeway to exercise his worst impulses. The situation is similar to a common family situation where an older child bullies the younger one. It's almost always a sign that the parents are neglecting to exercise proper authority.

Okay, so much for the lecture. Now the question is, what do you do? How can you restore morale to your firm and blunt the ugly effects of rivalries? First, you must have a long talk with Jim Morgan. Do it outside the office, and give yourself a day or two to prepare. Since you have a tendency to blow up, over-prepare: think out everything he might say to counter your points, and decide on calm and appropriate ways to respond. At the outset of your talk, be strong and frank: tell him exactly what is bothering you, but refuse to be drawn into the position of repeating what other people have said, which can only trivialize the problems and distract you from your major points.

Also, let Jim know that you are partly responsible for the level of interoffice rivalries and bickering because you have been reluctant to take an active role in personnel management. But let him know those days are over, that you're taking responsibility for improving office morale; and that you're counting on him to help you in this effort.

I recognize that it's going to be difficult to strike exactly the right note. You don't want to be accusatory, and you don't want to trade in rumors and gossip. But at the same time, you have to let him know that you understand that negative attitudes are tearing your company apart, and you will not stand by and let that happen.

Above all, appeal to his interests as a partner. I know you're sorry you made him one, but the fact that you did can work for you now. Certainly, given his liability and exposure, he does not want to lay the company open to the possibility of legal action by Marsha Fixby, or by women clients who have been made to feel uncomfortable. *That* is the direction the company is heading if Jim continues to make derogatory remarks and if Marsha continues to be undercompensated for her work.

Please, don't let Jim get away with the excuse that he was "only joking" when he was perceived to be patronizing and rude. Again, perception is most important in this regard. If he feels that other people in the company lack a sense of humor because they take offense at some of his remarks, that's *his* problem—and the

The leadership vacuum created by your ambivalence has given him the leeway to exercise his worst impulses.

problem of the firm in which he has an equity stake.

Now, on to the issue of Marsha Fixby. You need to fully accept that, given the quality of her work and her popularity with clients, you most certainly will lose her if you don't make her a partner soon. At its worst, her departure could have legal ramifications; failing that, it will surely result in lost business. And just as surely, it will create an atmosphere in which other women employees—whether fairly or not—begin to perceive your firm as an unsympathetic place for women to work. They will view it as a company in which the glass ceiling is impenetrable despite the talent and dedication that a woman might bring to her work.

These are terrible alternatives, so I strongly urge you to look at ways in which you might be able to promote Marsha to partner. Doing so will be a boon to your company in the long run, and should further serve to keep the Jim Morgans of the world in line. Bullies are at their worst when they perceive other people as lacking power.

Finally, you need to take a serious look at how your firm might restructure so that you don't have to deal with problems like this on a crisis basis. It's painfully obvious that the company needs channels for more open communication, so people don't have to resort to backbiting and gossiping in the rest room. You need to put people with real authority in place who can report to you on disputes as they arise, so you won't have to hear about them—after the fact—from your secretary.

Since you also need to create an area of common interest between Jim Morgan and Marsha Fixby, consider appointing the two of them to co-chair a small committee that will make recommendations on how fairness issues are affecting the staff. Being co-chairs will give them the opportunity they need to work openly together and to forge the kind of relationship they must develop if they are both to function as partners. Give them a chance to work the issue out together. If they disagree about something, ask them to decide how to handle it among themselves, and then to get back to you with their decision. The other side of exercising proper authority is knowing when to give other people responsibility for handling their problems.

As partners, both Marsha and Jim will have a long-term commitment to the firm. Unless Jim Morgan is absolutely out of control (in which case, you should review his contract), he will probably prove valuable once he recognizes that you are determined to put strong standards in

place and that you are serious about maintaining high morale. You've had a leadership problem in the firm, partly because you've been ambivalent about your role there. That's a problem only you can solve, Dick. Good luck!

Sincerely,

Sally Helgesen

Sally Helgesen

Respect, Respect, Respect

Mary Rowe, Ph.D.

Dr. Rowe teaches Negotiation and Conflict Management at the MIT Sloan School of Management, where she is also an ombudsperson for the MIT community.

BY EXPRESS—CONFIDENTIAL AND PERSONAL—FOR MR. RICHARD SHEW ONLY

Dear Richard:

I am honored that you ask my advice. I think of your firm as one of the best in the business. But I am not surprised by your question—nearly everyone who runs a small business has this kind of problem sooner or later. You ask what you should do. Well, I think we should begin by asking these questions:

- Is this an emergency?
- What do I really know? What will I need to know?
- Whose interests are at stake? What are their interests?
- Whose rights are at stake? How?
- How powerful is each major actor? In what ways?

Is this an emergency?

Helen certainly thinks it is pretty urgent. I think so too, which is why I am sending this answer back to you by express. (I hope you will feel free to telephone me. And by the way, do you have a private fax line?) I am worried about evidence of petty sabotage, intimidation and possible sex discrimination on the part of Jim Morgan. Most of all, I am concerned that Morgan may be acting as if he feels deeply humiliated. I believe that humiliation is the parent of destruc-

---

Take a serious look at how your firm might restructure so that you don't have to deal with problems like this on a crisis basis.

tive behavior, so to me this makes your question quite urgent. Morgan needs to be approached immediately—with respect—in order to prevent still more serious damage. He needs a chance to talk through his point of view for as long as he wishes.

I am very concerned about Marsha Fixby. Might she be working too hard? Is the firm recognizing her fairly? I wonder what *she* thinks is going on and how she feels about it. I think you are right to be worried about losing another "rising star." I also think this is not your only possible risk.

What do I really know? What will I need to know?

I know you have every confidence in Helen. She has always sounded to me like a gem. Moreover, as I read your letter, it was easy to believe what she told you. Nevertheless, let me back off just a little, and please bear with me if I ask you to check things out a bit more than you have.

You have always done superlative technical work. I know that you keep up scrupulously with changes in accounting law. (I loved the article you wrote on 1993 tax changes—and I want you to know that I did indeed move some flexible business expenses into 1993, after I read your piece in the *Forum.*) However—as you say yourself—you have not been able to keep up in this same thoughtful way with your staff and their interests. I am going to suggest to you—after we note your own accounting skills—that your *colleagues* are your most important resources, and that you must get to know more about them. Talking once with Helen is not a substitute for sitting down regularly with Jim and Marsha—and with a number of others, including your clients.

Whose interests are at stake? What are their interests?

You will, of course, want to make your own list of those whose interests are at stake in this situation. I hope you will begin the list with yourself, and, for that matter, include the interests of your wife and family if you think this is appropriate. I have added Jim and Marsha and Helen, the other staff and the secretaries that you mentioned. I would also add the other partners and your bank. And I am quite concerned about your clients. Am I missing someone else who matters? For example, are the interests of Hammerly and Jensen—or any other competitor—at stake, and could competitors possibly be playing a role in this difficult situation?

When you get this note, Richard, please make your own thoughtful list of all the possible stakeholders in this situation and what their interests are.

For example, begin with your own short- and long-run interests. Do you want to learn how to deal better with personnel matters on your own? You are only 55. You need to know whether you really are tired and are thinking about exploring a different career, or, whether you want to stay with your firm, but delegate personnel management. In either of these cases, consider having another partner—or possibly Helen, after a promotion to Executive Officer—deal now and later with these kinds of problems. Or, do you now want to learn to practice human resource management and quality management skills—in the same way you have learned and excelled in other areas?

What do the other partners think? *Is* there anyone else who could and would take on personnel oversight, now and in the future? What are the other partners' interests in this situation? Are the other partners also upset about Morgan? Does anyone know about the technical quality of his current work or his relationships with other clients?

My next question is about Helen. Your letter suggests that she has been handling responsibilities that you might well have thought your own. She has been listening carefully to client concerns and "facilitated" two clients going over to Fixby. Is her interest simply taking care of the firm? In this case you are probably very lucky and I wonder if Helen is being recognized appropriately. But—are you sure that there is no hidden agenda? The data you give me are consistent with appropriate—or inappropriate—lobbying by women for more recognition of women, and perhaps with some other laudable or problematic motivations, as well. What are her real interests?

The information you gave me about Jim could mean anything. Perhaps he is drinking too much, or having some other serious health problem, or is afraid of and resentful toward women, or is in over his head, or is being set up by someone and maligned. You need more information immediately. If you could quickly and quietly review any technical work he has done recently, you might get a handle on his situation. But some partner or you need to talk with him soon. Someone needs to sit down with him to listen carefully and draw him out. Please listen before you raise to him the concerns you have heard. Under all circumstances, give him an adequate chance to defend himself when the various concerns do come up.

Do you want to learn how to deal better with personnel matters on your own?

The staff has a right to a work environment that is free of intimidation and harassment.

By the same token, someone needs to pay a lot of attention right away to Marsha and draw her out in a supportive way. Did she want the last two clients? Does she feel she is doing okay? How does she feel about working with the *other* staff? I recommend doing a little homework before holding these conversations. Be prepared to discuss with her the classic performance evaluation questions: What assignments has she had? What has she gotten done? Where has she been doing well? Is there any way you could help her improve? How does she see her own interests in the next year or two? Listen carefully to see if by any chance she suggests that you talk with anyone else—a secretary, a client, a colleague. If so, follow up.

The interests of the rest of the staff may be very much at stake. You may want to talk with a number of people and ask them quite explicitly how they feel about their work environment and how it could be improved. I remember a time when a colleague from another business had a serious breakdown; I was surprised, but the cleaning person wasn't. She had known for months that something was very wrong, because the colleague had begun to treat her very disrespectfully.

Consider checking in with some or all of your relevant clients. I am thinking about the two that have been moved over to Marsha, but also of others. This is a very competitive economy and I think you or a partner or Executive Officer need to establish relationships that will provide feedback. At the very least, your clients have an interest in being treated professionally. Of course, you will want to ask about work quality and the timeliness of your firm's service to them.

Finally—did you include someone on your list that I do not know about? Please go over your list several times. All the major mistakes that I have made in life (those I know about, at least!) come from failures to think through whose interests were at stake and what those interests actually were.

Whose rights are at stake? How?

Next to each person's name on your list, include a column about "rights" and fill it in. Here are some examples: Do you and the other partners have a right in the Partnership Agreement to ask for a certain level of work? How is this right specified?

Jim would probably think he has a right to know if his relationships are thought to be unprofessional and so poor that clients are "facilitated" away from him. And of course he has a right not to be slandered (in case the story you have been told is not true).

The staff has a right to a work environment that is free of intimidation and harassment. Marsha had a right to be treated equally, and to have an environment that is free of demeaning comments about her clothes. The clients also have a right to service that is not sexist.

How powerful is each major actor? In what ways?

Each person has different kinds of power to use, whether responsibly or irresponsibly. So, make a third column of what each actor has the power to do and then think about whether they would use that power. The most important groups seem to be you, the other partners, Jim, Marsha, Helen and your clients. You may very well need an hour or two with your attorney, but first try this yourself on the list in front of you.

Do you have the formal power to remove or constrain Jim? To make Marsha a partner? Do you have enough *informal* influence, alone or together with your other partners to change or stop Jim's behavior? Is there any other partner who has a close relationship with Jim? What would you need to know, for example, about Jim's work performance in order to have more power in this situation?

Jim may have some formal powers of his own, in your Partnership Agreement and in law. He might be able to sue for defamation or interference with his business relationships. Marsha (and Helen and the secretaries) might be able to sue for sexual harassment or other forms of sex discrimination, depending on what facts you uncover.

I am also concerned about the informal power of each actor. Jim could mess up the data in your computers, or cause trouble for a client. He might even assault someone in the firm—a secretary, Helen, Marsha—if he is really falling apart and sees no way out. Marsha might leave with vital private information about the firm and take a number of clients with her. Clients might hear of trouble and leave your firm. Helen already appears to have had enough informal power to facilitate client moves in the firm. You may want to consider this point carefully. Should Helen be promoted? Or was she overstepping in an inappropriate way? What might she do next?

Obviously, you have not yet had a chance to think this through and to collect information. Also, I do not mean to unduly discourage you. (Remember that I am always looking for ways to minimize the worst possible losses as well as to maximize the best possible gains!) Would you want to call as soon as you have had a chance to think this through a bit, so we can work out long-term and short-term strategies that make sense? You may want to do a bit more nosing around before you make any decisions, or you might need to ask someone else to gather more information.

In the meantime, old friend, please remember: respect, respect, respect. Everyone in your firm matters to you. And all may be doing the best they can. So—begin by listening *a lot*, before you make the next decision.

Sincerely,

Mary Rowe

Respect, respect, respect.

Chapter 6

"I Want to Hire a Top-Level Employee. How Do I Go about It?"

Catherine Stover

David McLimans

K im Williford, Ph.D., owner of Custom Software, Inc., was pleased to see that there were no pink tablecloths this time at the annual Women in Business Awards Banquet. Last year, the hotel's dining hall had been decorated with pink flowers, pink napkins, pink name cards. The only decoration that had been missing, Kim thought, was a row of rosy-cheeked bridesmaids.

This year, the banquet organizers must have gotten the message that the business women in this community should be taken seriously. Kim and her peers sat at a white-and-gold table that was decidedly elegant. She was glad that she had made the effort to attend the awards ceremony, and she was enjoying the after-dinner conversation at her table.

But when her friend Rhonda asked what was new at Custom Software, Kim sighed and said, "I've decided to hire a financial expert so that I can spend more time on marketing. This will be my first top-level employee."

Rhonda said, "Sounds great. So why the heavy sigh?"

"The worst mistakes I've made in the history of managing my company have been in hiring. It's been my biggest headache. I've hired technicians who were stuck in 1980s technol-

Catherine Stover is the editor of the Small Business Forum.

ogy, clerical people who spent most of their time selling beauty aids over the phone, and an accountant who went through a mid-life crisis at my expense. I can't afford to make a mistake this time. This person will have a lot of responsibility—which means he or she could really improve my company or really mess it up."

Janet said, "I know what you're going through. Ever since I hired a senior accountant who turned out to have a fake college diploma, fake references, and less understanding of accounting than I have, I've used a recruiting firm for all of my professional-level hires."

"Really?" Kim asked. "Has it been successful?"

"Well, yes. It means that you have to give up some control, and it's expensive, but it's not as expensive as making a big mistake."

Rhonda said, "Control might be a legitimate issue if you are looking for someone you have to be able to trust. Do you want to delegate the hiring of your number two person to someone else?"

"I know someone who hired a graphologist," Sharon said.

"What's a graphologist?"

"A handwriting expert. This friend of mine had narrowed her search down to two people. She gave a graphologist writing samples from both, and the graphologist told her about the applicants' personality traits. It turns out that she was pretty accurate."

Diane said, "I guess I would try some of those psychological tests before I would try graphology."

Sharon said, "I have an Ouija board you could consult."

Kim said, "It would probably be more accurate than the dart board that I used last time. But seriously, I have to be concerned about the legal issues involved too. I know that applicants have certain rights, though I don't know what those rights are. And I know that the Americans with Disabilities Act is taking effect now for companies with 15 or more employees. Depending on how you count them, I have either 16 or 12 employees."

Theresa said, "Which is why I still haven't replaced one of my top people who left six months ago. It's a headache. People who have big businesses and can afford a human resources department don't know how lucky they are. There are endless ways to really make a mess of things."

Rhonda said, "But think of how much better off your company will be if you hire a top-notch financial officer. Kim, you are a natural marketer because you are a design wiz. You know what your clients need even before they do. That's what you should be doing with your time. Didn't your sales

almost double last year? Things could *really* take off if you could spend your time doing what you're best at. If I were you, I'd bite the bullet and get serious about hiring someone now."

Sharon said, "And in the meantime, we'll all keep in mind that you're looking for someone. Who knows? Maybe someone here will happen to come across the right person."

Theresa said, "What kind of person are you looking for, anyway? I know you said you wanted a financial officer, but this person will have to do more than just the books, right?"

Kim said, "Well, yes. I want someone who can be in charge of all the numbers—everything from calculating a new pricing structure to conducting a budgetary analysis to supervising the pay roll. I guess it sounds pretty broad, but people who work for small businesses have to be versatile."

Rhonda said, "Sounds to me like you want a vice president who runs the office while you make the sales."

Kim laughed. "That's right. I'd like someone who could take care of things so that I can concentrate on growing the company. It's not that I have math anxiety—I've taken care of the budget for years myself—it's just that I don't think it's the best use of my time."

Diane said, "I hope you don't make the same mistake that I made a few years ago when I hired someone to run things for me. I didn't write a job description because I wasn't sure at the time what I wanted my new manager to do. So I hired a very ambitious go-getter who just took over. I had to get rid of him in about a year because we didn't have the same goals or the same philosophy. I hope you don't have to learn that lesson the hard way."

Kim said, "I'll keep that in mind. I guess I'm going to have to do some soul-searching to find out what kind of person I really should be looking for."

Diane said, "And if you find a sure-fire way to hire someone, you have to let us know. We're all in the same boat."

Theresa said, "If you get it figured out, you could sell your company and make a living at teaching people like us how to do it right."

Rhonda said, "Kim, you've solved tough problems before. I'm sure you'll figure this one out too. When we were in high school, they didn't have any computers in the building. You were the only girl in your college computer classes. Your company has a great reputation. You've been in business too long to let something like this slow you down."

"Thanks, Rhonda. I feel like I just won one of the awards that they were handing out. I'm

The worst mistakes I've made in the history of managing my company have been in hiring.

going to contact as many experts as I can and learn as much as I can about hiring professionals. I'm sure it will pay off in the long run."

What advice would you give Kim Williford? *We asked a number of experts to offer advice and suggestions.*

Write a Results-Oriented Job Description

Roger J. Plachy

Author of Results-Oriented Job Descriptions, More Than 225 Models to Use or Adapt—With Guidelines for Creating Your Own *(AMACOM, 1993), Mr. Plachy is a principal of the Job Results Management Institute in Winston-Salem, North Carolina, and has consulted with managers for nearly 25 years.*

Dear Kim:

How nice to hear from you again. Congratulations on your successes, but then we who know you well are not surprised. Thanks for inviting me to offer some help as you expand Custom Software.

You wrote that the worst mistakes you've made in managing your company were in hiring. Join the ranks of the disappointed. Understanding people is still the bane of most managers. However, that's because most managers still approach relationships with employees as a voyage in uncharted territory.

One map for a relationship is a job description. A job description? you say. Isn't that what we write so that our personnel folders are up-to-date? Generally that's the way a job description is used, but successful managers know better.

Hiring is only one step in the management process. Your friend Diane discovered that the person she hired did not have the same goals or philosophy that she had. She learned that she should have identified her requirements before she made a job offer.

Message #1: Define the results the job must accomplish. Diane said she didn't write a job description because she wasn't sure what she wanted her new manager to do. That's very understandable. Who among us can predict the

future? (When you learn to do *that*, start your road show immediately.)

Prepare a temporary job description. Mark it "TEMPORARY" at the top. Schedule a review of the job description at four months into the new relationship. Make sure that your new employee understands and agrees with the plan.

Kim, in your letter you said, "I have to do some soul-searching to find out what kind of person I really should be looking for." Soul-searching, yes, but let me suggest a different ending to that statement: "... to find out what *work I want this person to accomplish*." Concentrate first on what the person will be expected to accomplish.

Message #2: Focus on the work instead of on the person. You said that taking care of the budget is not the best use of your time. Analyzing your own job is an excellent place to begin thinking about the work that will augment yours. Ask yourself:

- What work needs to be accomplished for Custom Software to continue its growth?
- What directions are defined in your strategic plan?
- What are your talents?
- What is the best application of your talents?
- How much time are you spending on your various responsibilities?
- Where should you be spending your time? (You mentioned marketing.)
- Where do you need help?

You suggested, for example, calculating the price structure, conducting budget analysis, and supervising the payroll preparation. Think of writing a job description as clarifying a new division of responsibilities. The new executive should have some ideas. You may even negotiate a new job description at the time of hire, but at least you will have a solid basis for the discussion.

Because I know you and other entrepreneurs like you, let me remind you that Custom Software is your baby. You are not likely to give up control easily. After all, you've done it all and you are successful. But you're at a new stage in the development of your company, Kim. Other people will have to help you grow your company.

Still, dividing the responsibilities is not the same as giving up control. *You* will control how your company proceeds, I'll bet on that. However, now you need a more complex map based on different people sharing the work.

Message #3: Focus on the results to be achieved. Earlier I asked you to focus on the work instead of on the person. Let's magnify that concept. Traditionally work has been described as what

Define the results the job must accomplish.

people do. A new, results-oriented style emphasizes the *results* people must accomplish.

The point is that people can *do* what we ask of them yet not *accomplish* the results we want.

Using some of the examples you gave me, here's what I mean by adding results to the duties:

Maintains Competitive Marketing Posture
by
calculating the price structure.

Provides Managers with Planning and Control Information
by
conducting budget analysis.

Pays Employees and Complies Payroll Information
by
supervising the payroll and preparation.

Notice the three-part structure with the word "by" always separating the result from the duty. This structure helps us think more clearly about a job's real purpose.

Message #4: Define why work is important. Don't let me put words to your plans. The results in the examples are only ideas to illustrate the difference between results and duties. The important commitment for you is to define the results that you need to have accomplished. Results explain why work is important to the business. Here's a trick to clarify the results and duties you have in mind: transpose your ideas both before and after the "by."

You mentioned some legal concerns, specifically the Americans with Disabilities Act (ADA). You're right to be concerned and I know that you are seeking advice elsewhere, so I won't dwell on the topic.

The concept of the ADA reinforces a focus on job results instead of on job duties. The ADA language is: "... able to perform the essential functions of the job." I prefer the words: "... able to *accomplish* the essential functions of the job."

The results-oriented style focuses on whether or not the person can *accomplish* job results. It opens the possibility that the person may not *do* the job the way others would. The law aims us at allowing for individual differences that do not substantially affect job outcomes.

Message #5: Define job qualifications. Identifying results helps clarify the specific qualifications candidates need to fulfill our needs successfully. For example, the result "to provide managers with planning and control information" suggests a different ability than the duty "to conduct budget analysis." Focusing on job

results helps us clarify the kind of person we want.

Message #6: Manage job results. The job description is also valuable as a reference for charting work plans that aim at fulfilling the business objectives established in your strategic plan. Work plans are guides for preventing individual job results from drifting off-course.

Let me conclude this way, Kim: Your concern is that the person you hire could either improve your company, or mess it up. We all face these concerns when we decide to involve others in our business. We start our business, nurture it, and want it to succeed. If we want our business to grow, eventually we will need help from others. We can't do it all by ourselves.

You need to set the stage for people, give them your support and guidance, and turn them loose in the same way that you set out freely when you started Custom Software. The trick, however, is to give them your vision for the company, and specifically, the results you need to continue to be successful.

Do keep me posted on your progress.

Best regards.

Roger J. Plachy

Roger J. Plachy

Take it From Me: Write a Job Description

Jim Johnson

As CEO of White Glove Service Systems, Inc.

 *with approximately 300 employees throughout the country, Mr. Johnson has 18 years of experience in solving human resources problems.*

Dear Kim:

Let me tell you what happened to me one time with one of my new hires. I hired a workaholic to be a manager of a large contract for our company. He was eager to catch our attention and to please his immediate supervisor. He not only did his assigned job well, he volunteered for almost everything that came up. His attitude was, "I'll handle this, and that, and I'll go here and there."

Well, it was very nice for a while to have someone around who did everything. But,

---

after a few months, we found that we had to "reel him back in." We had to set him down and get him refocused. He had lost his focus because he was doing too much. He would not delegate responsibilities—he was doing everything himself. He became ineffective as a manager, even though he was an outstanding employee.

But we needed a manager. So we decided to write a job description for him—and what a difference this has made. He has become an effective manager and he is still with us. He sticks to his assigned duties, and he has learned to delegate. He is also helping to develop and write job descriptions for his job site.

He understands that once the job description is written, it is fairly easy to determine the personal qualifications that are important for the job.

I am telling you this because I hope that you will learn from my experience. Employees can do too much (though it's more common for them to do too little) if you don't describe what you want them to accomplish in detail.

I understand the situation you find yourself in pretty well. I've had to make important hiring decisions several times since I've been in business, and it's never easy.

When I spoke to you last week, we talked briefly about the type of person you would like to hire. I've had a chance to think about it, and I think I can give you some fairly good advice based on some of the things I've learned by going through the process.

I believe that before you hire this person, you should write a job description that covers all of the duties that the new employee will be expected to perform.

List the duties you expect the employee to do, then write out why, and how they are to be done. This will help you to determine what qualifications to look for in the employee, and whether or not the duties you want performed are broad enough, clear enough or fair.

When writing the job description, I use the following order:

- Job identification,
- Job summary,
- Duties to be performed,
- Supervision to be given,
- Relation to other jobs,
- Working conditions,
- Definitions of unusual terms, and
- Comments that add to and clarify the above.

Since the person you choose has probably not been exposed to your type of business, you should explain some of the terms or jargon used in the computer software business, so that the new employee will feel comfortable as quickly as possible.

When we spoke last week, you mentioned that the new employee should have a strong background in finance. That being the case, I would suggest that you include a section concerning the goals you would like to accomplish with his or her help. Since marketing is your strong suit, I think this new employee should be able to help you establish policies, objectives, and plans for overall company profitability and productivity.

Most experienced employees tend to carry their work pattern with them into new jobs, which will then modify their new job drastically. So if I were you, Kim, I would rewrite the job description after he or she has had time to alter the job. I've found that job descriptions can quickly get out of date. Out-of-date job descriptions can cause lots of problems, as you can imagine.

Another thing to remember about job descriptions: if you are going to use it as a tool for job evaluation, make sure that you and your new employee agree that the job description is fair for the wages being paid. Otherwise, the job description and the job evaluation will both be considered unfair.

Kim, you've done an outstanding job in managing and growing your company, so there is no doubt that you know exactly what duties you want the new employee to perform. Carefully consider these duties, and write them out.

But you should always remember that when it comes to hiring the right employee, there are no sure fire formulas. Hiring is ultimately a matter of predicting human behavior. I suggest you go with your gut feelings—after interviewing several qualified candidates and after diligently doing your reference checks.

The many years of experience I've had in dealing with our staff, and all of the different job classifications we use out in the field, has taught me well. Of course, my staff and I have had our share of mistakes. We've taken what we have learned through trial and error, and have developed a pretty good method of writing job descriptions.

I hope that these suggestions will help you. Don't hesitate to call me with questions.

Best wishes and continued success.

I remain always your friend,

Jim Johnson

It was very nice for a while to have someone around who did everything. But, after a few months, we found that we had to "reel him back in."

Consider These Guidelines on Conducting Interviews

Michael W. Mercer, Ph.D.

Author of Hire the Best ... and Avoid the Rest *(AMACOM, 1993) Dr. Mercer is an industrial psychologist and professional speaker with the Mercer Group, Inc., Chicago.*

Dear Kim:

When we talked on the phone today about interview techniques, I promised I would send you some information from my new book *Hire the Best ... and Avoid the Rest*.

Before I begin, however, I'd like to say that interviewing is one part of the hiring *process*. It's also important to test your candidates and check their references. I hope that you will consider the other steps of the process as well.

For now, however, I would like to share some information with you on the essential elements and the potential traps of interviewing.

Six Essentials of all Effective Interviews

The six essentials of all effective interviews are as follows:

Do a quick, yet exacting, job analysis. This specifies the six to nine job-related criteria required of a candidate who is capable of succeeding in a par-ticular job. Such job analyses can be accomplished easily with the help of a job analysis checklist.

Take notes during the interview. It is amazing how often managers fail to take notes during interviews. Or if they take them, their comments turn out to be useless. Why does this happen? Some interviewers simply do not know what to write. Yet this problem vanishes when a customized Interview Guide Form is used.

Other interviewers figure that they can take notes after the interview. Lots of luck! Often after an interview, a busy manager forgets key points or gets distracted by a rash of conversations, meetings, or phone calls. By the next day, that manager won't have a clue as to what to write about an applicant.

Both excuses for not taking notes must be avoided. It is necessary to take notes so that a useful record of the interview will be available for a later discussion and rating of each candidate.

Remember the principle that past behavior is the best predictor of future behavior. How can you spot behavior patterns relevant to the job? Continually:

- Ask for specific *examples* of projects, tasks, or assignments the candidate has handled.
- Probe for *details* on how the candidate actually went about this work.
- Look for *patterns* in how the candidate accomplished these tasks.

For instance, imagine that you want to hire someone for a job in which creative problem solving is crucial. When you ask Candidate A to describe projects she did, she repeatedly describes carrying out projects by conscientiously following step-by-step procedures laid out by someone else. In contrast, Candidate B continually talks about tackling projects by conjuring up new methods or variations of previously used procedures. Question: Given their answers, which candidate would be more likely to use creative problem solving on the job? Of course, Candidate B emerges as much more likely than Candidate A to use creative problem solving. After all, Candidate B's interview responses reveal a pattern of giving specific, detailed examples of having used creative problem solving, whereas Candidate A's responses reveal the opposite.

Observe the candidate's nonverbal behavior. Another way of putting this is, ask yourself: Do the words go with the music? I once interviewed a management applicant who repeatedly mentioned how much he "loved dealing with people," and that this was partly why he sought the management position; yet he avoided most eye contact; often put his hands over his mouth while talking; and periodically spoke so softly that he was hard to hear. In this case, the words sounded on target for this particular management job, which required lots of personal interaction.

However, his "music" sang a different song. This music included (1) avoiding eye contact, (2) putting his hands over his mouth while talking, and (3) sometimes becoming difficult to hear. Such "music" betrays the candidate's game by showing that his words expressing how much he enjoyed contact with people are a sham. An interviewer who listened only to the words without taking the "music," or nonverbal behavior, into account would miss such make-or-break data about the candidate.

Consult other people who saw the candidate. During one of the first interviews I ever conducted, I felt awed by how sharp-witted and charming the job applicant seemed. After I showed him out the door following the interview, I exclaimed, "Wow, what a candidate!" (meaning what a great candidate) to which the receptionist replied, "Yeah, what a jerk!" The receptionist then revealed that while waiting for me to interview

Ask for specific examples of projects, tasks, or assignments the candidate has handled.

him, the applicant had *complained* about the magazines in the waiting room, the lighting level in that area, the coffee the receptionist gave him, and the attire of certain employees. The candidate had put on a magnificent show during the interview, and at that early point in my career I was not astute enough to detect the negative, complaining, grumbling behavior the receptionist immediately noticed.

Keep in mind that the behavior you see during the interview is likely to be the best behavior you'll ever see from that person. Why is this true? Because candidates usually are on their best behavior during the applicant screening process. After they are hired and have been on the job for a while, people get used to their boss and co-workers and resume habitual ways of acting.

For instance, let's say that you want to hire a mannerly person for a particular job. If Candidate A acts in a very mannerly fashion during the interview, then if you hire Candidate A you can expect her to act very mannerly—or worse—on the job. By the same token, if Candidate B acts in an unmannerly fashion during the interview, then you can expect her to act that unmannerly—or even worse—if hired. People tend to act the same or worse after they are hired. They seldom behave better on the job.

The Two Types of Interview Questions

There are only two types of questions—closed-ended questions and open-ended questions:

Closed-ended questions. (such as: "Did you like your last job?" "Was your boss helpful to you?" "Did you use creative problem solving in that job?" "Is this enjoyable work for you?") These ask the candidate to answer yes or no, think very little, and talk very little.

Open-ended questions. (such as: "Tell me about your last job." "What was your boss like?" "Describe specific problems you dealt with and how you handled them." "How do you feel about this sort of work?") These result in the candidate not being able to answer with a quick yes or no, which means that he or she talks more—especially about thoughts, needs, feelings, opinions, experiences, interests and goals.

Based on my experience training thousands of managers, it is apparent to me that prior to training, most interviewers (1) do not know what questions to ask, and (2) rely overwhelmingly on closed-ended questions.

Amazingly, many of the closed-ended questions that the average interviewer asks virtually give away the correct answer. For instance, a typical interviewer may ask the closed-ended question, "Did you use creative

problem solving in that job?" Any candidate with a modicum of intelligence instantly realizes the exact answer the interviewer wants to hear, namely, "Yes, I used creative problem solving." By asking such closed-ended questions, many interviewers unknowingly enable candidates to come across as vastly more capable than they really are. This, in turn, contributes to the typically poor ability of most interviewers to accurately predict on-the-job behavior.

A better way to discover the same information about a candidate's creative problem-solving ability would be to use an open-ended probe, such as "Describe some problems you dealt with and how you handled them." Then, listening for repeated patterns in what the candidate says, you can detect if the candidate used creative problem-solving techniques or noncreative problem-solving methods. The advantage of the open-ended inquiry is that it never reveals to the candidate that the interviewer wants to hire someone who is definitely experienced in creative problem solving.

Four Topics to Cover

What are the most important subjects an interviewer should ask about during an interview? The four that are the most basic, cover the greatest amount of territory, and are most likely to generate crucial information about the candidate are the following:

- Work history or experiences,
- Education and training,
- Career goals or aspirations, and
- Anything else the candidate wants to add or ask.

Answers to an array of questions on these four subjects yield information on and insights into the candidate in terms of the six to nine job-related criteria that you previously identified. The interviewer takes notes as this information unfolds.

The way to start the interview, after an initial couple of minutes devoted to helping the candidate feel comfortable, is to state:

"We'll delve into four main subjects in this interview: First is your work history or experiences, second is your education and training, third is your career goals or aspirations, and fourth is anything else you want to add or any questions you want to ask."

Use mainly open-ended questions and very few closed-ended questions. This works best, as we've seen, because open-ended questions make the candidate both think harder and reveal more information that is relevant to the crucial job-related criteria.

For instance, start interviewing on the first subject by stating to the candidate, "Tell me about your work history or experiences." After complet-

Most interviewers (1) do not know what questions to ask, and (2) rely overwhelmingly on closed-ended questions.

ing that topic, launch into the second topic with another open-ended inquiry, "Tell me about your education and training."

Use the same open-ended approach to initiate the other two interview subjects. For the third subject, start by asking, "What are your career goals or aspirations?" Later in the interview, lead into the fourth subject by asking, "What questions, if any, would you like to ask me? Or would you like to add to or clarify anything we've already talked about?"

As the candidate talks on each subject, focus particularly on and probe into his or her choice points and change points:

- *Choice points* These come up when the applicant mentions making a choice between alternatives or options, such as choosing a particular way to handle a project or assignment.

- *Change points* These arise when the applicant mentions altering course, such as changing jobs, careers, or academic majors.

The pattern of how and why a candidate makes choices or changes can reveal a good deal about certain job-related criteria, such as thinking style, personality, and motivations.

When the candidate mentions a choice or change, probe how she came to make that decision. For instance, the candidate may say, "After my first job as a bookkeeper, I got a job as a salesperson." This indicates both a job choice and a career change. So, probe that. A good query could consist of either of the following:

"How did you land the sales job?"

"Why did you decide to switch from bookkeeping or financial work to sales work?"

The applicant may go on to say, "I began my job at that company as an inside salesperson. But, after six months, I started doing outside sales." As this represents still another change, investigate it. Ask, "How did you happen to make that change?" or "How did you feel about making such a change?"

Give lots of time to management and executive candidates:

- Spend at least two hours per interview.
- Schedule multiple interviews with each finalist.
- Have several of your employees interview each finalist.
- Cease to consider any candidate who refuses to endure such heavy interviewing as that candidate would probably balk at other high-intensity situations on the job.

Traps Set by Applicants

Interviewers may fall into some common traps laid by candidates. Dodging these traps boils down to heeding three *avoid* warnings.

Using the word *we*. Don't let them do it. Applicants commonly, sometimes deceptively,

overuse the word *we*, as in "*We* planned and implemented such and such a program" or "*We* succeeded in carrying out that assignment." Often this is a truthful statement that a group of people—not just the candidate—did the work. However, the interviewer is not concerned with hiring an entire group. The interviewer needs only to resolve whether or not to hire the one individual candidate who is being interviewed.

So, it often proves necessary to tell candidates politely to refrain from using the word *we*. When a candidate says *We*, in a context that makes it hard to discern specifically what the candidate did, the interviewer can say:

"I understand that you did this project with other people. However, I'm particularly interested in what *you* did on the project you are describing. So, please tell me what *you* did, use the word *I*, and, except when absolutely necessary, avoid using the word *we*."

The candidate may respond that a group or team really did do the project. When this occurs, the interviewer can reply:

"I appreciate that fact. However, I need to get to know *you* and what *you* did. So, please use the word *I* most of the time and refrain from using the word *we*."

Offering generalities. Don't let them get away with it. Pin them down. Candidates often gloss over the specifics of what they did on a job or project. Instead, they offer generalities, such as, "I succeeded in implementing the such and such program." Naive interviewers often accept at face value that the candidate is successful or results-oriented. However, a more astute interviewer will realize that this generality may not tell the whole story. For instance, how *specifically* did the candidate implement the program? And did the program achieve its goals?

The prescription to get candidates beyond generalities and into specifics is this: When an applicant gives a generality, follow up with open-ended probes:

"Tell me specifically what you did."

"Give me some examples of how you implemented the program."

"Explain exactly how you managed to do that."

"I'd like to hear about the results of the program in detail."

Giving only positive answers. Be cynical about candidates who appear too perfect, too gung ho. Of course, every outstanding job prospect has done a lot of wonderful things. However, some applicants artfully phrase every response in glowing, positive terms. While they may be telling the truth for the most part, a shrewd interviewer will realize that any negative information is being downplayed. If a well-

---

When the candidate mentions a choice or change, probe how she came to make that decision.

rehearsed candidate faces an overly trusting interviewer, that interviewer may never uncover how human—with all the weaknesses that implies—the candidate really is. To avoid falling into this trap, you could ask the overly positive-talking candidate questions like this:

"You described your success on that project. What problems did you encounter?"

"What did you not do as well as you might have?"

"In retrospect, what would have been an even better way of carrying out that assignment?"

"Tell me about a time you goofed up. Describe it in detail."

After asking such questions, you can then observe whether the applicant's answers meet such job-related criteria as:

- Being candid or open in discussing problems,
- Being detail-focused,
- Being able to handle stress.

Kim, I hope you will find this useful. Please don't hesitate to call me to discuss this further.

Best wishes,

Michael Mercer

Michael W. Mercer

This contains excerpts from the book Hire the Best ... and Avoid the Rest *by Michael W. Mercer. Copyright 1993 by Michael W. Mercer. Reprinted by permission.*

You Need Personnel Testing in Your Selection Process

Ramzi B. Baydoun, Ph.D.
John W. Jones, Ph.D., ABPP

Dr. Baydoun is a management assessment consultant at London House, a leading test publisher located in Rosemont, Illinois. He has over five years of applied experience in testing and selection. Dr. Jones is vice president of research at London House. He is the Editor-in-Chief of the Journal of Business and Psychology *(Plenum Press).*

Dear Kim:

It was a pleasure to hear from you again. We were quite flattered that you asked for our advice and feel that we can help clarify the issues you must address. As you are no doubt beginning to realize, successfully identifying and selecting qualified managers and employees can be a process fraught with pitfalls. However, there *are* ways that you can ensure success in this endeavor, even if you don't hire people on a routine basis.

Kim, a small company like yours obviously does not require an "HR" person. Instead, you should take it upon yourself to become familiar with the basics of the selection process. Before you recoil in horror at such a thought, let us assure you. We are not saying that you need to become an expert in personnel selection. You just need to know enough to effectively cover the basics. In general, the same general hiring procedures can be used regardless of an organization's size.

Conducting a Job Analysis

Judging from the discussion with your colleagues that you relayed to us, you are already becoming aware of some of the primary factors to consider when selecting someone into your organ-ization. First, you must ensure that the techniques you use are accurate or *valid*. That is, the procedures you use should have *proven* effectiveness for identifying those individuals who will succeed in the position for which they are applying.

For example, almost everyone uses an interview when hiring; however, most people do not realize that decisions based solely on interview performance are notoriously inaccurate. We know you have experienced this problem firsthand, Kim, in your own organization. Sometimes an interviewing "star" turns out to be an ineffective or unreliable employee. We are not saying you shouldn't interview; interviewing can help address such factors as interpersonal skill and demeanor. Instead, we suggest you supplement what you currently do by using a more scientific and objective approach to selection.

Second, you must ensure that the selection tech-niques you plan to implement are able to accurate-ly predict success *in the position for which you are hiring*. This is an important point, Kim, that we cannot overemphasize. From our previous discussions it is apparent that you don't exactly know what the functions of your "financial expert" will be. If you don't know what you are looking for, you are guaranteed to never find it! You should sit down and spend some serious time thinking about the most important requirements of this position and what capabilities a successful individual would possess. Write those parameters down. Specifi-

Most people do not realize that decisions based solely on interview performance are notoriously inaccurate.

cally, you should begin to collect the following basic information:

- What are the minimum educational and work experience requirements for this position?
- What job-related knowledge, skills, and abilities would be required for success in this position?
- What duties would this person have to successfully complete on a routine basis?
- What work-related traits would this person have to possess in order to smoothly interact with you and your coworkers?
- Who would this individual report to?
- Would other employees report to this person?

In essence, what you are doing is documenting the job in terms of the behaviors necessary to perform it. This is called *job analysis*. What you are creating is a narrative-based job analysis for the position under examination.

Although a narrative is a good start for analyzing a job, we suggest that you supplement it with a structured job analysis questionnaire. Such questionnaires are typically developed by psychologists and other experts in the field of personnel selection. These inventories ask a series of questions about the position which is being assessed and are typically completed by individuals who are familiar with the position under examination.

In your case, several of your work colleagues and you could complete the instrument. One instrument which has been developed specifically to assess managerial and professional positions is the *Managerial and Professional-Job Functions Inventory* (MP-JFI). The MP-JFI has been researched extensively and its cost is very reasonable. This 140-item instrument assesses and empirically documents the importance of the following areas:

- Setting organizational objectives,
- Financial planning and review,
- Improving work procedures and practices,
- Interdepartmental coordination,
- Developing technical ideas,
- Judgment and decision making,
- Developing group cooperation and teamwork,
- Coping with difficulties and emergencies,
- Promoting safety attitudes and practices,
- Communications,
- Developing employee potential,
- Supervisory practices,
- Self development and improvement,
- Personnel practices,
- Promoting community/organizational relations, and
- Handling outside contacts.

Testing is a scientific method for determining how suited different people are for different positions.

Typically, six or seven of these factors will be found to be critically important in any one position. These results can be combined with a narrative description to derive a well-rounded view of the position. In brief, a thorough job analysis serves two important functions: (1) it documents the requirements for the position, and (2) it determines what factors need to be examined in the hiring process.

Selecting a Personnel Test

Once you have successfully defined the requirements of the job, you are ready to choose selection procedures or instruments to help you in the hiring process. A smaller employer such as yourself would most likely desire techniques which are reasonably cost effective (i.e., between $25 and $150 per applicant) and easy to administer and interpret. Although there are a variety of methods available to assist in selection (such as structured interviews, reference checks, job sample exercises, etc.) we recommend some type of personnel testing.

Testing is a scientific method for determining how suited different people are for different positions. Although testing does not provide "perfect" prediction, no method does. What testing *can* provide is an increase in the probability of hiring someone who is successful compared to less scientific and subjective methods (e.g., interview, resume review, etc.). Professionally-developed tests have the following benefits:

- Accurate (valid) measures of future job performance,
- Developed to comply with all legal and professional requirements,
- Quick and easy to administer and interpret,
- Questions and scoring are standardized across all applicants, and
- Comparatively low cost.

Employment testing can focus on such job-relevant characteristics as knowledge, ability, personality and motivation. However, before you will be able to determine what type of tests you wish to administer, you should seek out a reputable test publisher whom you feel comfortable interacting with. A reputable publisher will be willing to supply you with the following information regarding their testing programs:

- Evidence that the test complies with all relevant professional (e.g. the American Psychological Association's standards) and legal standards (such as EEOC and ADA),
- Copies of the test booklet,
- Copies of the test report,
- Examiner's/interpretation manual,

- Copies of validation studies,
- Description of test scoring and decision-making procedures,
- Adverse impact/legal compliance reports,
- Test user training programs, and
- Other available user support services (e.g., computerized testing).

Since smaller companies such as yours typically do not employ industrial psychologists, a reputable publisher will allow you to use their staff psychologists to help you set up, administer, score and interpret a screening procedure. They can help conduct the job analysis or help interpret existing job analysis information and then offer expert advice on the best instruments for your situation. This is the point at which the accurate job analysis information you have collected becomes vital, since selection of the appropriate measures should be based upon the job analysis results.

Selecting your Financial Expert

An example can help clarify this process. The MP-JFI job analysis questionnaire described earlier is specifically designed to be used with the *LH-System for Testing and Evaluating Potential* (LH-STEP). The LH-STEP is a comprehensive assessment system designed for managerial and professional positions (including financial) that can be used for selection, training or placement. The instrument contains 50 measures of skills, abilities, personality, and aptitudes that are broken into the following five general areas:

- **Personal Background** including career advancement, financial responsibility, and leadership,
- **Mental Abilities** such as language facility, deductive and analytical reasoning, and visual perceptual skills,
- **Aptitudes** such as sales potential and creative/innovative behavior,
- **Temperament** including self reliance, the ability to work under pressure, personal insight, emotional responsiveness, and extroversion, and
- **Emotional Adjustment** including tendencies or factors which might hinder productivity or disrupt interpersonal relations.

Although the LH-STEP contains 50 measures, all are not typically administered when selecting into any one position. This is where the MP-JFI comes into play. It is used to match the job you are examining with similar positions that have been previously validated using LH-STEP. Once a match has been made, only the measures found to be predictive in similar positions are used for

assessment. Thus, you end up using the appropriate combination of predictors for your particular situation.

Let's look at the position you wish to fill, *financial expert*. The LH-STEP is designed to assess potential in the following four broad hierarchies (which represent most business and industrial organizations): *Line*, including production and operation positions; *Professional*, which entails health care professionals, scientists, and lawyers, to name a few; *Sales*, which entails professional sales positions; and *Technical*, which includes such positions as actuaries, accountants, and programmers.

Within each hierarchy LH-STEP can assess the positions mentioned as well as the middle managers and executives of these personnel. Although a final determination of the hierarchy *financial expert* matches would have to wait until the MP-JFI was completed, we would predict this position would fall into the Technical hierarchy. This, then, would determine the exact battery of LH-STEP subtests to be administered.

The LH-STEP takes about two hours to complete. Results are sent to a psychologist for next day computer scoring. The LH-STEP subtests are combined into an overall rating of "success potential" which you can use to make your hiring decisions. In fact, comprehensive subtest results are available for you to compare the strengths and weaknesses of different individuals. By using the standardized and scientifically-based LH-STEP, you will maximize your chances of making an accurate hiring decision.

In brief, a testing system provides you with information about applicants that you would have not otherwise acquired. The greater the amount of high-quality information you have, the better your hiring decisions will become.

Let us caution you, Kim, that we are not implying that you should use selection testing as your sole criterion for hiring. Instead, you should continue to utilize the other methods at your disposal, including resume review and interviews, and then *combine* this information with the testing results. This will allow you to get a much more well-rounded picture of the individuals you are considering.

We also empathize with your concerns regarding adherence to legal guidelines. You should realize that federal and state legislation and professional standards apply to *all* methods of selection—not just testing. You should do the following:

- Treat all applicants equally throughout the selection process,
- Request only job relevant information from applicants (do not request such information as income, number of children, marital status, etc.),

A testing system provides you with information about applicants that you would have not otherwise acquired.

- Ensure all of your selection procedures adhere to your state's privacy laws, and
- Always treat test results as confidential information. Test results should be divulged to others only on a "need to know" basis.

Should you personally implement a testing program to select future employees, consider the following:

- Ensure you receive training on test administration and interpretation,
- Be sure the testing area is free from distraction and that lighting, seating, etc. are satisfactory,
- Follow all administration instructions; strictly adhere to all time limits, and
- Ensure the applicant understands the instructions.

We hope this letter will serve as an introduction to the area of scientific personnel selection. Although you may feel you have a good deal of work ahead, Kim, let us assure you future benefits will far outweigh any costs.

If you are interested in reading more about testing, we recommend these two books: *Personnel Testing: A Manager's Guide*, by J. W. Jones, (1994), Menlo Park, CA: CRISP Publications, Inc. and *Test Scores and What They Mean*, by H. B. Lyman, (1991), Englewood Cliffs, NJ: Prentice Hall.

Let's get together soon to discuss this further.

Sincerely,

Ramzi B. Baydoun, Ph.D.

John W. Jones, Ph.D., ABPP

Handwriting Analysis Can Be an Important Tool

Debbie Berk, MHA, MA

Ms. Berk is president of Signature Dynamics, Inc., an internationally recognized handwriting analysis/executive assessment firm headquartered in Morristown, New Jersey. A former personnel director, she is certified as a Master Handwriting Analyst, has a master's degree in psychology and is developer of The Four Corners of the Page theory.

Dear Kim:

It was nice to hear from you and learn of your interest in seeing what handwriting analysis can do for you and your company. Handwriting analysis is a tool used by about 2,500 firms in the U.S. and by about 80 percent of all companies in Western Europe. (These figures come from *Human Resource Selection*, third edition, by Robert D. Gatewood and Hubert S. Feild.)

I want you to know from the start that I'm not going to tell you to replace your current hiring process with handwriting analysis. It would be a mistake to rely on only one source of information. Ideally, you should be equipped with many tools.

I first began using handwriting analysis when I was a human resources director. It helped me to target areas of concern before I did the interviews and reference checking. It is one step in the hiring process that can give you important information. It is not a replacement for the other steps.

Skepticism about the accuracy of handwriting analysis is not uncommon. Probably the direct experience of having your writing analyzed will have the greatest impact in increasing your confidence in the tool. It also may help to know that AT&T, Westinghouse, many other Fortune 500 firms and small businesses have hired me to provide handwriting analysis.

For about $100 to $300, (depending on the depth of the analysis), handwriting analysis can identify personality characteristics such as drive, creativity, intelligence, motivation, sense of humor, organization, ability to work with others, and working style. We get this information by examining hundreds of factors, including the size, slant, spacing and pressure of someone's handwriting.

Handwriting analysis can help you double-check your hunches by guiding you in targeting questions in interviews to gain an even broader perspective of the applicants. This allows you to spend your time most productively in interviewing and reference checking. I have found that when references believe that you have a firm understanding of candidates, they are usually more willing to make candid comments.

Handwriting is easily acquired by simply asking candidates to fill out an application

---

Handwriting analysis can help you double-check your hunches by guiding you in targeting questions in interviews to gain an even broader perspective of the applicants.

form or by writing an essay or two. I have found that questions such as "Why do you want this position?" and "What are your goals for the next five years?" can reveal a lot.

To find a good analyst, it is always best to get a referral. It should be the skill and experience of the analyst—rather than the location—that counts. Remember that geography plays little part in an analyst's work because writing can be sent via mail, overnight express courier or even fax when time is of the essence.

Questions to consider asking an analyst include:

- What is your area of specialization?
- What is your client base, business experience and extent of training?
- Are you certified from an accredited school?
- Have you had any apprenticeships? (Some programs are three to four years in length, while others are considerably shorter.)
- What additional special skills or services can you provide that might be helpful?

Once you have located an analyst, you can have your own handwriting analyzed. You may also wish to have a close friend's handwriting analyzed. That way, you can get a feel for the scope of information available to you and can see the difference between two profiles. In addition, you can use the information as a team development tool, further providing an incentive to your company's growth. Your analyst can be a strong ally, providing impartial yet qualified counsel for employment and management decisions so that objectivity can be maximized.

As an illustration, let me share with you the experience of one client who wanted to promote from within. I helped her review the personality profiles, behavioral patterns and management skills of the leading candidates. In addition, we examined her company position requirements. In the end, she decided to promote two candidates by creating two new jobs, instead of the one she had originally intended. (Incidentally, both did so well in their new positions that they have each been promoted again.)

Since what people say and what they mean aren't always the same thing, handwriting analysis guides you in cross-checking information, providing you with greater peace of mind in knowing that you are making an informed decision.

I've enclosed some sample illustrations. I hope that if you have any further questions, you'll feel welcome to call me.

Sincerely,

Debbie Berk

Debbie Berk

Maybe this will do for my handwriting analysis.

First Handwriting Sample

The rightward slant coupled with the fast and free-flowing movement of this writing sample is typical of an extroverted and dynamic, people-oriented person. The writer surpassed all quotas, becoming the leading salesperson in a Fortune 500 company in a territory previously considered the company's worst.

His style is responsive, aggressive and tailored. He is able to roll with the punches, seen in the easy flow along the baseline. In addition, he has a sense of humor, seen in the curved lead-in stroke on the "m" in "my," and coupled with the overall flexibility exhibited in the writing.

The yellow paper has a sample of the "subject's" handwriting. Please put your analysis in a sealed

Second Handwriting Sample

The upright slant and slower, more controlled writing seen here is typical of an introspective, reflective person who works well with detailed data and information. The writer proceeds logically in a reserved manner, carefully examining the facts before reaching a conclusion.

He is respected for his ability to remain calm under pressure and put mind over matter. Although he did reasonably well in sales for a small company, he chose to enter the legal profession after a few years and has been promoted several times since.

The tall height of the "h" in "the" shows ambitious ideals, while the simplified "n" letter formation in "analysis" shows the ability to create legible short cuts, a sign of superior intelligence.

Handwriting analysis guides you in cross-checking information, providing you with greater peace of mind in knowing that you are making an informed decision.

The Hiring Process Has Become a Legal Minefield

Julie M. Buchanan, JD

Attorney Buchanan is a shareholder in the Milwaukee law firm of Buchanan & Barry, S.C., which specializes in representing business in employment and labor law matters. The author of a variety of articles on employment and labor law issues, Ms. Buchanan is a member of the Labor and Employment and Litigation sections of the American, Wisconsin and Arizona Bar Associations.

Dear Kim:

The hiring process has become a legal minefield, and the number of tripwires has increased dramatically over the last several years. I know that you strive to do the right thing. However, like many business owners, you want to know what that is. I hope that I can help you.

From a legal standpoint, you should have the following areas reviewed: the job criteria and qualifications; the search process; the employment application form; the interview, and the selection and offer processes. Laws surrounding the hiring process affect each of these areas. In this letter I will summarize some of the more important and recent developments.

In hiring, particularly a top-level employee, you may give some thought to having an employment agreement, outlining terms and conditions of employment. The concern with employment agreements is that an agreement may place restrictions on your ability to end the employment relationship at any time for any reason.

Generally, employers strive to maintain an "at-will" relationship with employees. An "at-will" relationship means that either you or your employee may end the relationship at any time for any reason. To maintain an at-will relationship, all communications, verbal and written, should be reviewed to make sure that the at-will relationship is not altered by promises made by the employer. Such communications that may be found to alter an at-will relationship include offers of employment and employee handbooks. These documents should not include any

guarantees of employment, as some courts may find they constitute a contract that may be breached by your company should you terminate the employee.

I know that you are familiar with longstanding anti-discrimination laws relating to the hiring process. However, it is just as crucial to become familiar with some of the newer and lesser-known areas.

I'm happy to see that your company is expanding. Even if you haven't surpassed the 15-employee level, I'm confident that your company will grow. This, of course, means that you will be covered under the Americans with Disabilities Act (ADA), which affects employers of 15 or more, effective July 26, 1994. This includes part-time employees. You should assume your company will be covered.

No other recent law has affected the hiring process like the ADA. Here are a number of unwitting mistakes being made by employers:

Not realizing what is a covered disability. The definition of disability is very broad, and can include, for example, obesity, AIDS, alcoholism, a history of drug abuse, unusual sensitivity to tobacco smoke, and mental impairments. The law can also protect someone who is not disabled at all, but who is "regarded as" disabled by the employer.

Using "loaded" inquiries in screening processes. It is very important that you review your job applications and interview questions to make sure that they do not ask about impairments. Even the question, "Do you have a physical or mental impairment that may interfere with your ability to safely perform the job?" is now unlawful because it is framed in terms of "impairment." While you may ask about someone's ability to perform job-related functions, do not phrase questions in terms of a medical condition. Asking about back problems, vision impairments or history of workers compensation injuries are a few examples.

Not understanding restrictions on pre-employment physicals. While you may not ask applicants whether they have impairments, many questions may be lawful if done pursuant to a physical examination that is given *after* the person has been conditionally offered employment. In other words, the offer must be made first and then the hiring is contingent upon the person passing the physical. Such exams, if given, must be given to all entering employees in the particular category. However, if a disabil-ity is revealed, you still have a duty to accommodate the disability unless it is an undue hardship.

Playing doctor. While you may be understandably concerned that an applicant who is conditionally offered employment may pose a safety risk, the ADA limits employers' interests to risks that pose a "direct threat," which is defined as a "significant risk of substantial harm." It is wise to get a medical opinion before deciding someone's condition poses this kind of a risk.

Generalizing. The ADA imposes a case-by-case analysis of disabilities. Your company may not, for example, adopt a policy of excluding *all* epileptics or *all* diabetics. An individual assessment must be made.

The ADA makes it unlawful to refuse to hire someone because of a fear that insurance premiums will rise as a result. In addition, the ADA requires employers to accommodate interviewees who are disabled.

Other new laws are being passed at the state level. A number of states protect applicants and employees against discrimination based on certain "lifestyles," including smoking. For example, here in Wisconsin, it is unlawful to discriminate against someone on the basis of use of lawful products. This includes persons who smoke, although you may completely ban smoking at work or while on duty. This means you may not ask an applicant whether he or she smokes, although you can inform him or her of smoking bans you may have. A number of states make it unlawful to discriminate against persons with conviction records, unless they are job-related.

As you can see, it is very important that you become familiar with the laws in the particular states in which you are hiring people.

It is important also to keep these legal restrictions in mind when checking job references and verifying background information. Reference and background checking are important as well as verifying degrees and licenses held by the applicant so that you can avoid the situation of hiring someone with fraudulent credentials, as our friend Janet did. You should always review the information provided carefully so that you can seek clarification for any gaps in employment so that you can have a full view of their employment history and level of experience.

When checking references, be sure not to ask questions that you cannot legally ask the applicant. Also, when conducting background checks, you may wish to inform the applicant that you are doing so and obtain a waiver of any liability that may arise due to the background check.

In developing job criteria and qualifications, the key issue is that they be job-related. In fact,

the job-relatedness of any criteria, interview question, advertisement statement and selection decision will be key in defending any kind of discrimination-in-hiring lawsuit.

A number of other pre-employment inquiries should not be asked during an interview or on employment applications. These include questions relating to pregnancy, marital status, future childbearing plans, U.S. citizenship, religion, union affiliation, national origin, ancestry, age, and, in a growing number of states, sexual orientation. Everyone interviewed should be interviewed in a consistent manner.

As your company grows, it is likely that you will delegate more of the interviewing tasks to your managers. It is crucial that these persons become familiar with the applicable laws and are trained to do interviews properly and legally.

The same restrictions that apply to interviewing apply to advertising. You may not indicate any type of preference for individuals if it is based on a protected class or unlawful inquiry. It goes without question that "wanted: young, aggressive salesmen" is unlawful. Hiring a younger financial officer because you fear another one who is over 40 might go through a mid-life crisis is just as illegal.

Be aware that delegating the hiring decision to a recruiter doesn't necessarily absolve you of legal concerns. If you place illegal hiring parameters on the recruiter, your company and the recruiting firm could both have liability.

You should also know that a growing number of legal challenges are being made to psychological and integrity testing. More employers are turning to these tests in the aftermath of legal restrictions on polygraph testing. However, an increasing number of legal challenges are being made to these tests. In addition, a major study on integrity testing found that the research on such tests does not clearly confirm or refute that honesty tests accurately predict dishonest behavior.

On the legal front, integrity and psychological testing has been challenged under the ADA, privacy lawsuits and discrimination laws. Recently, Target stores in California agreed to pay $2 million to settle a lawsuit brought by applicants for security guard positions. They had been required to undergo the Minnesota Multiphasic Personality Inventory, and their lawsuit charged an invasion of privacy under the California constitution. In settling the Target case, the concern was that the test might violate the ADA. If you are contemplating the use of such tests, it may be best to get a legal opinion first, as this is a developing area.

On the legal front, integrity and psychological testing has been challenged under the ADA, privacy lawsuits and discrimination laws.

A word on handwriting analysis: A number of psychologists discount the credibility of graphology entirely and one report states that no graphology system has been scientifically validated. One leading psychologist has stated that the only thing one can tell better than a guess from handwriting analysis is the sex of the person, and there are better ways of determining that. I would advise against using graphology as an employee selection tool.

Even though the law restricts what employers may ask and do during the hiring process, you should not despair. There are many lawful and effective interviewing and selection techniques that employers often overlook. Countless books and reference materials are available, and consultants can also effectively assist companies in this area.

I hope this has been helpful. If I can be of further assistance, please don't hesitate to call.

Very truly yours,

Julie M. Buchanan

Julie M. Buchanan

The author wishes to thank Attorney Ann M. Barry for her contribution to this article.

> *You don't want to rule out random opportunities, but don't get caught depending on them.*

Consider Using an Executive Search Firm

David A. Lord

Mr. Lord is the editor of Kennedy Publications, which publishes Executive Recruiter News, The Directory of Executive Recruiters, Consultants News, The Directory of Management Consultants and The Directory of Outplacement Firms.

Dear Kim:

You've made a good decision right off by doing some research about recruitment before jumping in. I'm happy to fill you in on how to select and use an executive recruiter. But let's take a look at whether executive search is the way to go here.

You seem clear about your need for a CFO and you have at least a general idea of what responsibilities you want the person to handle. You also have a commendable appreciation for the importance of the hiring process and the resources required to make it successful. Remember when Sharon said, "Maybe someone here will happen to come across the right person"? In fact, it would be dangerous to rely on such informal approaches. You don't want to rule out random opportunities, but don't get caught depending on them.

So, given the significance of this move for both you and Custom Software, it's clear that the hiring process warrants *someone's* full attention. It's going to take at least a couple of months for anyone to do this properly, so you might begin by asking yourself:

- Am I prepared to drop everything for at least a month and spend at least part of my time for an additional month or two (or three, or four, or more) to do this myself?
- If not, who can?
- Or, if I do have the time, do I have all the skills I need to assure success?
- If not, who does?

If your answers here include an "if not," you probably want to consider using an executive search firm. Delegating this task to someone who lacks either the time or skills could be a big mistake.

An executive search firm can help you in several basic ways:

- Defining your need and how it translates into a specific job description, including developing a solid understanding of you, your goals, the culture of Custom Software and other intangibles that may play into the hiring decision,
- Offering ideas about where the ideal person can be found and what level of compensation will be needed to attract him or her,
- Conducting a thorough candidate identification and screening process,
- Interviewing candidates to determine their suitability and interest,
- Communicating regularly with you to keep you informed and make mid-course corrections to avoid costly and unpleasant surprises,
- Preparing you fully for interviews with final candidates,
- Thoroughly checking the references of final candidates,
- Negotiating an offer and persuading the preferred candidate to accept it, and
- Helping you get the person off to a great start.

In addition to all this, a good search consultant will address other specific needs along the way. How much control would you like to have over the process? You can, in fact, establish a fairly high level of control even though the search consultant is doing the work—if you and the search consultant agree to address that concern together.

You can also explore personality testing with your search consultant, and you may choose one search firm over another because of its impressive candidate testing procedures. Or, the search consultant you select may persuade you that other screening techniques are more valuable.

You mentioned legal issues. Good search consultants know the law and abide by it. Further, a good search consultant won't simply do whatever you ask, but will let you know if there's something in your request that could raise a legal problem. (For example, you may have in mind that you'd prefer a man in this job. A good search consultant will advise you to consider the best available candidates, regardless of gender, even though gender may figure in your final hiring decision.)

Now, how do you go about selecting an executive recruiter?

First, some background on what kinds of search consultants we have to choose from. In the United States, there are three basic levels of personnel selection services. At the low end, employment agencies help corporations fill entry-level and occasionally higher level positions by sending along candidates who may or may not be qualified. Employment agencies are sometimes paid by the candidate and sometimes paid by the hiring organization. Either way, they do not, as a rule, conduct a search; they simply send you candidates who become available to them.

At the mid-range of executive hiring are contingency search firms, which work generally in the $30,000 to $85,000 salary range. Contingency firms are paid to conduct a search for you, but their fee is contingent on hiring. The effect of that is, the contingency firm may not devote a great deal of time to your search because it's not being paid for the process, only the result— a sort of prize for being there first with an acceptable candidate. Contingency recruiters tend to work on dozens of job openings simultaneously, sending out lots of resumes to hiring authorities in hopes that a few will connect. (More on this in a minute.)

At the high end of the salary scale, beginning at about $75,000 and extending to the multimillion-dollar compensation packages used to fill the corner offices of the world's largest corporations, are retained search firms. Retainer firms are paid by the hiring organization in advance to conduct a search; they are paid for the process, regardless of whether it's successful (although good search consultants don't leave good clients unsatisfied).

For your need, Kim, let's rule out employment agencies and look more carefully at contingency and retainer firms. But before we do, I want to consider again the services recruiters offer and what you need. It's my opinion that for a position so important to the future of Custom Software, and given the fact that your company doesn't have a human resources department that might be able to carry out parts of the process, you should seek a search firm that can provide all of those services.

But you could decide to contract out only part of the process: You might decide, for example, that you need help writing the job description and identifying candidates, but that you'd like to do the interviewing and reference-checking, develop the offer and make the hire. In that case, you could look for a search firm willing to "unbundle" its services and sell you only what you need. Or, you may decide you need only a research firm that can identify candidates that meet certain basic specifications, leaving the rest of the process to you. In your case, however, my advice is to hire the best search firm you can find and make use of its full capabilities. This is the best way to guarantee a satisfactory result, and to hold a search firm accountable for it.

Next: Shall it be a retainer or contingency firm? From what you've told me, it seems we could be talking about a salary level near the high end of the contingency market and the low end of the retainer market—somewhere between $50,000 and $100,000, right?

Then before making this choice, let's take a more general look at what kinds of searches are best suited for the two kinds of firms. Retainer firms are best suited to top-level management assignments. These are positions for which confidentiality may be an issue, it's a tough one-of-a-kind search, the company's long-term success is at stake, executives may be weighing internal versus external candidates, or the position is new and requires skills new to the hiring organization.

Contingency firms are best suited to assignments in which the job is in middle-management, several similar positions are being filled, immediate placement is needed, the hiring firm is willing to do the interviewing, evaluation and referencing. Contingency firms are also used when cost is a key concern or the post should be filled locally.

In your case, Kim, I'd lean toward a retainer firm but not rule out working with a contingency firm if you find an especially appropriate one.

You can, in fact, establish a fairly high level of control even though the search consultant is doing the work.

About fees: You should expect to pay a retainer firm one-third of the new employee's guaranteed first-year compensation. The fee is usually paid out in monthly installments, with an invoice for one-third of the fee at the outset. In the final bill, an adjustment is made to reflect the actual compensation package. But there are variations on this. You might negotiate a different percentage fee or you may agree on a fixed fee not tied to the exact pay level of the hired executive. You should also expect to pay expenses such as candidate travel. Some search firms will ask you to pay other expenses; make sure you understand what they are.

Contingency firms operate on a similar salary-percentage or fixed-fee basis, but the percentage may be slightly lower and expenses are likely to be less because contingency firms don't usually travel to interview candidates before presenting them to you.

Do you know about off-limits? In order to guarantee that, after completing your search, the search firm doesn't take advantage of its knowledge of your organization to recruit people away from you, a good retained search firm will promise not to take people out of your company for at least two years after completing your most recent assignment. Again, make sure you have a clear understanding on this.

Are there any guarantees? If a candidate is hired but fails within the first year for any reason that could have been determined before hiring, a good search firm will replace that candidate for expenses only. Get it in writing.

Now, you may be wondering how long the search will take. On average, retainer searches take three to four months. A shorter time line is possible and should be negotiated, with trade-offs for speed fully understood.

Those are the basic ground rules. Now, where will you find the right search consultant? The best resource is our own *Directory of Executive Recruiters*, widely acknowledged as the leading reference in the field, now in its 23rd annual edition. It profiles more than 2,800 retainer and contingency firms in more than 4,000 locations in North America. It's available both in paperback ($39.95) and on disk as SearchSelect ($195): an automated directory that produces lists and reports based on your specified criteria. For more information, please call 1-800-531-0007.

Available with both directories is *Kennedy's Pocket Guide to Working With Executive Recruiters*. Using the directory, you can quickly develop a list of search firms in your area that have strength in finding CFOs for the computer services industry.

Finally, Kim, here are a few hints on how to select and use the right search firm:

- Although experience in your field and in the CFO function will be important, skills and integrity in the search process are even more important to the success of your assignment. So don't rule out the generalist whose methods and professionalism are outstanding, even if he or she lacks experience in your industry.

- If you select a retainer firm, ask if the firm is a member of the Association of Executive Search Consultants. Its members follow a Code of Ethics and Professional Practice Guidelines. (The guidelines are included in the *Kennedy Pocket Guide* and make a good checklist for your search process.)

- Run through the list of ways search firms can serve you (above) and check the search firm's credentials on each point.

- Make sure you know who'll be doing the work on your assignment; check their credentials and references.

- Make sure the firm has experience working with smaller firms. Large search firms tend to work with large clients, but so do small search firms. It's most important that you're seen as an *important* client.

- Do your part. Although you're delegating the recruitment to professionals, they can't do their job without your enthusiastic participation.

Good luck, Kim. You're well on your way to finding the right person.

Sincerely,

David A. Lord

David A. Lord

Be Sure to Include All Three of These Steps in Your Hiring Process

Edward M. Pickett

Mr. Pickett, professor of small business, directs the Business Outreach programs at the University of Wisconsin—Milwaukee's Small Business Development Center and teaches person-

> You should expect to pay a retainer firm one-third of the new employee's guaranteed first-year compensation.

nel and management throughout Wisconsin. He also worked for ten years in personnel and management in the private sector.

Dear Dr. Williford:

I well understand your need to hire a financial type. After all the advice you received at your awards banquet, and the recommendations from seven or eight experts, you will need to boil all of this into a hiring strategy. I will try to add to—rather than duplicate—what others have discussed with you.

The process I recommend you follow has three distinct steps: searching, screening and selling.

Step One: Searching

You are really searching for two things: the type of position you should fill, and the type of employee you need.

Since this is a new position, you have no previous job description to guide you. That's good and bad. It's good because you need to define what hasn't yet been defined. Some items that you might wish to consider:

- Will your new person be an officer of your corporation?
- Will the title convey status and position significance to the appropriate external financial community, i.e., banks, your CPA firm, etc.?
- Duties and responsibilities: You say you want someone to be in charge of all the numbers. What does that mean? I suggest you detail it. For example:
- Calculating a new price structure;
- Conducting budgetary analysis, developing cost systems, profit and loss centers;
- Supervising the payroll;
- Bank relations;
- Contact point with your CPA firm; and
- Personnel, benefits, risk management, facilities, etc.

In addition to the responsibilities, you should also consider the behaviors that you are looking for. Obviously, you want someone who performs accurately, shows up on time every day and is free of any conviction for financial improprieties. Do you wish someone to take charge or someone to tend the store? Should she or he be capable of selling banks on the need for a loan? Kim, this is important because if you are to spend your time in marketing, you will need this employee to perform certain roles that you are now performing. Keep this in mind when you are down to your short list of candidates.

Step Two: Screening

Next, you need to consider the nature of the market for financial people. In this area, you are fortunate because at this time there are many competent financial people seeking employment. Here are some decision points to consider:

First, do you plan to conduct the search yourself or do you plan to hire a search firm to do it? If you decide to do it yourself, plan to spend a fair amount of time. Recently a major publishing firm showed me the result of focus groups run with CEOs of small corporations. They stated that a major concern was the hiring of employees. I'm afraid many CEOs do not spend the time to plan and implement a successful search. Since this is your first senior management position, I cannot stress how important this hiring decision is. Do it right or hire someone to do it for you.

If you elect to do it yourself, several issues must be answered. How will you write up the announcement? That's where the homework you previously did will pay off. Where will you announce the position—local papers, *The Wall Street Journal* and/or Sunday's edition of *The New York Times*, financial papers? Will your search be local, regional or national?

Do you want your bank and/or CPA firm to announce it through their contacts in professional associations? Maybe they can recommend someone.

How about your colleagues—Women in Business—can they help?

Lastly, do you know someone you want who is employed? Would you consider calling him or her to tell about your position?

If you elect to do the hiring yourself, who—in addition to you—will interview the candidates? Consider: employees of your company, your banker, your CPA, owners from Women in Business, and someone who knows you well, such as a spouse or significant other and will truly tell you whether or not you can work with this applicant.

Another approach is to hire a search firm that will present you a "short list of candidates" for your consideration, and you would just need to interview them. This would probably cost you 30 percent of the first year's salary plus their out-of-pocket expenses. This may be a good choice if you don't have the time to do all the groundwork.

Once you make this decision you will need to make additional decisions:

- What salary will you pay? Is it competitive in the financial market? Can you afford it? Is the job worth that amount of money to you?

On average, retainer searches take three to four months.

- What benefits will you offer? Will this package impact other key employees, especially higher-level software development types?
- Do you plan to give now or in the future (a promise for) an equity position?
- Will this be "contract" or at-will employment?
- Are you prepared to battle another firm for the person you want? What is your competitive advantage?
- If the candidate is an out-of-towner, what relocation benefits will you offer?
- If the person you want is married and has an employed spouse who wants to continue his or her career, are you prepared to help the spouse find work?

Step Three: Selling

Once the applicant has accepted your offer, there is a great tendency to think that your work is over. However, there are three reasons for you to continue to sell.

First, while it is not common for someone to back out after accepting an offer, it does happen. This type of disaster can often be prevented if you take the time to keep in contact with your new hire.

Second, you should use this time to orient your new financial officer about your business and if necessary, your industry. Some information you might send:

- A copy of your current business plan,
- Appropriate financial documents,
- Personnel policies/employee handbook,
- Your product line information,
- An organization chart, and
- Your plan for the first few months of employment.

Recently, *The Wall Street Journal* ran an article on a corporate trend that expects new key people to hit the deck running and impact the organization very rapidly or get fired.

Remember, Kim, your goal is to spend your time marketing, but this won't happen until you develop confidence and trust in your new associate. So use this interim to build on this critical aspect of the boss-subordinate relationship, and to pave the way for a fast start.

The third reason to continue to sell your company is one that I hope will never come into play at your company. In the unlikely event that as you get to know your candidate

The process I recommend you follow has three distinct steps: searching, screening and selling.

better, you decide that you made the wrong hiring decision, it is possible to withdraw your offer. If this occurs, I would recommend that you consult with your attorney to mitigate damages.

The last point I wish to discuss is getting ready for the first day.

There is a tragic story of a vice president who, wanting to do an outstanding job, reported to work on his first day; highly motivated, he arrived 30 minutes prior to the starting time. Unfortunately, the president (who had interviewed and hired him) was out of town on business and neglected to tell anybody about his new hire and the agreed-upon start date and time. The new vice president sat in an outer lobby for three hours until the president's secretary located him about 10:30 a.m. He was then allowed entry into the business.

The vice president's attitude about the company, its president and his aspirations of doing an outstanding job underwent a significant negative change. They separated shortly. I would call it a failed hiring situation.

I know you couldn't be that insensitive, but let's examine that first day.

- How much time will you have?
- Should any meeting for that day or first week (such as CPA firm, banks, key customers, significant inside people) be arranged in advance?
- Issues after the hire (like office, desks, telephone and office support) all have to be thought out.
- How will your new associate describe his or her first day that evening at home?

Additionally, I recommend that you develop a list/schedule of tasks you are currently doing that you wish to delegate to your new financial officer, so that your confidence in his competency is reinforced and you build up your level of trust in the advice you receive.

When you reach this level of confidence and can trust his or her advice, I would say the hiring process is finished. Now your leadership/manager role becomes paramount.

I hope that this overview of the hiring process will be useful to you. Of course, I am always available to talk with you about it further.

Cordially,

Edward M Pickett

Edward M. Pickett

Chapter 7

Quality Improvement: Too Much? Too Little? Or, Too Late?

David S. Krause and Catherine Stover

David McLimans

Dr. Krause is part-owner of several small businesses. He is also a financial consultant for large and small manufacturing companies and is on the faculty of Cardinal Stritch College in Milwaukee.

Catherine Stover is the editor of the Small Business Forum.

Sixteen months have passed since the untimely death of Scott Burton, Sr., president and owner of Burton Screw Machine Company, Inc. No one has taken his place, literally or figuratively, and his desk still looks exactly the way it did the day he died. Both of his sons—Scott, Jr., and Peter—now co-manage the business, but neither has had the heart or the time to clean out the most cluttered desk in the building.

When her husband died last year, Shelly Burton inherited his stock and his title. But she had no hands-on experience in the business, so she decided somewhat impulsively that her sons should run the shop as equals. She couldn't decide which son was better qualified to be in charge. Scott, Jr., an M.B.A., was a long-range planner for a Fortune 500 computer firm. At first, he resisted the idea of moving back home to Midvale, Indiana, but finally Shelly's wishes

They decided they couldn't postpone discussing the firm's condition with their mother any longer.

prevailed. She told Scott that his father would have wanted it that way.

Peter, on the other hand, had always worked at Burton Screw. He had spent his first ten years there as a machinist on the shop floor, then spent six years as the company's purchasing manager. His knowledge of the company and its 40 employees was second to none. He had always assumed that he would take over the shop, even though his father had never talked in those terms. Peter, 34, is five years younger than Scott, Jr.

The brothers have not fought over the title of president or over their father's desk. However, they've drawn battle lines around just about everything else. Their company is in bad shape. The firm's cash flow and financial situation have deteriorated to the point where the brothers wonder how much longer they will be able to stay in business. Even thought the U.S. economy was strong during the 16 months following their father's death, the business has suffered.

When their mother inherited the business a year ago last November, it was operating smoothly. Thirty-five of the firm's 45 screw machines were always running, which is well above the business's break-even point of about 25 machines. In recent weeks, it is rare when more than 26 machines are operating. And the brothers—who had always been on agreeable terms—now battle with each other every day because they can't agree on what they should have done, or worse yet, what they should do next. It's reached the point where they can no longer hide their differences from their mother. Though she had sensed that things between them hadn't been running smoothly lately, she still finds it hard to believe that they have anything to fight about.

Yesterday, they decided they couldn't postpone discussing the firm's condition with their mother any longer, so they scheduled a meeting with her at the factory.

When she stood outside their office door, she could hear them yelling at each other.

She opened the door. "That's enough from both of you! For God's sake, you're both almost 40 years old and you are acting like children!"

No one said anything for a moment. "Now," she said, sitting at Scott, Sr.'s, old desk, "bring your chairs over here and sit down. There's no excuse for this fighting."

The men did as they were told.

"Do you think this company has never had hard times?" She looked at Scott first, then at Peter. "From the day your grandfather founded this company, there have been bumps in the road. Now, tell me what's going on."

Neither responded.

"Your father always told me everything. Even in 1974, which was a very bad year for our business, he told me everything."

"He did?" Scott responded.

"Yes. I've missed hearing about the business. Now come on."

"Everything was fine," Peter said, "until Scott decided to take control—"

"It wasn't fine. This business was being run like it was still 1950—"

"Mr. M.B.A. just couldn't resist—"

"Stop it! We're not going to argue about who has the college degrees and who doesn't. And we're not going to argue over who knows more about this business. I want the facts about what's going on. Give me some numbers. What are the receivables?"

"About $250,000."

"Two-fifty? They were nearly 400 a few years ago! How many machines are you running?"

"We average 24.6," Scott said, pointing to a wall chart that was hanging on his side of the office.

"But 25 is break-even! What happened?"

"Mr. University here shuts down a machine whenever it is out-of-control. His fancy quality control system has choked off our production. We can't keep our machines running."

"Let me tell her." Scott stood up. "We were making too many bad parts. About a year ago we were spending 30 percent of our time re-working parts that we had gotten back from our customers. Now we've cut that down to ten percent," he said, pointing at another computer-generated chart.

"But we were making money before, and we've cut that too!"

"Peter!" Shelly Burton slammed her fist down on the desk.

"All right! I'll shut up."

"We were losing orders," Scott, Jr., said. "Our major customers told us that if we couldn't send good parts, we shouldn't bother. The world is changing, Mom. People want quality. They don't want the stuff we used to make."

"Listen, young man. Your father was as quality-conscious as everyone else was."

"You're right. He was. Americans as a group have let quality control slide during the last 40 years. After the Second World War, there was such a pent-up demand for goods, that U.S. production couldn't keep up. We could sell the world anything we made, and we didn't have to focus on quality. But along came the Japanese. They instituted very tight quality-improvement standards and kicked our butts. It didn't take consumers very long to figure out that Japanese cars and TVs don't break down as often as American-made products."

"So what are you getting at?"

"If we can tell our clients that we document our inspections and use statistical process control and that we really care about making good products, we will get more business. If we don't take major steps to improve our quality, no one is going to want our parts a year from now."

"So what? We'll be broke by then anyway," Peter said.

"Give me more information."

Scott returned from his desk with a ring binder full of charts and graphs, and sat down. "I'll give you the good news and the bad news. First, the good news. As I mentioned earlier, we're spending ten percent instead of 30 percent of our factory labor hours on rework. Our shipments past due are down to 25 percent from 36 percent six months ago. We don't need to buy any more quality-control equipment and we really are producing better parts than we did last year at this time.

"The bad news is that we had to spend $100,000 on computers, electronic gauges, and the training of our quality improvement inspectors. The main reason our quality systems have slowed production down by about 40 percent since a couple of years ago is because the guys on the floor don't want to change. They say, 'We've been doing our job for 20 years and now some hotshot thinks he can tell us what to do.' So, when their machines get shut down, the guys just screw around for a while. Then, instead of making minor adjustments, they waste a couple of hours by re-setting the whole machine. They just don't care if they get anything done that day or not. They don't have a work ethic anymore."

"Can't you get rid of these people, Scott?"

"I went to high school with those clowns. If we sack them, the whole town will be outraged. Besides, the unemployment rate is two percent here. Where will I find sober people who can read and write well enough to learn how to run a $100,000 machine?"

Shelly Burton closed her eyes and groaned. "So you can't go back to what you were doing because you already spent the money on the equipment. You've promised your customers that you'll do statistical process control and your slick new brochure advertises your commitment to quality. Yet you're losing money because production is so low because your machines shut themselves off when they make bad parts. Is that right?"

"I don't know," Peter said, "how I let him fast-talk me into this. It sounded so good back

then. Concentrate on quality, so we can cut costs and increase our sales. We'll be known as a quality shop. Problem is, I don't think our quality is really any better and we're always barely getting the parts out the door because there are so many production delays. The employees are fed up with quality."

"What about the Bennoit shop?" Shelly asked. "They always kept only half of the machines busy this time of the year."

"They're out of business," Peter said. "The whole plant was shut down in '92 because the labor was so cheap in Hong Kong. The same thing happened to Jako. Remember Jako? The company Dad was so impressed with up in Gary?"

"Is Schertz still your largest customer?"

"Schertz is on C.O.D., Mom," Scott said, "Their business is a tenth of what it used to be. Nobody buys American anymore—the Japanese have taken the market almost completely away."

"Peter, who are we selling to?"

"Our customer base isn't what it used to be. With the auto and consumer products industries way off, we've had to go after more defense and aerospace. Problem with that is, we no longer get the easy, long-running jobs. The average order size is way down. The parts are much more complex, too."

"Today, the average job is only for 5,000 parts compared to about 20,000 a few years ago," Scott added, looking at a chart.

"Peter, why do you think that a greater emphasis on quality improvement has resulted in decreased production?"

"The biggest surprise to me in this whole thing was the huge drop in production. Quality, according to Scott and his dear Dr. Deming, is actually supposed to increase production because less time is spent redoing things. It's supposed to actually save us money because we inspect the parts during the entire process and not just at the end, so we end up wasting less material and time. The theory sounds good and, supposedly, that's how the Japanese did it. But I don't see results."

"Do you expect things to turn around?"

"I don't know, Mom. I really don't like what I see. You know that Dad always said he'd shut down if he couldn't keep 25 machines up and running."

"Scott, what do you think?"

"Mother, it's tough to see only 25 machines running, but we can't make bad parts. If we were to ignore what our customers wanted, we'd be out of business next week. I'm convinced that, in the long run, we will have to go this way."

The main reason our quality control systems have slowed production down by about 40 percent . . . is because the guys on the floor don't want to change.

Burton Screw Machine Company
Exhibit 1 SUMMARY OF OPERATIONS

March 1994

	1991	1992	1993	YTD
Gross Sales (000)	$4,298	$4,563	$3,884	$ 804
Customer Returns	6.3%	6.1%	3.7%	2.5%
Gross Margin	31.2%	30.1%	30.6%	30.8%
Earnings Before Taxes, Interest and Depreciation	17.4%	17.0%	14.2%	12.0%
Net Profit	6.6%	5.6%	1.8%	(0.1%)
Dividend Payout	70.5%	78.3%	286.1%	

Exhibit 2 PRODUCTION AND QUALITY CONTROL MEASURES

	Q1'93	Q2'93	Q3'93	Q4'93	Q1'94
Production Scrap	3.5%	3.4%	3.0%	2.7%	2.6%
Past Due Shipments	36%	34%	36%	30%	25%
Production Hours Spent on Rework	30%	26%	24%	16%	10%
Avg. Machines Producing/Shift	34.7	32.2	29.6	25.7	24.6

Exhibit 3 CUSTOMER RETURNS

% of Total Returns

Cause of Return	1992	1993	1994 YTD
Dimension Out of Tolerance	54%	42%	37%
Raw Material/Plating/ Heat Treating Problems (Outside Vendors)	27%	35%	44%
Parts Made to Wrong Print Revision	12%	16%	15%
Other	7%	7%	4%

Exhibit 4 1993 CUSTOMER/INDUSTRY MIX

	% of Sales
Electronics and Controls	30.5%
Automotive	24.3
Defense/Aerospace	12.6
Medical Equipment	11.6
Consumer Products	9.4
Other	11.6
	100%

Exhibit 5 BALANCE SHEET - MARCH 31, 1994

Assets		Liabilities	
Cash	25.1	Accounts Payable	52.7
Accounts Receivable	247.8	Notes Payable	251.2
Inventory	769.3	Accruals	23.7
Net Fixed Assets	1027.8	Long-term Debt	954.8
		Equity	787.6
	2070.0		2070.0

"If you look at the checking account balance, we might not make it until next week," Peter chided.

"The problem we have is that in the short run you pay a price—lower production. But in the long run, we'll have lower costs and a better chance to land new customers."

"Why?"

"Because we are spending less time re-working bad parts and we'll be scrapping less material. So we'll see our margins improve soon. We'll get more productivity for each input dollar we spend. Also, since most major companies are demanding higher tolerance requirements, we'll be able to meet their needs. We'll pick up new business."

"How do you know this works?" Shelly asked.

"It's supposed to!" Scott said between clenched teeth.

"All right, Scott. The big question, then, is where are we now? Have we hit bottom? Are we on our way up? Or should we cut our losses and sell the company? Remember, borrowing more money is out of the question. All the assets are already collateralized."

She looked at her sons, at the big dusty desk, at the desk calendar which said March 19, 1994, at the room she had helped decorate during the last 40 years. No one spoke.

"Scott, give me that big binder of yours. I want to look at it. I'll give it back to you tomorrow." She walked to the door. "We'll decide what to do tomorrow. Keep your afternoon open and get some sleep tonight. I have some numbers to look at."

What should the Burtons do? Experts in the fields of quality improvement, family business, finance, and employee education, provide a range of perspectives on the Burtons' predicament in the letters that follow.

Stay the Course: Quality Takes Time

Norman E. Rickard

Norman E. Rickard is the Vice President of Quality Improvement at Xerox Corporation. In 1991, President Bush presented Xerox with the Malcolm Baldrige National Quality Award.

Dear Scott:

I had dinner the other night with your mother and she brought me up to date on the condition of the company. You may know that I've been with Xerox for the past ten years and I was struck by the similarities between Xerox and Burton Screw Machine.

That's not as bizarre as it may sound. Like you, we were doing quite well and then along came foreign competition. In fact, the Japanese took about half of our market share away during the late 1970s and early 1980s. They did it by focusing on quality.

We eventually beat them at their own game. In fact, we believe we are the only American company in an industry targeted to the Japanese to regain market share without the support of tariffs or other import quotas. I tell you not to boast, but to let you know that it is feasible and that we did it by focusing on quality. I encourage you to stay the course! The data your mother shared with me indicates that you are on the right track. Production scrap is down. Past due shipments are down. And production hours spend on rework are down.

The financial results will follow. If there is one thing we have learned from the Japanese, it's that improved quality reduces cost. You may have heard of Philip Crosby, author of *Quality is Free*. He estimates that large companies waste about 25 percent of their revenue by not focusing on quality. That was true at Xerox and my hunch is that it's also true at Burton Screw Machine. Another thing we learned from the Japanese is that quality strategies take patience and discipline. It took us three or four years of hard work before we saw quality improvement reflected in the bottom line.

That's the good news. The bad news from what your mother tells me is that you are overly focused on only one aspect of quality—manufacturing. That's only part of what TQC or Total Quality is all about. My recollection is that you have an excellent work force. Use them!

The focus on quality that we initiated four years ago was built on some very fundamental assumptions about the American worker:

- That management does not have all the answers.
- That all people have ideas about how their work can be done effectively.
- That people closest to the problems often have the best solutions.
- That this almost unlimited source of knowledge and creativity can be tapped through employee involvement.
- And that people are willing and eager to share their thoughts and participate in developing solutions to business problems.

Your brother Peter knows the workers a lot better than you do. I strongly suggest that you give him the freedom to design a strategy to get your workers involved in problem solving and quality improvement. This will probably involve some quality training and some new reward and recognition programs, but they'll be worth it.

I know you are going through some tough times now, but your approach is sound. Incidentally, we define quality as meeting customer requirements. It's an axiom of business that's as old as business itself. Make sure you know exactly what your customers want and then harness the energies and talents of your people in making sure you give the customer what they want—each time and every time.

Good luck.

Sincerely,

Norman E. Rickard

Start by Writing a Business Plan

Randall W. Hackbarth, CPA

Mr. Hackbarth is a partner with the CPA/Business Consulting firm of Smith and Gesteland. The firm's practice is built upon serving closely held, family-owned businesses; Mr. Hackbarth heads up the firm's Manufacturing Group.

Dear Shelly:

There are many hard questions which need to be answered:

Another thing we learned from the Japanese is that quality strategies take patience and discipline.

- Who will run the company?
- Can the company develop and maintain quality?
- Will the employees cooperate?
- Can the company increase productivity?
- Will customers come back?
- Should the company be sold?
- Can the company survive?

Decisions should not be made in a vacuum. It's important to get input and involvement from all areas of the company through an organized approach. I would suggest a business plan approach that addresses all factors.

The business plan development process includes gathering information, identifying strengths and weaknesses, preparing an industry/market analysis, and preparing an economic/financial analysis. *Some of the company's strengths include:*

- A history of a successful and stable company.
- The company is still in business even though some competitors have failed.
- An investment in quality control equipment and training.
- Major improvements in reworking time, control over past due shipments, customer returns, scrap reduction, and out of tolerance variations.
- Gross margins maintained even during a period of decreasing sales.

Some of the company's weaknesses include:

- A production reduction of 40 percent from just a couple of years ago.
- A history of past due shipments and customer perception of poor quality.
- An eroding customer base.
- Vendor problems, including low-quality raw material and an apparent lack of credit.
- The company is in a position that it can't borrow additional funds.

From an industry/market analysis standpoint, several things are happening. The company is in transition from competing in a national marketplace to competing in a global marketplace. A higher emphasis is being placed on quality, i.e. providing customers with products and services that meet customers' expectations at a price that represents value. Two of the company's major competitors, Bennoit and Jako, have gone out of business due to foreign competition. A major customer, Schertz, is having financial difficulties due to foreign competition. Burton's customer base is eroding and shifting to different industries.

The economy has been strong over the last 16 months. It is important to determine what the economy might do over the next few years. Financial analysis can be done by developing financial trends, calculating key ratios, and comparing the data to industry standards. These industry standards are available in Robert Morris Associates' *Annual Statement Studies, The Almanac of Business Industrial Financial Ratios*, and Financial Research Associates' *Financial Studies of the Small Business*. The inventory percentages, current ratio and inventory turnover ratio indicate that your inventory is higher than the industry average. Potentially, inventory could be reached by as much as $200,000 to $300,000. Fixed asset percentages and other ratios point out the high investment that you have already made in property and equipment. The accounts payable percentages and payable turnover ratio indicate that your accounts payable are very low. They're showing on average that payables are being paid within seven to nine days. This would indicate that the company is on C.O.D. with a number of its suppliers. If your credit terms could be extended up to 30 days, an additional $100,000 of working capital could be generated. On the other hand, the receivable turnover ratio indicates that your company is collecting receivables faster than the industry. The industry average is around 43 days, while the company is collecting receivables in 23-28 days. This could mean that Burton Screw has some customers in financial difficulty and is not extending credit to them, that the company's not taking enough credit risk, or that the company is not extending credit terms to the extent of some of its competitors. These can all lead to reduced sales and lost customers. The industry data also indicates that your gross margins are strong and that the historical profits of the company have been good in comparison to the industry. Lastly, the debt ratios indicate that while there may not be additional capacity for new borrowing, the bank is more than adequately collateralized and the company should be able to serve its debt as long as there is an adequate cash flow.

Once this fact-gathering process is completed, putting together the business plan will help you face the crucial issues of determining business goals and objectives and strategies to meet these objectives in at least the areas of facilities, marketing, technology, manufacturing operations, financial operations, and personnel. Four areas in particular are key to Burton right now: marketing, manufacturing operations, financial operations and personnel.

Marketing. Can the company compete in a global marketplace? Can it develop and maintain high quality standards? Perhaps your company should differentiate its product and develop a distinctive

Large companies waste about 25 percent of their revenue by not focusing on quality.

competence in a particular area. This is called "niche marketing." Whatever markets the company selects, it must determine customer needs. A customer needs assessment could be conducted to identify customer requirements for quality, cost, and value. The marketing plan must then be developed to identify key issues such as quality standards, timeliness of delivery, credit terms, etc. This marketing plan must also receive the commitment from top management. Whatever the company is doing to meet customer needs must be continually communicated to customers.

Manufacturing operations. At the present time, this seems to be one of the key problem areas of the company. There has been poor communication of customer needs and expectations to the production people. There seems to be a lack of adequate training and clear lines of authority. There is mistrust and a lack of cooperation. A lot of jargon is thrown about today in the manufacturing environment including MRP, TQC, JIT, CIM, SPC, etc. The major intent of all of these is to develop a continuous improvement process. This process must involve everyone, including the production people. Production people must be involved to help remove barriers and mistrust. The organizational chart should be examined to determine if all the bases are covered with skilled personnel. Key positions include production control, purchasing, and materials management.

The company seems to be having major problems with the quality of the materials received from its vendors. While the company's quality efforts seem to be improving, the quality of the vendor materials is getting worse. Problems must be communicated to the company's vendors and resolved. The cost of materials includes the cost of reruns, returns, and scrap. A vendor certification program could be undertaken which would review vendor qualifications. Additionally, better payment terms must be negotiated with the company's suppliers. A formal business plan will help with these negotiations.

Financial operations. The company is having cash flow problems. One part of the business plan can be to prepare projected financial statements and cash flow information for the company. The assumptions for these projections are derived from the other parts of the business plan. Some of these key assumptions include sales volume, gross margin, equipment needs, marketing costs, personnel needs, debt requirements, etc. A number of alternatives are usually looked at to determine if the business plan is feasible. It appears that the company's additional debt capacity is quite low, however, our financial analysis indi-

cated that additional working capital might be available by increasing accounts payable (borrowing from creditors) and by reducing inventory.

Additionally, the company has been paying dividends of $200,000 per year, for at least the last three years. This is a very expensive way of taking money out of the company unless the company is an S corporation. For a C corporation, there is currently no deduction for those dividend payouts and the income is basically taxed twice; once at the corporate level and once at the individual level. This dividend payout mechanism should be examined to determine if it is necessary or if it can be restructured. Since many of the goals of the business plan are quantified in dollars and percentages, finance should develop ways of monitoring these goals and communicating them with the company. This will keep the continuous improvement process moving forward.

Personnel. The area of personnel includes management, organization structure, ownership, board of directors, key employees, and professional advisors. There is currently much turmoil in the company. Who is in charge? A 50-50 management relationship is difficult for a company. Scott seems to have some of the necessary skills to help the company out of its crisis; however, Peter knows the company well and has a good relationship with the employees. Perhaps you, Shelly, should run the company for a while until a succession plan is developed. Had a succession plan been developed, while Scott, Sr., was still around, perhaps some of these problems would not exist. In order for personnel to function at their best, they must understand the company's situation and plans. These plans must be communicated to employees throughout the organization. Adequate training must always exist to keep the company current. When changing to a global marketplace and instituting more quality control standards, the old, long-term employees may not have the necessary skills to run the company. Key employee involvement is critical to the success of any business. This can be done through participative management and if necessary, financial incentives. Another key ingredient to a successful company is to surround itself with strong professional advisors and if possible, an outside board of directors that can bring in new and fresh ideas.

The development of a business plan is a large undertaking. It seems to be warranted in this case, however, due to the number of issues involved and the interrelationship of the issues. In the development of a business plan, you can be as thorough as you like, and get as many people involved as you

Whatever the company is doing to meet the customer needs must be continually communicated to customers.

wish. The important thing is to get started, get key people throughout the organization involved, and get all the facts on the table.

The benefits of having a business plan include:

- Improved resource utilization.
- Increased employee motivation.
- Improved understanding of opportunities, problems and weaknesses.
- Greater organizational control.
- Source of information for third parties.
- An educational tool.
- Can assist with raising money.
- Helps deal with uncertainties.
- Prepares for contingencies.
- Allows for smooth transition of management personnel and succession planning.

Approaching the problem this way will give you the greatest chance at success and will involve many people throughout the organization. Had this process been undertaken while Scott, Sr., was still around, the current situation might be quite different than it is now. Once the process is competed, it is important to continually update and revise the plan.

Sincerely,

Randall W. Hackbarth

Randall W. Hackbarth

You Have a Management Problem, Not a Quality Problem

Ronald L. Heilmann

 *Dr. Heilmann is the Director of the Center for Quality, Productivity, and Economic Development at the University of Wisconsin-Milwaukee. He also chairs the Education Committee of the Continuous Quality Improvement Project Team of the Automotive Action Group in Detroit.*

Dear Mrs. Burton:

Thank you for providing me with this opportunity to be of service to you. Please find below my analysis and recommendations for returning Burton Screw Machine Company to being both competitive and profitable.

The starting point for this analysis is to assemble the facts. Exhibits 1-5 which you provided establish the basis for the analysis. Your Exhibits 1, 2 and 3 have been reworked and expanded into Exhibits 1R, 2R and 3R respectively, and are attached to this letter.

As is demonstrated below, those eight exhibits support the basic conclusion that Burton Screw Machine Company has a management problem rather than a quality problem. The argument between your sons concerning the extent of the effort to improve quality is evidence that their attention is misdirected. The facts do not support the negative statements either has made regarding the quality improvement effort. Nor does the evidence indicate that a causal relationship exists between the investment in improving quality and the deterioration in economic performance. Indeed, the evidence shows clearly that the quality effort has benefitted Burton Screw. For example, in Exhibit 1 it is shown that customer returns have fallen from 6.3 percent in 1991 to 2.5 percent for the first quarter of 1994. This is a dramatic improvement in excess of 60 percent and is attributable to improved quality. As shown in Exhibit 1R the dollar value of these returned goods has fallen from $278,000 in 1992 to an estimated $80,000 during 1994. Over $130,000 of that improvement occurred during 1993 alone. This real reduction more than pays for the "bad news" expressed by Scott of having spent $100,000 on computers, gauges and training. Clearly, this was money well spent.

Further support for the soundness of the investment made in improving quality is found in Exhibits 2, 2R, 3 and 3R. In Exhibit 2 it is shown that production scrap, past due shipments and production hours spent on rework have all declined. Those declines are quantified in Exhibit 2R. These improvements are all the direct result of focusing the attention of the work force on quality. And, they enhance Burton Screw's economic performance. Exhibit 3 presents percentage distributions of the reasons for customer returns. The dollar values attributed to each reason are shown in Exhibit 3R. As seen, all categories show improvement. However, the area of slowest improvement is new materials and vendor's services, i.e., the one area for which Burton Screw's work force is *not* directly responsible.

In summary, the shop workers have made significant contributions to improving the performance of Burton Screw. Thus, attention must be focused on management's contribution to Burton Screw's performance.

It is your management's responsibility to know your competitive environment and devise a strategy to satisfy the firm's customers in a manner superior to that of the competition.

Quality, and its companion, productivity, are the shared responsibility of everyone in the firm.

Exhibits 1 and 1R reveal a serious deterioration of gross sales. Assuming 1994 performance stabilizes at the pace of the first quarter, the fall in gross sales will exceed 25 percent over the 1991-94 period and approach 30 percent if the peak sales of 1992 are used as the base. None of the markets in which Burton Screw participates has exhibited such serious contractions. Therefore, your sales decline represents a loss of market to your competition which is evidence of serving those markets in an inferior manner. It is your management's responsibility to know your competitive environment and devise a strategy to satisfy the firm's customers in a manner superior to that of the competition.

In addition to knowing the competitive environment, you must know the needs of the customers that constitute your market. Peter indicated that a change has occurred in Burton Screw's customer base with automotive and consumer products currently being "way off." In Exhibit 4, you show that these two weakening markets accounted for approximately 33 percent of Burton Screw's sales during 1993. Although no comparative data from other years were provided, this degree of concentration in weakening markets appears to create an undesirable vulnerability. Such a situation is usually addressed by having the flexibility to increase sales in other markets.

Peter identified the defense and aerospace industry as the market chosen to offset the softening automotive and consumer product markets. Current market conditions suggest this is a strategic error. The defense and aerospace industry is facing difficult times. This is an inopportune time to attempt to establish a greater dependence on that industry. Exhibit 4 shows that defense and aerospace accounted for 12 percent of Burton Screw's sales during 1993, which is as much exposure as you should accept. Furthermore, you need to be aware that this industry is placing demands for continuous quality improvement similar to those faced in the automotive market. Indeed, defense contracts are requiring that bidders have established Total Quality Management (TQM) systems. Therefore, pursuing defense industry business does not change the necessity for successfully implementing a total commitment to quality at Burton Screw.

Automotive OEMs and major manufacturers are reducing their supply bases through the implementation of supplier certification programs. Thus, as Scott has indicated, the ability to produce and deliver a quality product is essential to getting more business in the future. He is partially correct. In the 1994s and beyond, it will require continuously increasing quality to remain competitive and profitable. Therefore, arguing about the quality effort indicates blindness to the realities of the marketplace in which Burton Screw competes.

The key word in the above paragraph is *profitable*. Every firm's long-term survival is based upon making a profit. Making a profit in your highly competitive industry requires that the entire organization work efficiently together in a highly coordinated manner to achieve common, well-understood objectives that focus on satisfying the customer. Burton Screw is not operating in this manner. The productivity gains that have been realized as a by-product of the quality improvements to date have been limited to the shop floor. The quality effort must pervade the entire organization. Quality, and its companion, productivity, are the shared responsibility of everyone in the firm. The focus must be on satisfying customers. None of the material you provided indicates this is being done. Indeed, a major concern was expressed about the average number of machines running in the shop, with a break-even of 25 cited as a primary performance measure. This is indicative of a focus inward rather than on the customer. And, as demonstrated in Exhibit 2R, it is a meaningless measure. Note, for example, that during the first quarter of 1993 an average of 34.7 machines were running. However, 30 percent were performing rework. Therefore, 70 percent, or an average of 24.3 machines, were effectively producing per shift. The 30 percent, or 10.4 machines, were contributing extra cost and lowering profitability.

From the data you present in Exhibit 5 two ratios have been calculated to assess the financial status of Burton Screw. The current ratio of 3.18 appears strong. However, inventory is the dominant asset. The quick ratio is 0.33 which is far short of the standard for financial health of 1.0. Management's attention should have been devoted to this developing financial situation much earlier. Further damage was done by a policy of maintaining a constant dividend payout (Exhibit 1R) regardless of economic performance. The withdrawal of $200,000 in 1993 when net profit contributed $70,000 has greatly diminished Burton Screw's resiliency. This constitutes a management decision that does not serve well the long-term interests of Burton Screw.

In summary, the management team of Peter and Scott Jr., has not performed well. Burton Screw has been damaged, but not destroyed. Based upon the above analysis, the following recommendations are offered to return Burton Screw to being both competitive and profitable.

Burton Screw Machine Co.
Heilmann Exhibits

Exhibit 1R REVISED SUMMARY OF OPERATIONS ($000)

	1991	1992	1993	(est.) 1994	% Change 1991-94
Gross Sales	$4,298	4,563	3,884	3,216	(25.2%)
Customer Returns	$271	278	144	80	(70.5%)
Net Sales	$4,027	4,285	3,740	3,136	(22.1%)
Cost of Goods Sold	$2,686	2,912	2,552	2,146	(20.1%)
Gross Margin	$1,341	1,373	1,188	990	(26.2%)
Selling & Adm.	$593	597	636	604	1.8%
Earnings Before Taxes, Interest and Depreciation	$748	776	522	386	(48.4%)
Tax, Int. & Depr.	$464	521	452	389	(16.2%)
Net Profit	$284	255	70	(3)	(101.0%)
Dividend Payout	$200	200	200	???	??
Retained Earnings	$84	55	(130)	???	??

Exhibit 2R REVISED SUMMARY OF PRODUCTION AND QUALITY CONTROL MEASURES

	Q1'93	Q2'93	Q3'93	Q4'93	Q1'94	% Change Q1'93-'94
Production Scrap	3.5%	3.4%	3.0%	2.7%	2.6%	(25.7%)
Past Due Shipments	36.0%	34.0%	36.0%	36.0%	25.0%	(30.5%)
Production Hours Spent on Rework	30.0%	26.0%	24.0%	16.0%	10.0%	(66.7%)
Avg. Machines *Running*/Shift	34.7	32.2	29.6	25.7	24.6	(29.1%)
Avg. Machines *Effectively* Producing/Shift	24.3	23.8	22.5	21.6	23.1	(4.9%)
Avg. Machines contributing to Extra Cost/Shift	10.4	8.4	7.1	4.0	1.5	(85.6%)

Exhibit 3R REVISED SUMMARY OF CUSTOMER RETURNS

Cause of Return			Distribution of Returns	
	1992	1993	1994	% Change 1992-94
Dimension Out of Tolerance	$150	61	30	(80.0%)
Raw Material/Plating/Heat Treating Problems (Outside Vendors)	$75	50	35	(53.3%)
Parts Made to Wrong Print Revision	$33	23	12	(63.6%)
Other	$20	10	3	(85.0%)

. . . too much of an emphasis on statistical methods and not enough on team building and quality planning.

- Hire a president who has knowledge of the competitive environment in which Burton Screw exists and who will lead the entire organization into focusing its culture on satisfying the customer.
- Peter and Scott Jr., should continue with the firm with well-defined responsibilities. Peter should have responsibility for the manufacturing function, but he must gain an understanding of and become actively involved in the quality effort. Scott should coordinate the quality effort and use his planning capability to help develop a long-term strategy that provides for the flexibility to be responsive to changing economic trends. This should include identifying future markets in which Burton Screw should have a position.
- Broaden the quality effort to include the entire organization. The demonstrated benefits resulting from the achievements of the shop workers will expand to all of Burton Screw's employees.

Should you have any questions regarding my analysis or recommendations, please call. You have strengths to build upon and I wish you well in returning Burton Screw to competitiveness and profitability.

Sincerely,

Ronald L. Heilmann
Burton Screw Machine Company

Drastic Measures Can Turn Your Company Around

William A. Golomski

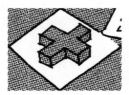 *Mr. Golomski is the President of W. A. Golomski and Associates, International Technical and Management Consultants, Chicago, He has also served as the President of the American Society for Quality Control.*

Dear Mrs. Burton:

Thank you for the opportunity to review the story of your company. The situation has gotten out of hand, but drastic measures can turn it around. I specialize in family-owned companies, and I have run into similar problems in the past.

Somehow the three of you in management believe that no news is good news. The market has changed in several ways and you were not aware of it.

First of all, the quality consciousness that your husband had isn't good enough for today. It shouldn't have existed at the current level in the past. You didn't know if processes were in control. Even if they were operating with no special causes for upsets, you didn't know if the end-product would meet specifications. The variability in the end-product is due to the variability of the manufacturing process. Your returns for an out-of-tolerance condition might be due to the inability to control the process economically. A second reason might be that you are taking orders with tolerances or designs that you can't meet regularly with your type of equipment. Separate the returns into these two categories.

Second, your raw materials and subcontracting are causing huge problems. Find the causes and remove them. Get new vendors quickly, if necessary.

Third, your husband's rule of thumb on 25 machines being the break-even point was based upon assumptions that no longer hold. Among them were:

- All competitors have the same percent scrap, rework, and the same operating costs.
- Customers will tolerate the back orders of the past.
- Slow-downs or soldiering do not occur.
- Raw materials and subcontracted work does not cause delays or increased costs.

Your current problems are not to be found by looking at old break-even figures.

Fourth, I can't figure out why you pay out dividends when you have such serious problems.

Fifth, there is a total lack of management awareness and support for the quality improvement efforts. The way the effort was introduced was all wrong. There was too much of an emphasis on statistical methods and not enough on team building and quality planning. Start out quickly with employee discussions on quality. Get them to help develop improvement plans. Teach them why a complete change in a set-up is wrong when a small deviation suggests a minor adjustment.

Finally, meet daily as a team of three to communicate, to plan, and eventually to celebrate success. You should be able to do this without further use of a consultant. This will also lead to a natural form of organization.

If, however, you believe you need a consultant to give management guidance, please call.

Sincerely,

Bill Golomski

William A. Golomski

A Well-Trained Work Force Can Be Your Competitive Edge

Pat Wolf and Judy Jorgensen

 *Pat Wolf is the Associate Dean of Continuing Education and Business Outreach in the Division of Liberal Arts and Science at the Milwaukee Area Technical College. She currently helps 12 businesses manage their Employee Education Centers.*

Judy Jorgensen is the Academic Support Manager at Waukesha County Technical College. Like Ms. Wolf, Ms. Jorgensen helps local businesses in their efforts to increase employee math and reading skills.

Dear Mrs. Burton:

Many companies are going through a scenario similar to yours at Burton Screw Machine Company, Inc. Manufacturing equipment and techniques have changed so that companies can maintain a competitive edge in the international market. Companies are also finding that their competitive edge is a well-trained work force that can handle the new technologies. The Business Council for Effective Literacy estimates that one in every eight employees reads at no better than a 4th grade level, and one in five is at a 5th grade level. But 70 percent of the reading materials in a national cross-section of jobs is between 9th and 12th grade level, and 15 percent is even higher. With the introduction of quality assurance programs, companies can expect a need to increase the math and reading skills of their employees to approximately a 10th grade level.

We are going to describe how you can increase your employees' skills by establishing an Employee Learning Center, and we will give you four guidelines to insure your Center's success.

Many employees and their unions or employee groups are joining in a partnership with their local vocational college to provide workplace literacy programs. The Employee Learning Centers, as most workplace literacy centers are called, are on the company's turf, at times convenient for the employees, and on terms that meet the particular needs of the employees and the employers. The purpose of the Employee Learning Centers is to help employees develop the necessary skills so that they can be successful at their current jobs and in the future. For example, an employee needs to be able to do statistical process control, which includes algebra; however, if the employee is only competent through fractions and decimals, additional training will be needed to bring him or her up to the competency level to implement SPC on the job. Employee Learning Centers assist employees with reading, writing, math, computer literacy and problem-solving skills. Employee Learning Centers do not supplement other training such as SPC but rather teach the basic skills necessary for employees to learn the advanced skills.

There are four keys to successful Employee Education Centers: job analysis, peer advising, the instructor, and the concept of being a good-faith partner.

Job analysis should be done during the planning stages so that everyone is aware of and can agree upon what needs to be taught at the site. Curriculum is then developed to meet the identified needs. An instructor competent in the areas can be chosen. Job analysis gives firm direction to the Employee Education Center and a base line for evaluation.

Peer advising is key because it allows for ownership of the program by the employees and serves as another conduit for evaluation. Peer advisors are selected through the union or the company, are trained, and are assigned a group of employees. Peer advisors contact their fellow employees to encourage use of the Employee Education Center. As evaluators, peer advisors keep the college aware of what is and isn't working and act as agents of change.

The right instructor is essential. It's important that the person be competent, and comfortable in the specific work environment. The best instructor is one who understands the mission of the company and is able to transfer that mission to the environment of the Employee Education Center. The instructor also needs to be comfortable on the shop floor and aware of the integration of basic skills and new technology.

In addition, there must be mutual trust embodied in the good-faith partner concept. It can be assumed that the company, the union, and the college are all interested in the improved learning capability of the individual employee so that each employee in turn will be more productive. Openness, honesty, and

Peer advising is key because it allows for ownership of the program by the employees and serves as another conduit for evaluation.

frequent communication are necessary elements of a successful partnership venture.

In the approximately 18 months that Wisconsin's vocational colleges have been involved in WPL programs, new emphases have emerged and change is continual. Companies are discovering the need for lifelong learners: employees who are able to spot the changes and trends in their industry and who will seek out the skills and knowledge they need to be able to keep themselves and their industry competitive. Labor unions are finding that they have to take the lead to encourage and enable their membership to pursue lifelong learning. The colleges have to continually update curriculum and methodology to meet these changes. The ability to read blueprints and math skills to the level of calculus are requisites in most manufacturing companies today.

Problem-solving, the ability to communicate the process, and being able to work together as a team are crucial skills in today's market.

Mrs. Burton, we would be happy to meet with you to discuss how we can help you improve your employees' math and reading skills. We are certain that you will discover how great an asset a well-trained work force can be. Call us at your convenience to arrange a meeting.

Sincerely,

Pat Wolf

Judy Jorgensen

> *Problem solving, the ability to communicate the process, and being able to work together as a team are crucial skills in today's market.*

Having an SPC Program Does Not Mean You Have Quality Production

Dennis Poeschel

Mr. Poeschel is the Senior Quality Assurance Engineer in the Electromechanical Systems Unit at Johnson Controls. An A.S.Q.C. Certified Quality Engineer, Mr. Poeschel's responsibilities include supplier audits, development of quality plans, interfacing various engineering functions with suppliers, and quality program development for new JCI products.

Mrs. Shelly Burton:

Thank you for the opportunity to offer you some of my thoughts about the situation at Burton Screw Machine Company. It is very apparent that many of the company's current financial problems are closely tied to problems with managing the quality function. Because quality assurance is my special area of expertise, I will offer you the following observations about the quality program at Burton.

A company's commitment to quality must start with its top management . Scott and Peter have different perspectives on quality, and that confuses your work force. The 1950s philosophies toward quality, shared by the machine operators and Peter, will never change under these conditions. Co-managerial positions will be successful only if both managers have the same goals. A clear-cut leader must be appointed. Whether you assume the president's position yourself, appoint Scott, or look outside, it must be done. Peter's current standards do not appear in line with the best future interests of Burton.

It is important that the workers know what is happening. Because of their current standards, Burton is losing customers.

Operators should be given specific examples of what their quality levels are doing to the company. This should include sharing financial information with them. Tell them that customer satisfaction is of prime importance. They need not worry about their jobs. Lost customer satisfaction can result in a loss of work, which may lead to lay-offs. When employees realize that their involvement can make a difference, they will have a higher level of commitment to the company's success.

Scott's implementation of SPC/SQC within the shop is noteworthy. However, it appears this was done with a shotgun approach. The use of SPC is only a tool for operators to monitor the process. It is not a method whereby quality parts are produced. Does the company understand the capabilities of its processes for its diverse customer base? As Peter pointed out, machines are often stopped and the "Q.C. system has choked off our production; we can't keep our machines running." The Q.C. Inspector received training but the machine operators didn't. The operators need to own the process, monitor it, control it with the SPC Charts and make adjustments before producing defectives. With the inspectors running the control process, the operators became frustrated. Tools like SPC are good only if the people know how to use them. Train the operators and give them ownership. Inspectors would better be used to monitor the procedures instead of the actual processes.

Operator involvement is not the only factor. To run a control chart, it is assumed a process is capable of producing the part. The constant shutting down of machines could be the result of process variability. Maybe the machines are set up wrong, which means they will continue to require adjustment. Or, maybe your machines are not capable of maintaining the requirements. No control chart in the world can product parts to .010 if the process can only hold .020. As part of the control process, machine capability and process capabilities need reviewing first. Simply having an SPC program does not mean you have quality production.

From the information supplied, Scott's efforts have been directed to in-house controls during manufacturing. The analysis of customer returns shows that the highest ranking factor is the material/services not controlled by Burton. These are centered around raw material, plating and heat-treating problems. Regardless of how well you run the in-house operation, these factors will not go away. Burton's suppliers must also take action. If suppliers can't meet your requirements or refuse to openly work with Burton, find someone who will.

Establish a quality plan with the supplier for the parts/services bought. Suppliers should outline, in writing, just how parts or processes will be monitored and controlled. By discussing these quality plans, both companies will understand exactly what is needed and how it will be monitored.

Documented procedures within the operation will assure consistency. Procedures should not only address the factory operations, but also engineering and business operations, such as purchased material control, operator work instructions, inspector/testers instructions, records of inspection-test results and final inspections. By addressing these issues, the problems related to wrong revision levels would be corrected. Although this is not the highest problem on the list, the reported 15 percent is very significant. This type of problem is eliminated by having a good check and balance system for reviewing revision levels when Burton receives customer orders.

I am looking forward to discussing these matters in detail when we meet next week.

Sincerely,

Dennis Poeschel

Commit to a Process That Takes the Emotion Out of Family Business Decisions

Paul W. Woerpel

Mr. Woerpel is the President of Family Business Dynamics, a company that helps owners of family businesses to successfully meet the relationship, managerial and organizational challenges unique to such enterprises. Services include: succession and transition planning, strategic planning, management team building, conflict resolution, and family consultation.

Dear Shelly, Scott and Peter:

Things at Burton Screw Machine may look bleak right now, but the situation is far from hopeless. The business and the family have experienced plenty of change in the last 16 months. Change, even positive change, is often unsettling. Time will be a factor in getting family relationships and the business back on an even keel.

First, I'm going to comment on key business issues. Then, I'm going to outline the process that I believe can help you resolve those issues.

Without question, efforts to improve quality have begun to pay off. Burton Screw Machine is shipping more of its product on time, and getting fewer customer returns. Gross margins are rising and with additional sales volume the company could be profitable. At the moment, there simply isn't enough volume to offset the cost of operations. Taking measures to increase sales and improve cash flow will have a positive impact on the company's financial health.

The business is experiencing significant operational and strategic difficulties. The situation is complicated by a lack of clear, consistent leadership.

Despite the achievements in improved product quality and manufacturing efficiency, there appears to be a lack of support for the internal changes which have been initiated. (Again, change can be unsettling.) The quality-improvement process questions the traditional assumptions about the nature of work and the roles and responsibilities of employees and managers. The challenge is to help employees understand what the firm is trying to accomplish, so that they can

When employees realize that their involvement can make a difference, they will have a higher level of commitment to the company's success.

The quality-improvement process questions the traditional assumptions about the nature of work and responsibilities of employers and managers.

appreciate the connection between their participation and the company's survival and success.

The market has changed; Burton Screw Machine's customer base has shifted. Customers are ordering in smaller quantities and certain segments of the market have declined. In addition, customers expect more and demand more. Offshore manufacturers have discovered ways to compete successfully with domestic producers. The challenge here is to rethink and revamp the firm's marketing strategy.

In a family business, the sudden death of the founder or president creates a void that is difficult to fill. Management succession at Burton Screw Machine has not been resolved. As a result, the conflicts between Peter and Scott, Jr., strain the family relations and create uncertainty that is detrimental to the business. The challenge will be to reach a fair and business-like conclusion about who will be the next president.

I suggest that you work on the business rather than managerial issues to begin with. Your objective will be to develop a plan to improve your sales and your operating efficiency. If these most pressing issues remain unresolved, the discussion of which brother becomes CEO will be purely academic.

A commitment to objectify and depersonalize the planning process will help the brothers to focus on what is best for the business rather than what is best for Scott or Peter. When agreement has been reached about the key initiatives, the responsibility can be divided according to natural inclination and ability. For instance, Peter's shop floor experience and history with the company make him the logical candidate to enlist employee support for the quality improvement efforts.

The plan becomes the vehicle by which Scott and Peter present a "united front" to the organization. Furthermore, each becomes accountable to the plan, rather than accountable to the other. Ultimately, the transition to a single president can become part of the plan.

What I am advocating is a commitment to a process that takes some of the emotion out of decision-making in the family business. Such a process results in clearer thinking and more systematic and effective problem-solving. What are the essential ingredients in this process?

Participation. Critical decisions are most likely to have broad support when the people affected are included in the process.

Separation of Family and Business. To avoid sacrificing the family for the business, or the business for the family, it's important to clarify which decisions are family decisions and which are business decisions.

Honesty and Forthrightness. Avoiding painful realities doesn't make them any less painful or real.

Consensus Decision-Making. When it comes to high-impact decisions, the time it takes to reach a shared understanding is a worthwhile investment.

Since it's obvious I'm not going to make a recommendation on a successor, here at least are some of the questions and considerations for the three of you to ponder:

- What kind of leadership will be required to run Burton Screw Machine now and in the future?
- What are the critical skills and abilities the next president must possess?
- What are Scott's and Peter's skills and abilities; managerial strengths and weaknesses?
- What does each of the brothers want for the business and from the business?
- Provided both choose to remain with the business on a long-term basis, what will be done to maximize each son's contribution to the business once a president has been named?

Finally, here are some thoughts on the circumstances in which you find yourselves today as a result of Scott Sr.'s, death. Families in business have a remarkable capacity to rise to the challenge in such instances and do what is necessary to insure the survival of the enterprise. Your family is no exception. When family members choose to work together, there are compelling reasons that go beyond the financial benefits and rewards. I am assuming in your case that the motivation includes a desire to preserve the legacy of two generations.

One way to complete the mourning process is to talk with one another about that legacy. The world is changing so the business must change. What is it that remains constant over time? What are the enduring family values which have become part of the fabric of this company? What are the critical ingredients in the culture that must be preserved? Sometimes, deciding what to hang on to facilitates the process of letting go. When you have become comfortable about letting go, it will be time to clean out Scott, Sr.'s, desk and redecorate the office.

During the past 16 months, individual sacrifices have been made for the sake of the family and the business. More will be required.

You shouldn't expect the transition to be painless. Since the discussions and decisions that lie ahead will be difficult, it's important that you agree on an approach and remind each other from time to time why you're going to all the trouble.

Sincerely,

Paul W. Woerpel

Paul W. Woerpel

Understanding the Philosophy is Critical

Thomas W. Davis, P.E.

Mr. Davis is the Senior Vice-President of Academics and Dean of Faculty at the Milwaukee School of Engineering. He has consulted with nearly 300 companies and specializes in working with manufacturing companies' quality and productivity improvement programs.

Dear Shelly:

Your recent visit gave me a lot to think about and I do appreciate your candor regarding your concerns about Scott, Jr., Peter, and the company. Having known all of you for years, I understand what you are going through. As I promised, I have given this considerable thought and have looked over all of the materials that you left with me. I am ready to offer my perspective.

First, let me say that I do believe that you are on the right track for the long-term success of Burton Screw Machine Company. Scott is right about the long-term consequences of short-term thinking; in the long run, the survivors will be those who invest in the future and quality. However, I also believe that you could use some help in understanding how some of the basic philosophies in a total quality control program work. Things like SPC, charts, graphs, computers, JIT, and electronic gauges are all part of the process, but not part of the philosophy. In order for the system to work, there must be a common understanding of the philosophy. Listed below are some suggestions which I hope will help.

Commitment from the top. Anyone will tell you that in order for the program to be effective, there must be commitment from the top of the organization. This means that you, Scott and Peter must believe that it is important and it will work. Perhaps a few visits to other companies will help. Or, attend some of the national quality program seminars. I have attached a suggested reading list that may help too.

Employee involvement. A philosophy that is critical to the success of this program is employee involvement. Many of the long-term employees have a lot to offer. Listen to them. Involve them in the process. Show them trust and respect. Their future depends upon the success of the company as much as yours does. Support them as much as possible and implement some of their ideas on how to keep the quality up and running. Most importantly, provide them the education to run the new $100,000 machines or to finish high school, if that's what it takes. Gain-sharing is another tactic which has been successful in other companies. Whatever approach you use, the employees must feel ownership of the program and the process. There must be a way to get them to buy into it.

Customer satisfaction. Another key element to this product is total customer satisfaction. Work closely with them, let them know what you are doing and what challenges you face. Maybe they can help you along the way. Similarly, work with your vendors to increase quality. (One of the sheets that you supplied showed that your problems with outside vendors are increasing.) Establish a close and intimate working relationship with each of your vendors. Invite them in to show them the problems you are having with their product, and help them to make improvements.

Continuous improvement. Adopt a philosophy of making small, continuous improvements. (Baseball games are won by base hits rather than by home runs, even though it's the home runs that get all the attention.) If you can help the employees make a couple of improvements each day, in six months you will see the difference.

For example, one continuous improvement topic you may want to look into is the reduction in set-up time. With your product mix changing and reducing in volume, set-up time may become a more critical factor.

Continuous improvement must be part of the process. Quality is process-oriented, not inspection-oriented. Monitor what you want to improve and determine the factors which will

Anyone will tell you that in order to be effective, there must be commitment from the top of the organization.

result in improvement. Ask your employees to help establish realistic goals and targets for continuous improvement so that they will take ownership.

Everyone needs to share the same vision of what needs to be done. This can be done only when everyone understands the basic philosophies. Other businesses have undergone this same process. Learn from them. Learn from their mistakes and learn from their successes. Perhaps it might even be advisable to ask several people to become outside directors of your company to get some objective advice and input.

New equipment, SPC and a slick brochure are not the way to true quality. Quality is a process which takes time to implement. The process is never completed because there is always room for improvement. Shelly, the people at Burton Screw Machine have taken the first step. If you can now get everyone working in the same direction, under the right philosophy, with trust and respect, you will succeed.

Sincerely,

Thomas W. Davis, P.E.

> *Everyone needs to share the same vision of what needs to be done.*

Recommended Reading

Spirit of Manufacturing Excellence, Ernst C. Huge, Dow Jones, 1988.

The Goal—A Process of Ongoing Improvement, Eliyahu M. Goldratt and Jeff Cox, North River Press, Inc., Croton-on-Hudson, New York, 1948.

Thriving on Chaos, Tom Peters, Alfred A. Knopf, New York, 1988.

World Class Manufacturing—The Lessons of Simplicity Applied, Richard J. Schonberger, The Free Press, New York, 1986.

The Team Handbook, Peter R. Scholtes, Joiner Associates Inc., Madison, Wisconsin, 1988.

Zapp!—The Human Lightning of Empowerment (and how to make it work for you), William Byham, Development Dimensions International Press, Pittsburgh, 1989.

Out of the Crisis, W. Edwards Deming, MIT Center For Advanced Engineering Study, Cambridge, Massachusetts, 1986.

The New Manufacturing Challenge: Techniques For Continuous Improvement, Kiyoshi Suzaki, The Free Press, New York, 1987.

The Japanese Educational Challenge, Merry White, The Free Press, Macmillan Inc., New York, 1987.

The Reckoning, David Halberstam, William Morrow, New York, 1986.

The Management Challenge: Japanese Views, Lester Thurow, MIT Press, Cambridge, Massachusetts, 1988.

Japanese Style Management—An Insider's Analysis, Keitaro Hasegawa, Kodansha International Ltd., New York, 1986.

The Art of Japanese Management, R. Pascale and A. Anthos, Simon and Schuster, New York, 1981.

Seven Arrows, Hyemeyohsts Storm, Ballantine Books, New York, 1972.

Kaizen, Masaaki Imai, Random House Business Division, New York, 1986.

Editor's Note: *This case study was based upon an actual screw machine manufacturing company. However, in the interest of privacy, the names of the people and location have been changed.*

Chapter 8

"I Want to Sell My Business. Where Do I Begin?"

Donald Reinardy, C.P.A., M.S., and Catherine Stover

David McLimans

E ven though it was only 6:00 pm, it was getting dark already as Ben Logan and his son, Michael, walked to the parking lot. The lights above the company sign—Logan Printing Company, Inc.—began to flicker on as the men approached the last two cars in the lot. Ben didn't know what bothered him the most: the fact that autumn was almost over, or the fact that it was Saturday and another exhausting week was over, or the fact that his son drove a Honda. A Honda Accord—when he himself had

driven nothing but Cadillacs for 30 years. Mike was different.

Ben's car, which was parked in the place reserved for the company president, was closest. Ben put his key in the door and turned to say goodnight.

"Dad," Michael said, putting his briefcase down on the pavement.

Ben braced himself, anticipating another lecture about why he should be using that remote control thing to unlock his car and start the engine. Mike was always promoting useless high tech gadgets. Ben liked keys, and

Donald Reinardy is a partner with the CPA/ business consulting firm of Smith & Gesteland.

Catherine Stover is the editor of the Small Business Forum.

he had spent too much time with his son today already.

Mike's pause was beginning to seem overly dramatic, when finally he said, "We have to talk. We haven't had five minutes alone together since you announced your retirement two weeks ago. If you want to get out in six months, we better start talking about the buy-sell agreements and the evaluation pro— "

"Later, Mike," Ben said, and turned the key and opened the car door. He was cold. He wanted to go home and eat.

"When, then? You and Mom could come over to the house after church—"

"Not tomorrow." Ben looked at his watch, and then at his son's exasperated expression. The last thing he wanted to do was to go over to Mike's spotless little house and listen to Mike's spotless little wife talk about her fax machine business. In Ben's opinion, that couple took themselves too seriously. They were 29, and what have they accomplished? When he, Ben, was 29, he had already fought in the Korean War and had come home and had founded a business. "We're having brunch with the Riversons at the club after church."

"Dad, look. We have a lot of talking to do."

"I told you I'd hire that valuation firm to take care of it."

"There are a few things we have to get straight first. Like where the company is heading. What kind of technology we're going to invest in. The results of our S.P.C.—"

"Not now, Mike." Ben put his briefcase on the passenger seat, and sat down behind the wheel. It seemed as though Mike had been trying to show him the error of his ways ever since he started working for Ben two years ago.

"Even this parking lot is falling apart, Dad. If you think I'm going to pay a fortune for your old, junky—"

"That's enough, Mike." Ben started the car. "When—and if—you purchase this company, you will be buying a generation of contacts, a good reputation, and loyal employees." The kid always expected things to be handed to him. He always expected things to be easy and accurate and on time. But life isn't like that. "You're not the only one who is interested in buying Logan Printing."

"What!"

"Don't get excited. We've had some inquiries, but I haven't promised anything to anyone yet."

"Dad, I can't believe I'm hearing you say this. This business belongs to the family—"

"Jim Webb has been with the company for 32 years, and that makes him family. I don't know

why he wants to buy the company at his age, but he does. The other interested party is American Printing, Inc. They have about 40 firms the size of ours across the country, and they've been interested in this place for several years."

"Why haven't you told me any of this before?"

"Would it have made a difference?"

"I'm your son, for godsakes, and I have a right to know what is going on!"

"You are 29 years old. You've worked here for two years. You don't have any rights. And I'm not interested in pursuing this conversation."

Mike picked up his briefcase.

"Goodnight, Mike." Ben closed the car door, and very slowly began to drive out of the lot.

Ben was tired. Tired of heavy traffic, tired of Mike, and tired even of the printing business.

Ever since his son had joined the firm—after finishing an M.B.A. and working in that place in Atlanta—it had stopped being fun.

It was getting hard to get to sleep at night. He would hear his son saying, "The new presses are much faster and more efficient," or "Statistical process control—known as S.P.C.—could reduce our direct costs by 30 percent," or "We can't do everything anymore. We have to find a niche. Let's specialize in one area, and be the best."

The most aggravating part of it all, Ben knew but wouldn't admit if his life depended upon it, was that Mike was usually right. Ben knew his equipment was out-of-date and that they probably should spend the $3 million on the high-tech stuff that Mike wanted.

But Ben wanted out. He didn't want to spend anything on anything until the business was sold. He had worked hard his whole life. He deserved to be comfortable.

He knew the time had come to retire when, two weeks ago, his major customer—the president of the firm that accounted for 25 percent of his sales—had phoned him to say that ten months of negotiations were over; he had sold his firm to one of the biggest corporations in the world. It wasn't a surprise to Ben—he had heard about the negotiations for months at the club—but it still was a big blow.

The fact that Ben Logan had printed books for this no-longer-local business for almost 30 years probably wouldn't matter at all to the new owners. The new people—who were headquartered in London—had not even bothered to return his calls. Would he ever get another order from them? He didn't know. Nobody seemed to know.

*When—and if—
you purchase this
company, you will
be buying a gen-
eration of contacts,
a good reputation,
and loyal
employees.*

Logan Printing Company, Inc.
Analysis of Asset Value
December 31, 1994

Assets	1990	1991	1992	1993	1994
Cash	598,400	515,660	190,509	228,611	487,342
Accounts receivable	991,780	968,047	1,055,754	1,266,905	1,434,335
Inventory	290,330	333,879	383,961	460,753	557,511
Marketable securities	389,781	448,248 0	100,000	263,773	
Prepaid expenses	26,400	30,360	34,914	41,897	49,019
Income tax refunds	0	0	152,848	0	0
Property and equipment	4,217,307	4,849,903	5,232,388	5,389,360	5,712,721
Accumulated depreciation	(1,850,692)	(2,128,296)	(2,447,540)	(2,863,622)	(3,207,710)
Cash value of life insurance	37,407	43,018	49,471	59,365	68,270
Receivable from officers	382,987	510,435	242,000	290,400	319,440
Total assets	5,083,700	5,571,254	4,894,305	4,973,669	5,684,701

Liabilities

	1990	1991	1992	1993	1994
Accounts payable	388,278	331,518	611,247	373,756	437,294
Accrued wages & vacations	159,428	183,343	210,844	187,242	187,242
Accrued payroll taxes	37,561	43,195	49,674	34,912	34,912
Accrued profit sharing and 401(k)	34,148	39,270	45,161	23,346	23,346
Accrued interest	14,442	16,609	19,100	14,338	14,338
Other accrued expenses	17,595	20,235	23,270	30,909	33,073
Income taxes payable	149,254	171,642	0	0	29,836
Deferred income taxes	166,300	191,240	0	31,880	88,200
Long term debt	2,238,752	1,999,564	3,449,499	3,342,172	3,197,060
Total liabilities	3,205,758	2,996,616	4,408,795	4,038,555	4,045,301

Stockholders' Equity

	1990	1991	1992	1993	1994
Common stock (10,000 shares, $100 par value)	1,000,000	1,000,000	1,000,000	1,000,000	1,000,000
Additional paid in capital	237,198	237,198	237,198	237,198	237,198
Retained earnings	640,744	1,337,440	(751,688)	(302,084)	402,202
Total equity	1,877,942	2,574,638	485,510	935,114	1,639,400
Total liabilities and equity	5,083,700	5,571,254	4,894,305	4,973,669	5,684,701

Logan Printing Company, Inc.
Analysis of Income

	1990	1991	1992	1993	1994
Sales	4,554,543	5,228,815	5,333,392	6,133,401	7,122,413
Cost of sales	2,342,712	2,660,973	2,873,851	3,362,405	3,765,894
Gross profit	2,211,831	2,567,842	2,459,541	2,770,996	3,356,519
Officer salaries	143,010	150,160	131,900	185,400	210,600
Office salaries	99,807	104,797	109,513	113,346	118,673
Payroll taxes	100,095	105,100	109,829	123,673	138,620
Auto expenses	4,419	4,640	4,848	5,018	7,377
Dues and subscriptions	6,424	6,745	7,048	7,295	7,724
Employee benefits	45,743	48,030	50,192	51,948	54,390
Insurance	38,270	40,184	41,992	63,461	73,288
Repairs and maintenance	33,085	34,740	36,303	199,573	93,373
Office supplies	20,144	21,151	22,103	22,877	33,629
Professional fees	24,343	25,560	326,710	120,335	46,892
Rent	180,000	180,000	180,000	180,000	180,000
Personal property taxes	1,507	1,583	1,654	1,712	1,859
Utilities	41,742	43,829	45,801	47,404	54,684
Advertising	45,222	47,483	49,620	66,987	98,471
Bad debts	34,184	35,893	37,508	50,636	74,435
Sales and travel expenses	27,552	28,929	30,231	81,289	119,495
Pension plan contributions	123,073	129,226	135,041	179,768	214,259
Director fees	10,000	10,000	10,000	10,000	15,000
Officers life insurance	11,500	11,500	11,500	11,500	11,500
Contributions	2,460	2,583	2,699	2,794	2,925
Cleaning and security	15,487	16,261	16,993	17,588	20,754
Depreciation	320,577	336,826	358,375	387,082	421,839
Total expenses	1,328,644	1,385,220	1,719,862	1,929,686	1,999,787
Net operating income	883,187	1,182,622	739,679	841,310	1,356,732
Other income and expense					
Interest income	41,182	51,860	17,492	22,956	28,102
Gain on sale of assets	17,287	7,918	86,752	7,250	9,836
Miscellaneous income	12,919	9,483	15,627	18,205	16,078
Interest expense	(199,333)	(188,264)	(270,894)	(383,827)	(294,638)
Miscellaneous expense	(5,436)	(24,848)	(21,873)	(24,408)	(30,182)
Pollution damages	0	0	(3,000,000)	0	0
Total other income and expense	(133,381)	(143,851)	(3,172,896)	(359,824)	(270,804)
Net income before taxes	749,806	1,038,771	(2,433,217)	481,486	1,085,928
Income taxes	249,882	342,075	(344,088)	31,880	381,641
Net income	499,924	696,696	(2,089,129)	449,606	704,287

Logan Printing Company, Inc.
Additional explanation

(1) Real estate owned by Ben Logan and leased to the company on a 5 year lease at $15,000 per month. Market rent is $5 per square foot for the 50,000 square foot building.

(2) Stock ownership   Ben - 40%
                        Wife - 20%
                        Mike - 20%
                        Sister - 10%
                        Jim Webb - 10%

(3) Officer salaries

	1990	1991	1992	1993	1994
Ben	143,010	150,160	131,900	148,320	168,480
Mike				37,080	42,120

(4) Pension and profit sharing plans cover officers and office. Production workers are covered by union retirement plans.

(5) Company uses last-in, first-out (LIFO) inventory method.

LIFO reserve	1990	1991	1992	1993	1994
	87,100	103,500	122,800	152,000	189,500

(6) Company paid $3 million in 1992 for cleanup of groundwater pollution as a negotiated settlement of an Environmental Protection Agency lawsuit. The company also bought $350,000 of equipment to prevent future incidents and paid $300,000 in legal fees in 1992 and $80,000 in 1993 in connection with this matter.

He did know that he was tired of hearing about his son's success with his new venture. Six months ago, Michael began printing the weekly advertisement sections for that big discount place on the edge of town. It seemed a little undesirable to Ben to be associated with that discount place.

He had approved funding the project just because he wanted to get Mike out of his hair— give the kid something of his own to do so he wouldn't keep talking to him about soy ink and employee training programs and recycled paper. He never dreamed it would work. It was going well—but it was hardly the direction he had ever envisioned taking the company himself. Those discount places are depressing. There is a big difference, he felt, between printing books and printing ads that end up in the garbage.

As Ben pulled into his driveway, he heard himself sigh. He was not looking forward to the valuation process. The thought of finding out how much his company was worth terrified him. It was like knowing that Judgement Day was just around the corner, and that everyone in town would find out that he was a sinner. Maybe it wasn't worth as much as he thought it was. He knew he'd probably end up selling it to Michael, but he didn't want the kid to be ungrateful. If he didn't let American Printing make an offer, the kid would probably spend the rest of his life thinking his old man had taken advantage of him.

Ben pulled himself away from unpleasant thoughts, and opened his car door. He was home. And he had six more months to sell his company.

What should Ben Logan do? We asked four valuation experts, "If Ben had consulted you, what advice would you offer?"

Authors' note: The authors would like to thank Michael Hoesly of Hoesly and Company, Inc., Mary Ellen Kinner of Printing Industries of America and Jack T. Hayes of Printing Industries of Wisconsin for the contributions they made to this case study.

He was not looking forward to the valuation process.

Capacity for Future Profit is What Counts

Theodore F. Gunkel, C.P.A.

Mr. Gunkel is the president and founder of Madison Valuation Associates, Inc. He has been involved with hundreds of valuations and transfers of ownerships of closely-held business equities over the last 20 years.

CONFIDENTIAL

Dear Ben:

I received your letter of May 1st requesting our assistance in establishing the fair market value of your firm, Logan Printing Company, Inc. (Logan Printing). Thank you for asking us to be a part of the process you and your wife are initiating.

As I understand, you are building a program for ownership and management succession for the business as a part of your overall retirement and estate distribution plan. Valuation is an important part of this planning process and we are pleased to help you with it. It is important that we define an approach and budget that will provide the information you need to make the decisions confronting you today. Here are some recommendations, observations, and questions that may be of some help to you in defining the approach you want us to follow.

First of all, I should disclose my own preconception of the business and financial situation existing for you and your wife, as you confront retirement and estate planning. These impressions are the result of our discussions over the past years.

Would Mike get a preference and/or price discount because he is your son?

- The majority stock position (60 percent) you and your wife own in Logan Printing, plus the commercial real estate you own and lease to the Company, represents at least 75 percent of your total personal estate value. You also have a profit sharing plan benefit that must have a $200,000 to $300,000 balance by now. If you were to retire today, you and your wife would need to rely heavily upon the value of the company stock and real estate for your personal security. These are very important dollars for the two of you.

- Your business is well established in its market and has a fine reputation for service and quality. It should be readily salable to several of your direct competitors as well as to one or more of the regional and national printers who are currently pursuing acquisition plans. These competitors and expanding acquirers tend to be the types of potential buyers who can justify paying the highest price for a business like yours. They usually bring efficiencies of scale and depth of management to the transaction. In a resulting merger, they tend to expand the products or services your sales staff can offer to your customer base and conversely bring your products and services to theirs. These buyers usually can take over your business at the lowest level of risk since they tend to have the best insight into your business and marketplace. In addition, they have the technical and general managerial talent and capital to support their business plan for your firm under their ownership. We often refer to them as "best fit" buyers.

- Logan Printing has a thin management team and has relied upon you and your right-hand man, Jim Webb, for the 20 years I have known you. Your son, Mike, has been with you for two years now and he appears to have the background and desire to manage a business like yours. You mentioned that both Jim and Mike have talked to you about buying the business. I wonder if they are qualified buyers. Do they have the money or credit? Do they have the knowledge? Do they have the entrepreneurial and managerial capacity to exploit the business opportunity? Can they match the price and terms you could get from the strategic best fit buyers discussed above?

- If you sought several offers from these strategic buyers, would their efforts form a floor that Jim and Mike would have to meet in order to buy the business? Would Mike get a preference and/or price discount because he is your son? Would Jim get a preference or price discount because of his long employment tenure and his key role in providing managerial continuity?

- If you were to seriously consider retaining your 60 percent ownership in the company as a long-term passive investment, you would need to prepare a business plan with the assistance of your chosen executive management team. Based upon this business plan, you could assess the potential return on your continued investment and the degree of risk (uncertainty) associated with this potential income stream. I doubt that you have prepared a formal business plan for the future of Logan Printing. You need a plan, as do

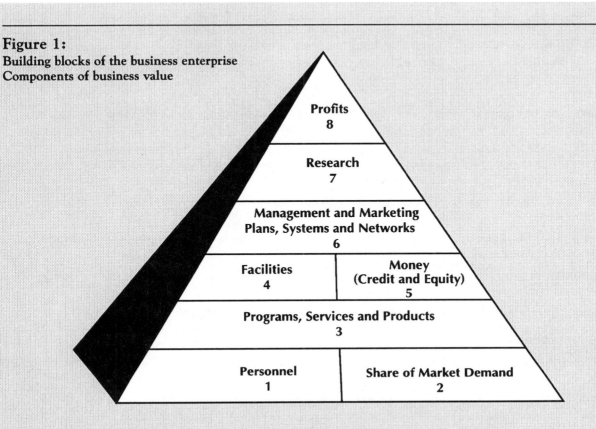

Figure 1:
Building blocks of the business enterprise
Components of business value

Profits
8

Research
7

Management and Marketing
Plans, Systems and Networks
6

Facilities
4

Money
(Credit and Equity)
5

Programs, Services and Products
3

Personnel
1

Share of Market Demand
2

Define the "capacity" of each component and the current level of utilization of its capacity by the current owners and management.

Copyright 1991 Madison Valuation Associates, Inc.

Mike, Jim, and Logan Printing. Business plans take time to prepare, but you and Jim are as qualified to prepare a plan as any managers I know. Mike's education has provided him the training to complete a formal business plan.

- Your recent outlay of $3 million for environmental remediation and the threat of losing 25 percent of your sales volume (due to acquisition of your major customer by an English conglomerate) will have an impact on the future of Logan Printing. You need to know what Logan Printing is worth to you as a continuing investment.

- Your six-month timetable for getting out of the business does not seem very realistic to me. The process of planning for management and ownership succession requires patience if you are to avoid upsetting your key people

and putting them and you at unnecessary risk. The whole process is less difficult and threatening than it may appear. Once your options are better defined, you will see whole new roles for yourself and your capital. Then you can set timetables for action that are less arbitrary than your current six-month deadline.

- The facts (as I understand them) concerning stock ownership, key people and their roles in your life, and your business are as follows:

  a. Stock Ownership (No buy sell agreement or stock transfer restrictions exist).
  Ben: 40 percent
  Mary (wife): 20 percent
  Mike (29-year-old son in the business): 20 percent (received as gift)
  Nancy (32-year-old daughter living in Alaska): 10 percent (received as gift)

Your six-month timetable for getting out of the business does not seem very realistic to me.

Figure 2: Business enterprise buyer's ranking (A Generalization)
Relative value of a business enterprise ranked by buyer's motivation to acquire a special benefit

Highest Value

A *Business* in the same industry or market which would employ its own business plan to: 1. Realize the added economic benefits of vertical or horizontal integration with the seller (synergy) or 2. Realize the added economic benefit of eliminating competition.

B *Business or investor group* with its own business plan to aggressively entercompetition in the seller's industry and which desires the seller's business and management as the nucleus of this planned growth.

C *Business* with the same industry concerned that sale of the business to a more aggressive competitor would adversely affect its market position and business plan.

D *Investors* who will be owners/managers organized to utilize the income tax and borrowing benefits of an Employee Stock Ownership Plan to enhance their proposed purchase plan.

E *Outside investors* who will be owners/managers and who possess deep management skill, knowledge, and experience within the seller's industry and markets.

F *Insider management group* who will be owners/managers and who have complete knowledge of the seller's business, which gives the group potentially intimidating leverage over seller, because it could become an owner without a management team.

G *Passive investors* with a diversified investment portfolio who will take on the seller's management and business plan.

H *Individual investor* who desires both the investment opportunity and an executive position within the seller's business.

I *Passive investors* without a diversified interest portfolio who will take on the seller's management and business plan.

Lowest Value

Copyright 1991 Madison Valuation Associates, Inc.

Capacity for future profit is what counts to a buyer.

Jim Webb (54-year-old key operational manager without non-compete agreement): 10 percent (received as bonus)

b. Key managers essential for smooth transition to new owners.

Ben—age 62, in good health with 35 years of managing and marketing the business. He would be needed as a consultant for six months to two years depending on the buyer's background and management depth. The buyer would require strong non-compete assurances.

Jim Webb—age 54, in good health, with 30 years experience in plant management operations. His desire to buy the company may make him an unwilling participant in a transfer to some other buyer if he feels he didn't get a fair shot at purchasing it himself.

It may take some serious money to assure his support and obtain his transitional services and a non-compete agreement.

Mike Logan—age 29, in good health, with two years on the job. He would probably be required to provide a non-compete to the buyer and some transitional services.

c. Your family wealth distribution concepts.

Upon the death of Ben or Mary, the surviving spouse is to have access to the entire financial value of the estate until his/her death.

Upon the death of surviving spouse, the estate is to be divided equally between your two children (Nancy and Mike).

Mike has joined the business as a manager with the impression that he will be given an opportunity to buy all or part of the business

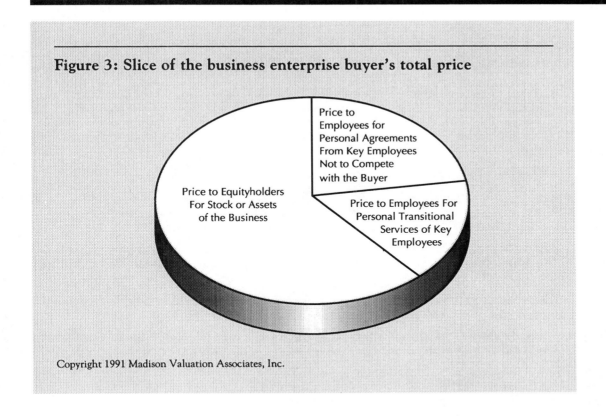

Figure 3: Slice of the business enterprise buyer's total price

Price to Employees for Personal Agreements From Key Employees Not to Compete with the Buyer

Price to Equityholders For Stock or Assets of the Business

Price to Employees For Personal Transitional Services of Key Employees

Copyright 1991 Madison Valuation Associates, Inc.

before it is sold to others. No price, terms, or timing has ever been discussed.

If these impressions of your personal and business situations are reasonably correct, I would suggest the following steps to establish the value of Logan Printing:

1. Meet with your attorney (with or without me) to discuss suggestions regarding this type of planning. Provide this letter if you think the general background would be of value. Ask your attorney if our firm should be engaged directly by them to gain any "confidential privilege" to our work product. This could be important in the event our valuation analysis should become the subject of a tax audit or some other legal process.

2. Meet with me to discuss our engagement. In particular, I would like to discuss your thoughts on the following topics. (I have enclosed some explanatory materials on each topic, which should help you to understand the thrust of our inquiry.)

a. What are the valuable components of your business that must be fully appreciated by any buyer to understand its capacity? To what extent have you utilized this capacity

under your ownership and management? Capacity for future profit is what counts to a buyer. It also counts to you if you keep the business yourself. (See Figure 1, p. 141)

b. Who are the potential buyers for the business enterprise? Rank them according to their probable willingness and ability to pay the highest price. Every buyer has some special benefits they are seeking through the purchase. It is critically important to understand what those benefits really are in order to ask and get the optimum price for your business. (See Figure 2)

c. How much of the enterprise price that you finally get out of your buyer will go to shareholders for their stock? How much will have to go to individuals to buy their transitional services and their non-compete covenants? (See Figure 3)

d. Once you decide upon the total value of the shareholders' equity interests, how will you allocate the value to individual shareholder blocks of stock in Logan Printing? Will every share be assigned the same value or will the control block that you and your wife own get a premium? Remember the minority block discount you took on the

Who are the potential buyers for the business enterprise?

Figure 4: Equity ownership interest value ranking

Relative value attributed to various size ownership interests in a closely held business enterprise, assuming only one equity ownership class outstanding and no restrictive or protective agreements governing ownership of these equity interests

Highest Pro Rata Value

A *Pivotal small block:* critical to buyer wanting control of business enterprise.

B *80% to 100% block:* possessing, at 100%, total authority over the business enterprise and, if a corporation, at 80%+, the power to elect income tax consolidation and assert other legal rights associated with squeeze-outs, liquidation, etc., and to dictate Board of Directors composition and management policy.

C *51% to 80% block:* possessing less than total control yet lacking only a few of the income tax and legal rights; able to elect the Board of Directors, officers, set salaries, hire, fire, expand or contract business activities, declare dividends, redeem or issue ownership interests.

D *50% block with more than one equityholder owning other 50%:* possessing only negative control, able to block but not to initiate action; potentially able to join with one or more other equityholders on key issues.

E *50% block with only one other equityholder:* possessing only negative control with high risk of a deadlock; see special Wisconsin statute enacted to allow petition for court action to break such deadlocks in a corporation.

F *49% or smaller block but relatively large compared to other block(s) and no one block over 50%:* possessing potential leadership power through assembly of other equityholders with sufficient vote to gain group control or to dominate in business affairs because of wide dispersal of other interests among satisfied or disinterested equityholders, thus gaining effective control with this block.

G *Small block among many small blocks: not a dominant block but not dominated by other blocks:* management may have significant control over equityholders.

H *Small block dominated by large block(s) with clear control:* dominated block at the mercy of those in control.

Lowest Pro Rata Value

I hope it is clear from this letter that I do not believe that there is just one correct current "fair market value" for your company or your shares.

shares you gave to your children in past years? Does that discount still apply? (See Figure 4)

3. Meet with me a second time, after you have digested our first discussion, to decide if you want to hire us to assist you in the following:

a. Determine the names of five or six strategic "best fit" buyers for Logan Printing. Then, we can either help you to pursue sale to them or estimate what they would be expected to pay if you did sell to them.

b. Determine the value of Logan Printing to you and your wife if you kept it as a continuing investment.

c. Determine the price and terms that Jim Webb or Mike Logan could be expected to pay if you sold to them.

d. Determine the price that would be assigned to transitional services and non-compete agreements required of key personnel under each sale alternative.

e. Determine the price assigned to each shareholder's block of stock in Logan Printing under each sale alternative.

I hope it is clear from this letter that I do not believe that there is just one correct current "fair market value" for your company or your shares. I do believe there is one price for every buyer based upon the benefits they expect to realize. I also believe that there is a determinable value of your company to you as a continuing investment.

Since I don't know who your strategic buyers are yet, or what benefits they seek, I can't tell you much about their pricing of your business at this point in time. If they exist in the marketplace, it would be worth more to them than to you, your son, or Jim.

Another important piece of information will be your five-year plan. Pricing a business based upon history alone is like buying an apple orchard based upon the quality of last year's crop. You need to check on the health of the trees. Analysis of Logan Printing's past performance, combined with projections of the future, provides the most meaningful insights into its value.

I am often asked if there is a "rule of thumb" when valuing a business. There is, but it is not accurate. Let me explain.

In your case, the rule would say that the enterprise has a value to you of four to five times the earnings before interest and taxes (EBIT) of the past year less interest- bearing debt.

It would be wrong for us to rely on this estimate because by relying on 1994 earnings as a base for value, we would ignore the potential loss of 25 percent of gross volume due to the recent acquisition of the customer entity by a British conglomerate. We also would ignore the extremely positive growth (21 percent) in gross profits from 1993 to 1994 which might easily justify a far higher multiple than the four or five multiples chosen from my "rule of thumb" references.

Now that I have given you a simplistic approach to valuation, I urge you to ignore it. If, after thoughtful analysis and pricing, the rule proves to be correct, it is by accident. Your business is too important and too valuable an asset to apply a "boiler plate" formula in determining value.

Please let me know if you have questions regarding this letter. I encourage your discussion of our engagement and this letter with your attorney. His questions, as well as yours, are welcome.

Thanks again for requesting our assistance in this important project.

Sincerely,

Theodore F. Gunkel

The Value Cannot be Determined by One Precise Mathematical Formula

Leonard J. Sliwoski, Ph.D., C.P.A., C.M.A.

Dr. Sliwoski is currently the director of the Small Business Development Center at Moorhead State University in Minnesota, where he is also a professor of accounting. Previously, as a senior tax accountant at Arthur Andersen and Co., he performed many business valuations.

Dear Mr. Logan:

Thank you for giving me the opportunity to describe the valuation process to you. The purpose of this report is to lay the groundwork for our future discussions of this complex process.

Definition of Value

Before a business can be valued, we must determine the purpose of the valuation. Different purposes require different values. For instance, valuing a business as a component of a property settlement in marital dissolution is governed by various state statutes. Many of these statutes fail to adequately define what constitutes value, and therefore value is established by case precedent. When valuing a minority interest in a closely held business, the value is often less than the minority shareholder's proportionate value of the total entity due to minority interest discounts applied. Therefore, the purpose of the business valuation defines the valuation concept and related methodology.

The most widely recognized and acceptable standard of value is fair market value. Fair market value for closely held businesses is defined as the price at which ownership would change hands between a willing buyer and a willing seller, with both parties possessing reasonable knowledge of the facts, and with neither party acting under compulsion to buy or sell. This is the valuation concept typically employed when businesses are purchased or sold, and I've used this concept in valuing Logan Printing Company, Inc.

An old adage states that every business has three values: the value to the current owner, the value to a unique or special purchaser, and the value to the "normal" or "general" purchaser. This adage is true and indicates that fair market

I am often asked if there is a "rule of thumb" when valuing a business. There is but it is not accurate.

value to some extent depends upon who is viewing the business. For purpose of valuing Logan Printing Company, Inc., the concept of fair market value is utilized with this value being the value to the "normal" purchaser.

Eight Important Factors

The fair market value of a closely held business without a public market cannot be determined by one precise mathematical formula. Exact comparison to other securities is seldom possible. The fair market value of a business lies in a range of possible values. Reasonable application of correct valuation techniques assist in narrowing that range. In recognition of this, a sound valuation should be based upon all relevant facts. In addition, elements of common sense, informed judgment, and reasonableness enter into the process of weighing the facts and determining their aggregate significance.

For closely held businesses, a valuation analysis generally includes examination of the eight factors listed in Internal Revenue Ruling 59-60 with appropriate modifications and updating as discussed in Internal Revenue Rulings 65-193 and 68-609. These eight factors, although not all-inclusive, are fundamental and require careful analysis in each case. These eight factors are as follows:

1. Nature and history of the business
2. General economic and industry outlook
3. Book value and financial condition
4. Earning capacity
5. Dividend payment capacity
6. Goodwill and other intangible values
7. Sales of stock and size of holding
8. Market prices of comparable stock (or similar companies that are actively traded)

I will discuss each of the eight factors in the following pages. Gathering information in each of the eight areas requires: (1) general investigative work in relation to the overall economy and the industry in which a business operates, (2) analysis and adjustment of the business' financial information, and (3) application of appropriate valuation techniques.

1. **Nature and history of the business.** Ben, here is a list of the relevant facts as I know them:

- The business has been in existence for over 30 years.
- You started the business in your twenties, and you are still a key manager.
- The business has good contracts, a good reputation, and loyal employees.

- The business equipment is old and appears to a large extent technologically obsolescent, and therefore will require replacement. Replacement equipment will cost $3 million.
- The business is a full-service printing business that prints books and has successfully entered the quick-print market.
- The business has had some difficulty with environmental issues, but appears to have funded the required environmental cleanup and to have purchased the appropriate equipment to avoid recurring problems of this nature.
- It is probable that the business will lose a major customer who accounts for 25 percent of total revenue.
- Here is a list of additional information that I need for the valuation:

    - An organizational diagram depicting the management structure.
    - A corporate minutes book documenting significant past business events.
    - Geographical location. Major competitor information.
    - Specific information concerning major types of printing revenue, and contribution of each to sales.
    - Detailed information related to specific components of the cost-of-goods sold account.

2. **General economic and industry outlook.** There are numerous sources that project key overall economic statistics for future periods. For purposes of this valuation, the assumption will be made that the economy will be in a slow growth pattern at the federal, state and local level.

I examined specific information relating to the printing industry. Most of the information located was found in a major study, "Printing 2000," by Printing Industries of America, Inc. This study offered a complete analysis of the printing industry nationally. It addressed prospective changes in 13 printing markets. The most pertinent information is as follows:

- Printing technologies will continue to evolve toward greater digitization (computerization) and automation.
- Stricter environmental regulation will become an increasing cost factor and barrier to expansion in urban areas.
- Continuing technological change will lower per-page costs, and hence increase overall competition.

Every business has three values: the value to the current owner, the value to a unique or special purchaser, and the value to the "normal" or "general" purchaser.

- Real wages will rise (due to slow growth in the labor market) for workers with information technology skills.
- As growth slows in the overall demand for printing services, industry consolidation is likely to increase.
- Competitive pressures will fall most heavily on the less profitable, less well-managed printers with revenues between $2 million and $50 million.
- Profitability will increasingly become a crucial issue with all printers. Crucial success factors include: increased efficiency and capacity utilization, precisely defined market niches, access to capital, and management capabilities.
- Printers in the medium-size range (between $2 million and $10 million in annual revenues) will have substantial opportunities. By maintaining flexible pricing structures, they can take business away from larger and smaller competitors. In addition, they can focus on specialized product needs and take advantage of the growing demand for shorter run and higher quality work.

3. **Book value and financial condition.** As indicated previously, a financial analysis was completed with specific information relating to past trends examined. The financial analysis of Logan Printing Company, Inc. revealed the following:

Income Statement
- Sales have risen at approximately a 7.2 percent annual rate over the five-year period.
- Cost of Goods Sold (CGS) is unusually low in relation to industry standards. As a percentage of sales over the five-year period, CGS varied from 50.9 percent to 54.8 percent. The industry standard for CGS as a percentage of sales for businesses categorized in SIC 40 as depicted in the RMA Financial Statement Studies: 19902 is 70.2 percent. We need to determine why CGS was so low. Based upon the fact that both Ben and Mike are working six days a week and are tired, it could be due to lack of sufficient production staff.
- Selling, general, and administrative expenses over the five-year period as a percentage of sales varied from 13.7 percent to 19.2 percent, which is similar to the industry average.
- Owner's compensation as a percentage of sales is higher than the industry average. Between officer salaries, director fees, offer

pension plan, and rent, the owner's compensation in 1994 was $542,512 or 7.6 percent of sales. The industry median officers compensation as a percentage of sales was 4.3 percent.
- Overall, the business was unusually profitable over the entire five-year period, except for 1992 when it had environmental problems. In 1994, the net profit before taxes as a percentage of sales was 15.2 percent as compared to the industry average of 3.3 percent.

Balance Sheet
- The company collects slowly with accounts receivable taking between 67 and 78 days over the five-year period. The industry norm is 50 days.
- The company pays slowly with days accounts payable between 40 and 77 over the five-year period. The industry norm is 27 days.
- The company's inventory management appears questionable, with days inventory ranging from 45 to 53 over the five-year period. The industry norm is 25 days.
- The officers appear committed. The debt-to-equity ratio varied, but in 1994 it was 2.47 when the industry average was 2.10. There is a large officer receivable, which is of some concern. It might exist for a variety of reasons, possibly to defer paying income taxes. Adjusting for the officer note receivable makes the 1994 tangible debt-to-equity ratio equal to 3.06, which is still reasonable.
- In 1994, the company had equipment with a book value of $2,505,011. However, you have indicated that approximately $3 million in new high technology equipment is needed to replace the existing equipment.
- The company has correctly structured its financing, matching long-term asset needs with long-term funding sources. In 1994 the company had adequate long-term debt financing of $3,197,060.

The company has been and continues to be highly profitable, with the exception of 1992. The company appears lax in the management of accounts receivable, accounts payable, and inventory, but can afford to be lax. Once again, the possible reason the company is lax might be due to the fact that your management team consists only of you, Mike and Jim Webb. Between cash on hand and marketable securities, the business had $1,044,853 in 1994 which represents 53.8 days of sales. This amount of days sales held in cash and marketable securities is unusually high for a small, closely held business. In addition,

Earning capacity for the near future appears favorable.

between officer salaries, directors fees, officer pension plan, and rent, the owners drew out $542,512 in cash from the business during 1994.

4. **Earning capacity.** Earning capacity for the near future appears favorable. As I indicated earlier, the 1990s will be a competitive period for the printing industry. However, well-managed, well-capitalized, medium-sized printers should fair well. In your case, Mike has had two years experience in the business, has earned an M.B.A., appears to be technology-oriented, has been successful in the discount printing endeavor, and appears to understand the importance of being in a market niche. Assuming Ben's buyout is funded correctly, there should be adequate cash for operation and expansion purposes.

A negative concern is the probable loss of your biggest customer. In addition, because I have not seen an aging of accounts receivable, it is difficult to determine if the remaining sales are highly concentrated in a small amount of accounts.

5. **Dividend paying capacity.** With your excess cash, and with the large owner distributions, the business clearly has dividend paying capacity. However, in closely held corporations, dividends are not usually paid due to adverse tax consequences. Although discretionary cash is available, Logan Printing reflects no dividend payments. This is typical for small, closely held businesses.

6. **Goodwill and other intangible assets.** Goodwill is generally defined as the "excess earnings" over and above a fair return on equity. While such factors as the prestige or renown of a business, the ownership of a trade or brand name, and the record of successful operation over a prolonged period and a particular locality are supportive, they must be able to be quantified in the form of excess earnings to substantiate marketable goodwill. In the case of Logan Printing, with its above-average profit, goodwill does exist. In an actual valuation engagement, the amount of goodwill would be estimated using a valuation technique, an example of which is the excess earnings method discussed later in this letter.

7. **Sales of stock and size of holding.** In considering actual stock sales made as a basis for valuation purposes, it must be determined that the ownership interest was traded in an arm's length transaction. Where trading of

ownership occurs between family members, an arm's length assumption is invalid. You indicated that no arm's length stock sales were made. Therefore, this criteria was of no use in determining the value of Logan Printing.

8. **Market prices of stock of comparable or similar companies which are actively traded.** Sales information relating to similar publicly traded companies sufficiently comparable to Logan Printing was not available. If this information was available, discounts would need to be applied to make the stock of Logan Printing comparable to the publicly traded companies stock. Discounts would typically be applied for key persons, minority interest, and/or lack of marketability.

Valuation Methods

There are numerous business valuation methods. All of these methods can be grouped into four major categories, as follows: *market-based methods, income-based methods, asset-based methods, and hybrid methods.*

The *market-based methods* involve using data from comparable business sales, and also involve using "rules of thumb" for valuing certain types of businesses. Actual data from sales of comparable closely held businesses is generally difficult to obtain. In addition, rules of thumb need to be taken "with a grain of salt" as in some instances they are valid, while in other instances they are invalid. For small, closely held businesses, market-based valuation methods, due to practical difficulties associated with their application, are not used frequently.

Income-based methods attempt to determine a probable future income stream for the business and capitalize this income stream to determine the business's value. The probable future income stream is called an adjusted or normalized income stream. It can be determined by adjusting each revenue and expense item on the income statement to its probable future value over the near term. Capitalizing the income stream means determining an appropriate discount rate to apply to the income stream to arrive at its present value. This capitalization rate adjusts for the risk inherent in the business. Capitalization rates of 20 percent to 50 percent are typical for small closely held businesses. There are several valuation methods that utilize an income-based approach to valuation. The discussion of specific income-based valuation methods is beyond the scope of this letter. However, in a profitable closely held business, income-based methods should be the predomi-

Capitalization rates of 20 percent to 50 percent are typical for small, closely held businesses.

nant valuation method employed. The present value of the income stream in a profitable business is in essence what gives the business its highest and best value.

Asset-based methods determine the value of a business through a summation process. Each asset and liability on the balance sheet is adjusted to fair market value, and then these values are summed. This approach to a large extent ignores the earnings of a business, and therefore in concept should receive minimal attention when valuing on-going closely held businesses which generate earnings by selling products or rendering services. It is a more appropriate valuation method for businesses such as bank holding companies whose principal function is to manage income-producing assets.

Hybrid methods normally take into account both income-based and asset-based valuation techniques. The most popular hybrid valuation method is the excess earnings method which is discussed in detail in Revenue Ruling 68-609. Under this method, a business's excess earnings, or earnings over the norm for a given business, are determined. These excess earnings are then capitalized to determine the goodwill present in the business. This goodwill value is added to the fair market value of the net tangible assets in the business to determine an overall business value.

If you would like me to, I can adjust your income statements and balance sheets and apply the appropriate valuation methodologies. If you would like me to pursue this, I would like you to keep the following in mind:

- Since this is an on-going business with a strong earnings pattern, income-based valuation methods would receive my primary attention.

- A capitalization rate of 20 percent to 25 percent is appropriate. This is a relatively low capitalization rate for a small, closely held business. Using this capitalization rate would lead to a relatively high business value. A low capitalization rate is appropriate due to the long standing profitable nature of Logan Printing.

- Since net fixed assets are such a significant item in a printing business, some consideration should be given to asset values when reaching the valuation conclusion. Given the nature of the business (both the strong historical income pattern and the importance of net fixed assets) the excess earnings approach would be one of the methods chosen.

- After all appropriate valuation methods are chosen and the resultant valuation numbers determined, the appraiser would need to reach a valuation conclusion. This conclusion would be determined by the appraiser after examining all the valuation numbers determined. The appraiser would reach a final valuation subjective conclusion using judgment and reasonableness.

- After the valuation is completed and a valuation conclusion has been reached, operating cash flow projections should be compiled based upon the proposed financing structure. The purpose of compiling the cash flow projections is to determine if the valuation conclusion is reasonable. The cash flow projections should determine if the buyer will receive a reasonable return on his/her down payment and a market salary for managing the business, and if income from the business is sufficient to provide for debt service. Compiling these cash flow projections is sometimes referred to as a "sanity check" or "proof of purchase test."

Conclusion

As can be gleaned from the above discussion, valuation of a closely held business is a complex topic involving different methodologies, assumptions about capitalization rates, and informed judgment. It is an iterative process. If you would like me to proceed, I would conduct more research and employ additional valuation methodology. Then, I would determine a numerical business value.

We should also note that the value chosen for Logan Printing Company, Inc. would be the cash equivalent price for the business at December 31, 1994. If your stock interest will be purchased and paid for with future profits from Logan Printing Company, Inc., then this cash price will need to be increased. The increase would be due to the fact that part of the purchase price would be paid in future periods. Appropriate mathematical techniques are available which could equate the valuation number or the cash equivalent price to proposed future payments.

We have covered a lot of ground in this letter. Please don't hesitate to call if you would like to discuss any of it further.

Sincerely,

Leonard J. Sliwoski

Leonard J. Sliwoski

A low capitalization rate is appropriate due to the longstanding profitable nature of Logan Printing.

Consider Establishing an E.S.O.P.

Bradley Van Horn, C.P.A., M.B.A.

Mr. Van Horn is the director of finance at Valuemetrics, Inc., a national valuation firm in Chicago. He has participated in over 150 valuation decisions.

Dear Ben:

I appreciate the opportunity to work with you and Logan Printing Company, Inc. in the capacity of financial advisor. Based upon our initial discussions and my on-site visit, I have conducted a preliminary investigation of the fair market value of the common stock of your company, and offer the following comments.

Overview of the Valuation Process

First, I would like to review the overall valuation process we have used. As you will recall, we started by requesting five years of financial statement data from you. We then compared your historical operating performance with your current operations. The objective was to identify any unusual or nonrecurring income or expense items that have been incorporated into your financial statements. We discussed our analysis with you, and I also had several good discussions with Mike and with your key salesperson and your production manager. This enabled me to adjust your financial statements to an economic basis. I accomplished this by restating your financial statements to what they would have been if the unusual or nonrecurring events had not occurred.

We contacted a few of your key vendors and customers. None of your vendors supply a major portion of your inventory. We were also able to speak with the previous owner of your major customer, XYZ Company. He indicated that, because of the new ownership of XYZ Company, there will be some consolidation of printing suppliers and therefore demand for printing services from Logan Printing Company might diminish in the future. However, he also felt strongly that XYZ would keep Logan as a supplier for at least 75 percent of the current printing services already being provided to XYZ. Much uncertainty still exists regarding the remaining 25 percent.

We also analyzed the current economics of the printing industry. We analyzed the economic state of the local, regional and national economies within which you operate. An important aspect of this analysis was to determine how these economies are expected to change, and how changes in these economies impact your operations.

Your competitive analysis provided a great deal of useful information about how your market functions and who your major competitors are, both publicly traded and privately held. Since your list of publicly traded competitors included only two companies, we expanded your list to include several other printing companies whose stocks are actively traded over the public stock exchanges. Our search for publicly traded comparable companies resulted in a total of eight publicly traded companies which operate in the same or similar industries to yours. The selection of publicly traded comparable companies is important to the overall valuation process. Since we are readily able to develop the market value of a publicly traded stock by looking at its current trading price, we can use this information to develop an estimate of Logan Printing's market value. The use of publicly traded comparable companies in building a defensible valuation conclusion is listed as a requirement of the Internal Revenue Service in their Revenue Ruling 59-60. We realize that no public company will exactly match your operating characteristics, products, services, growth characteristics, or depth of management. And certainly the public companies are much larger than Logan Printing. Therefore, we conducted a thorough ratio analysis and made allowances for important differences between your company and these public companies in our conclusion on value.

Two Methodologies

Once we completed our preliminary study of the economy, your operations, your financial condition, and publicly traded comparable companies, we then were able to complete our preliminary valuation investigation. Since potential investors in your stock would be buying the right to earn after tax earnings and cash flows in the future, we concentrated on the methodologies that are based on earnings and cash flows. We used two primary methodologies: the capitalized earnings methodology and the comparable public companies methodology. Because you do not prepare forecasts of your future operating cash flows, we were unable to perform a discounted cash flow analysis.

The *capitalized earnings methodology* uses adjusted historical earnings and price-to-

> *We used new primary methodologies: the capitalized earnings methodologies and the comparable public companies methodology.*

earnings ratios derived from stocks of similar publicly traded companies to estimate the market value of Logan Printing Company's stock. The *comparable public companies methodology* compares several earnings and cash flow multiples derived from stocks of publicly traded companies directly to Logan's corresponding earnings and cash flows to arrive at a value for your common stock. If you are able to prepare a detailed five year forecast of Logan Printing's income statement and operating cash flows, we can also estimate your stock value with a *discounted cash flow methodology*. This is an excellent methodology because it incorporates an estimate of the future cash flows which are expected to be generated by the business. We can tell you what the value today is of these future cash flows by determining an appropriate discount rate from the publicly traded comparable companies. Unfortunately, your sales manager explained that it would be very difficult to prepare a meaningful five-year forecast of sales and earnings.

Capitalized earnings methodology. In the capitalized earnings methodology, historical financial data is adjusted, as mentioned before, to eliminate the effects of unusual or nonrecurring events. We then weigh each of the historical years included in our analysis, resulting in a weighted average historical earnings figure. The adjusted earnings of your company are then multiplied by the price to earnings ratio derived from the comparable publicly traded companies to obtain the market value of Logan Printing's common stock.

Because we use an earnings multiplier obtained from the comparable companies, we need to restate your historical earnings to eliminate revenues or expenses that would not be part of the earnings of the comparable companies. Through discussions with you and comparisons with the publicly traded companies, we determined that the following adjustments should be made to your historical financial statements.

Officers compensation. We compared the level of total compensation for Ben Logan with the total compensation being paid to Chief Executive Officers at private manufacturing organizations that have a similar sales level. We found that your total compensation is higher than the industry average. We have added back to income your excess annual compensation.

LIFO adjustment. Logan accounts for its inventory by using the Last-In First-Out

(LIFO) method. LIFO is an accounting method that decreases pretax income during periods of rising prices by increasing the cost of goods sold expense. It usually does not approximate the true economic value of inventory used in the printing operations. To arrive at a more accurate measure of income from the "normal" operations, we restated cost of goods sold in each year to what it would have been under the First-In First-Out (FIFO) method of inventory accounting.

Rent adjustment. From 1990 through 1994, Logan Printing has leased its 50,000 square foot operating facility from you for $180,000. Market studies indicate that the fair market lease rate is $5 per square foot, or $250,000 per year. We have subtracted from pretax income $70,000 for each year in our analysis.

EPA lawsuit settlement. Logan Printing paid $3 million in 1992 for cleanup of groundwater pollution as a negotiated settlement of an EPA lawsuit. This item has been added back to 1992's pretax income as a nonrecurring expense.

EPA lawsuit legal fees. In conjunction with the EPA lawsuit, nonrecurring legal fees of $350,000 in 1992 and $80,000 in 1993 were incurred, which were added back to income for those years.

Repairs and maintenance expense adjustment. In 1993, Logan Printing incurred extraordinary expenses in connection with the repair of some equipment that was not under warranty. Repairs and Maintenance Expense for 1993 was $200,000. For 1994, these expenses were $93,000. The production manager of the company has indicated that the expected level of annual expenditures in the future is around $100,000. We have added back to pretax income $100,000 for nonrecurring repairs and maintenance for 1993.

Gain on sale of assets. In 1992, the company sold a printing press at a gain of $75,000. The company's primary business is not equipment sales, and an investor would not purchase stock in the company in order to earn an economic return from equipment sales. Therefore, we have excluded this gain from our calculation of "normal" earnings for 1992.

Interest expense adjustment. The comparable companies and Logan Printing each have differing debt levels, and differing mixtures of debt and equity. These differences are important because they impact value. In order to account for differences in debt levels, we have added interest expense back to pretax income for each year. We also added back interest expense for

We found that your total compensation is higher than the industry average.

The replacement of the worn-out equipment represents a cash drain without any increase in the future earnings or cash flows of the business.

each comparable company when determining the price-to-earnings multiple. In this manner, we are able to determine the price that an investor would pay for the earnings of Logan Printing, before the payment of any debt obligations. From this figure, we must subtract Logan's total debt of $3.2 million to obtain the market value of the common stock.

The earnings of the comparable companies were also restated to eliminate the effects of nonrecurring items, special items, minority interests, and discounted operations.

Summary of capitalized earnings methodology. In summary, the pretax income for each historical year is adjusted for the nonrecurring items identified earlier. The adjusted pretax income for each year is given a weight, with more weight given to the most recent years. The result is a weighted average historical pretax income figure that has been adjusted for nonrecurring events. This number is then taxed at the prevailing state and federal tax rates to arrive at a net income figure which an investor can reasonably expect Logan Printing to generate.

The earnings multiple obtained from the comparable companies is applied to the weighted average net income of Logan Printing, resulting in the market value of both the debt and equity of the company. By subtracting the total debt of $3.2 million, we have our estimate of the market value of Logan's common stock before considering the company's non-operating assets.

Nonoperating assets. The December 31, 1994, balance sheet indicates that Logan Printing has $820,000 in cash, marketable securities and the cash surrender value of life insurance. A comparison of working capital requirements with the comparable companies indicates that a normal level of cash for a business of Logan's size would be approximately $270,000. In addition, you indicated in our discussions that a cash balance of $270,000 would be sufficient to fund your normal operating requirements. Therefore, we have determined that Logan Printing has excess cash of $550,000. Ben, you are a minority stockholder. Minority stockholders cannot control how this cash is utilized or whether this cash is paid out as a dividend to shareholders, so we deduct a minority interest discount of 20 percent in arriving at net nonoperating assets of $440,000. This cash creates value above and beyond the value an investor would pay for the earnings of the company, and we have added this amount in

calculating the total value of the company. If a controlling interest were being sold, a minority interest discount would not be applied to the excess cash.

The December 31, 1994, balance sheet shows a Receivable from Officers of $319,440. You mentioned that you would not intend to repay this loan from the company in cash. One strategy would be for the company to take a tax deduction for the loss from the non-repayment of this loan. You must, in turn, include the non-repayment of the loan as income. The corporate tax savings resulting from this deduction can be bonused to you to cover the taxes you must pay as an individual. The non-repayment of this note receivable has no impact on value.

Future equipment purchases. Ben, both you and your production manager mentioned that the need exists at Logan to replace some out-of-date printing equipment with newer technology. Upon further review, the production manager indicated that the equipment purchase could be broken down into two segments: (1) $1 million required to remain at current sales and production levels. This new equipment will replace existing equipment which is worn out, where some maintenance has been deferred pending the decision to purchase new equipment.; and (2) $2 million required to purchase new technology which will give Logan Printing the capability to add new product lines, and hence new sales, or will greatly increase the operating efficiency of the company, thereby improving the bottom-line profitability of Logan.

The replacement of the worn-out equipment represents a cash drain without any increase in the future earnings or cash flows of the business. Therefore, $1 million should be deducted from the value of Logan Printing in arriving at the value of the common stock. Because the purchase of $2 million in higher technology equipment will result in improved operating results, this prospective purchase would have no impact on the current market value of the common stock.

Marketability discount. One important difference between Logan and the comparable companies is that the publicly traded companies have a readily accessible public stock exchange which stock owners can utilize at any time to sell their stock. Logan Printing stockholders have no such stock exchange at their disposal. Therefore, the Logan Printing common stock is much less marketable than publicly traded stock, and much less attractive to a potential investor. Studies indicate that the price difference between publicly traded stock and privately held stock, such as Logan's, generally ranges between 25 and 40 percent. In our opinion, the appropriate discount for the lack of a ready market for Logan stock is 30 percent.

Control premium. Ben, since you own 40 percent of the company's common stock outstanding, individually you do not own a controlling interest (defined as greater than 50 percent). Therefore, although you exert great influence over the operating policies of Logan Printing, you cannot, by yourself, elect the board of directors, change salary levels, or change other important operating policies of the company. Only a person with a controlling stock interest can do these things. However, your wife also owns 20 percent of Logan's stock. By acting together to sell your stock, you can sell a total of 60 percent of the common stock of the company. Together, you and your wife do have a controlling interest, and potential investors are willing to pay more for this controlling interest. The term used to describe the extra amount which investors are willing to pay for a controlling interest is called a "control premium." We reviewed recent transactions involving printing companies where a controlling interest was being sold, and concluded that an appropriate control premium for Logan Printing would be 25 percent. Furthermore, the extent of the marketability discount is different when a controlling interest is being sold. Controlling interests are much more marketable than minority interests. We would apply a 10 percent marketability discount to Logan Printing if a controlling interest were being sold. A good case in point is American Printers, whose offer you mentioned is dependent on whether both you and your wife sell your stock. If you and your wife together sell 60 percent of the company's stock, the value of each share of stock is much greater than if you alone sell your stock.

Comparable public companies methodology. A second valuation methodology is used as a confirmation of the capitalized earnings methodology. In the Comparable Public Companies methodology, we first select several operating results which, in our opinion, would be predictive of the market value of your stock. In the case of Logan Printing, we selected the following data:

- Current Book value
- Current Sales
- Current, Three-Year Weighted Average and Five-Year Weighted Average Net Earnings
- Current, Three-Year Weighted Average and Five-Year Weighted Average Cash Flow

We have calculated the current value of the stock of the comparable companies as a multiple of each of these data points. We then applied these multiples to the corresponding data points of Logan Printing. The result of this methodology is similar to the result obtained from the capitalized earnings methodology.

As in the Capitalized Earnings methodology, we made several adjustments to Logan's earnings and cash flows, including the adjustment to eliminate interest expense during each year. We made similar adjustments to the comparable companies' income and cash flows in developing the multiples. When we applied the multiples developed from the comparable companies, the resulting values reflected what a willing investor would pay for Logan Printing if it had no debt in its capital structure. Again, we must subtract your total debt of $3.2 million, and add the value of your non-operating assets in determining the value of the common stock of your company.

Consider Establishing an E.S.O.P.

You asked me if there were any other strategies which may make sense in light of your current circumstances. I would like to suggest that you pursue one additional avenue involving the sale of your stock and your wife's stock to the Logan Printing employees. This would be accomplished by establishing a Logan Printing Company Employee Stock Ownership Plan ("E.S.O.P."), having the E.S.O.P. borrow the money required to buy your stock, and having Logan Printing guarantee the repayment of the debt.

There are at least two good reasons to do this. First, if an E.S.O.P. is established and an employee eventually retires or terminates from the company, the company is required to buy the employee's stock back. This makes E.S.O.P. stock more marketable than the other common stock of Logan Printing. Therefore, the stock can initially be sold at a higher price to account for its greater marketability. Second, if greater than 30 percent of the company's stock is sold to an E.S.O.P., the proceeds from the sale can be sheltered from capital gains taxes, perhaps forever. This situation occurs because of some favorable tax laws regarding E.S.O.P.s which were passed by Congress. We can discuss the particulars at our next meeting, Ben, but what I think you should realize is that by selling your stock to an E.S.O.P., the favorable tax treat-

If greater than 30 percent of the company's stock is sold to an E.S.O.P., the proceeds from the sale can be sheltered from capital gains taxes.

Chart 1

	NonESOP Minority	NonESOP Control	ESOP Minority	ESOP Control
Hypothetical Starting Point of Marketable Minority Value	$100	$100	$100	$100
Premium for Control	$0	$25	$0	$25
Marketable Control Value	$100	$125	$100	$125
Add Hypothetical Value of Nonoperating Assets	$10	$12	$10	$12
Marketable Control Value, Including Nonoperating Assets	$110	$137	$110	$137
Less Discount for Lack of Marketability	($33)	($41)	($11)	($14)
Hypothetical Nonmarketable Minority Interest Value	$77	$96	$99	$123
Analysis of Proceeds to Selling Shareholder(s): Pretax Proceeds	77	96	99	123
Less Personal Taxes at 30%	(23)	(29)	0	0
After Tax Proceeds from Sale	54	67	99	123

The friction that exists between you and Mike will not easily go away.

ment you can get will greatly enhance your net cash position immediately after the sale when compared to a sale to a different third party investor.

To illustrate this point, I have put together a chart which compares some sample values calculated under the following assumptions:

- Non-E.S.O.P. minority interest is being sold.
- Non-E.S.O.P. controlling interest is being sold.
- E.S.O.P. minority interest is being sold.
- E.S.O.P. controlling interest is being sold.

Note that the following numbers are for illustrative purposes only, and bear no relationship to the numbers which would be derived for Logan Printing Company.

When we look at the after-tax proceeds from the sale of the stock, we see that if a shareholder is able to defer or eliminate personal taxes from the transaction, the after tax proceeds are much greater. An E.S.O.P. is one alternative way to accomplish this.

Obviously, many more questions must be answered before you will be in a position to determine which alternative fits your particular circumstances best. Please give me a call at your convenience to discuss these ideas further.

Sincerely,

Brad Van Horn

Bradley Van Horn

Assessing the Future is Critical

W. Michael Donovan, CMA

W. Michael Donovan is president of Small Point Management Services and is affiliated with Corporate Finance Associates, both of Portland, Maine. Mr. Donovan advises owners of smaller firms on matters of general management, including assistance with valuation, mergers and acquisitions.

Dear Ben:

Lunch was enjoyable on Tuesday. After working with you for many years, it saddens me to hear that you are finally considering retiring. I appreciate your confidence in asking me for advice about your predicament. Let me see if I can shed some light on your questions, and help you think through the decisions that you need to make.

At the beginning, I must say that there are no easy solutions. The friction that exists between you and Mike will not easily go away. Indeed, no matter what you decide to do, there is the risk that you two will always be at odds about the final deal and the philosophy that guides Logan Printing's future. If you can let me say this now, then perhaps my comments below will sound more encouraging.

I will organize my thoughts as follows. First, I will discuss the nature of the process that affects both the buyer and seller whenever a merger, acquisition, or divestiture occurs. In particular, I will try to point out the pitfalls that your situation faces, given the possibility of selling either to a family member or an existing employee. Second, I will briefly outline my approach to valuing a business, which may run counter to some techniques that you have already seen. Finally, I will also discuss the concept of an offering price, as well as what I think a sophisticated buyer might bid for the business. Clearly, the three raw numbers—valuation, offering price, bid price—may differ. Since each number is used by different people, and since people are different, it seems that the numbers should also be different.

Perceptions of the Future

It distresses me that Mike has challenged you so forcibly in the management of the business. I find that such an attitude is prevalent among recent graduates from business school. Mike simply does not show tact and patience as he develops the ability to wield those new-found technical skills. Even though many of his actions might be sound, he simply is not looking at the business in a family way. Instead, he is attempting to be detached and cold, just as he learned he must be when negotiating.

And yet, Ben, Mike's actions really represent those found in the type of people that you would normally confront in an arms-length transaction. Potential buyers would attempt to whittle down the perceived value of Logan Printing. Mike is looking to the future and asking whether Logan can continue to produce the earnings that you have enjoyed over the recent years. You, in contrast, might be looking to the past and attempting to recoup what you have spent, both in time and money.

Let me explain.

When buyers and sellers come to the table to negotiate a deal, they have different goals and different perceptions of the future. The future is unknown, so the future holds risk. If buyers believe that there is significant risk, they will want to spend as little money as possible to minimize the chance of not recouping the investment. However, when the perception of risk is low—for example, if the buyers are experts at either the business or the markets being pursued—then the likelihood of recouping the investment in the future seems good and the willingness to part with money now to get a future return goes up. Clearly, from a seller's point of view, there is a need to find buyers who have confidence and experience. They will see less risk in a transaction and increase their bid.

Sellers also must look into the future. The sellers' decision to sell is based on a desire to cash out, to take the earnings that might come in the future and walk away from the business. In essence, sellers borrow on the future earnings and want as much of that future as possible. If the sellers' perception of the future is rosy, and if they want to continue working into the future, then they will hold out for a high price and continue to take wages from the business. However, if the perception of the future is not so good, or if the sellers want to get out as soon as possible, then they will lower the offering price to move the business. Sounds simple, and yet these ideas are really quite fundamental to any attempt to value the operations of a business!

This short analysis shows us that there are four types of situations: buyers who have low or high risk perceptions and sellers who have low or high risk perceptions. You might try to think

First, where will your markets be in one, three, or five years?

where you sit, and where Mike sits. Recognize that there is a significant difference between an individual who is closely involved with the business and a large corporate buyer with national markets and broad experience.

Deals can occur with any type of buyer or seller, but it is highly unlikely to have a successful deal if the buyer sees much risk and the seller sees little risk in holding on. The difference between an offering and a bid price will probably not narrow. The fast deals occur when the buyer sees great potential and has high confidence in the future, and the seller wants to get out. There is a question when both the buyer and the seller have the same perceptions of the future. The buyer may want to pay a higher price than others do, but the seller may still hold out. Or, the seller may be willing to start dropping the price, but a buyer just cannot see a good future and waits for more price declines.

Forecasting the Future

If you accept my arguments that perceptions of the future are important in valuing a business, then let me continue by looking at some key items that must be predicted, because they will affect a buyer or seller's perception of risk.

Future markets. First, where will your markets be in one, three, or five years? It seems that Mike has already identified some opportunities that he wants to pursue. Your original markets might move away, as indicated by the change in ownership of your prime customer. If your markets change and the new owner must invest his or her money to capture new markets, why will they want to pay you for a task you will not perform?

Stable prices. Second, can your products hold price, even if your markets are secure? I see from the numbers you gave me, that your gross margin has shrunk slowly over the past four years. Have you had to cut prices recently?

Controllable costs. Third, can you remain cost efficient? Will either your direct costs of doing business or your overhead remain in control? Mike is trying to see if your costs are controllable through the quality research he is performing. The technique is okay; he must not be doing a good job of pointing out its benefits. (But that does not surprise me!)

You and the buyer must assess what these and other variables will do down the road. Your assessments will determine how much someone is willing to pay, and how much you are willing to accept. I hope from what I have said so far that you can see the importance I place on forecasting the future. No matter how much

money or time has been invested up to now, a sophisticated buyer will ask only "what can my investments do for me in the future?"

P/E ratios. You might be wondering why I have not yet mentioned the fine earnings you have achieved during the past few years—especially the good operating results achieved three years ago when the firm was fined for environmental damages? Many analysts do look at current earnings and attempt to value a business solely on that number. This is where the term price/earnings (or P/E) ratio comes into play. P/E ratios are valuable tools, especially when compared among other firms in the same industry. A ratio is multiplied against a firm's current earnings and the result is used to set a selling price. However, Logan Printing is not a large firm, and its market is fairly narrow. It is not a national company. Attempting to compare its earnings with those of another company, especially a larger company in another jurisdiction, is faulty.

Such comparisons are faulty because Logan Printing will most likely be very different than the large firm. Perhaps there is a chance that Logan could grow to be like the large firm, or even be incorporated into the operations of a particular large firm, but what is the probability of being similar? Does Logan, with sales of just over $7 million, really have the skill to grow to be a $100 million firm? Would an acquirer of Logan be able to stimulate growth without any additional investment in tangible or intangible assets? I sincerely doubt it. Are the markets the same? Is the experience the same? It seems clear to me that Logan is not the same as a large, national firm, and thus should not be valued using the same ratios. Those who argue to the contrary do not show an understanding of risk and probability. They are oversimplifying critical assumptions about the future.

I must also say that P/E ratios are nothing more than shorthand attempts to translate current earnings into some future flow of earnings that has a total current value. Remember when we were talking insurance last year, and I explained annuities by asking "How much are you willing to pay now to get annual income of $10,000 each year?" You correctly saw that the amount you would pay depended upon interest rates. Well, saying that a firm has a P/E ratio of ten simply translates to saying that if I pay ten times earnings now, and my earnings grow slowly year after year, I will earn a little over 10 percent on my money. In brief, P/E ratios are short cuts to valuing a business and, significantly, do not take in unique characteristics of a small, local firm. In those cases where P/E ratios are very high, there is an assumption that earnings will grow tremendously in future years and that a high investment now will still reap a handsome reward.

The bottom line is that many popular valuation techniques are shortcuts and do not take into consideration the unique characteristics of a small, local firm.

A Valuation Overview

The key concept to remember is: you are asking someone to invest in a business with the prospect of earning a suitable return on their investment, given the risk involved. Buyers are concerned with the initial outlay, and with the prospect of how much more cash they will need to inject during the coming years. Any future investments will offset the returns. Examples of future investments include increases in inventory, accounts receivable, or cash. Don't be lulled into thinking investments are only bricks and mortar. I see, for example, that your accounts receivable have risen from $991,780 in 1990 to $1,434,335 in 1994. That cash has to come from somewhere.

Further, investors are interested in the cash that is generated by the operations of the business, which is why they will not look only at accounting earnings. Adjustments will be made for depreciation, which helps to generate cash to maintain asset levels, as well as for LIFO techniques, which is merely an accounting entry.

And finally, the buyers will assume that certain expenses are associated with you and not with them. For example, if a large corporation were to buy the business, they would put a general manager in place. The general manager would most likely not earn the pay and perks you get. As a result, adjustments must be made to add back part of your salary to the cash flow. The rent that is paid by the firm to you is below market prices. Hence, an adjustment must be made to reduce cash flow appropriately. Some of these adjustments will depend upon who the buyer is, but it is always safe to assume first that the buyer is an outsider who is driven solely by economic interests.

Once these adjustments have been made, the fun begins. Here is what I do:

- Assume a growth rate of sales from the most current year, and project sales growth for five years. Your analysis of income shows a compound growth rate since 1990 of about 11 percent. This assumption would be based on the recent trend and information about new

markets or products that might develop. After the fifth year, I assume that growth will stop.

- Assume a ratio of costs to sales for those costs that vary with sales. In 1994, the ratio of cost of sales to sales is 53 percent. I usually am conservative and use recent history. However, if changes are taking place, I will be sure to vary the number and test the sensitivity of the results.

- Assume a rate of growth of cash overhead. From your analysis of income, general overhead grew at about 11 percent compounded, without adjustments for depreciation. We hope that the cash overhead will not climb as fast as sales do. In your case, your overhead and sales have grown at the same rate.

- Assume a relationship between assets and sales, and a relationship between growth in assets and growth in sales. To the extent that assets do not grow at the same rate as sales, cash is conserved and the business has greater value. Your assets have climbed at less than a compounded three percent growth rate since 1990, based on the balance sheets that you gave me.

- Assume a tax rate. In 1994, your income taxes were 35 percent of net income before taxes. I feel quite strongly that valuations must be performed after tax. Too often I have seen transactions occur where the business was overvalued through a before-tax valuation, and the after-tax cash flow for the buyer was not sufficient to cover obligations. If the seller financed the deal, the results were a horror.

- Since I am analyzing after-tax cash flows, I assume a debt-to-asset ratio to approximate the cash flow effects of interest deductibility. In 1994, your debt as a percentage of total assets was 71 percent.

- Finally, I assume an after-tax rate of return that a buyer might want (25 percent). The question is "How much am I willing to pay to get a particular return on my money, given the future cash flows I am projecting?" The higher the rate, the higher the perception of risk. In your case I would start at 20 percent, and work up to 35 percent to see the effects of assuming more risk.

Next, we place these assumptions into a model that links the value of the future cash flows with an amount expressed in dollars in hand today. The difference between future dollars and today's dollars is signified by the rate of return. For example, $100 today and $110

The buyers will assume that more investment is needed and that there is risk to keep the business growing at the 10 percent annual rate.

received in one year is different by 10 percent, which is an expression of a rate of return. The computed amount becomes a valuation.

You have a great gross margin and handsome final earnings. What will buyers say? Based on what Mike has discovered, I suspect that sophisticated buyers might see problems. The buyers will assume that more investment is needed and that there is risk to keep the business growing at the 10 percent annual rate. Thus, buyers may bid less than what you might think is the appropriate price, if they have analyzed your business much as I have, but with greater conservatism. You should recognize that negotiations will be long and tedious. Therefore, you should start with a price that assumes a rosy future.

I must conclude by discussing the amount of money you will receive when a deal is completed. Is it clear to you that the firm currently owes money in various formats? As of the end of your most recent financial year, liabilities exceeded $4,000,000. These obligations must be paid, as well as any other contingent liabilities that exist (legal obligations, future pollution fines, etc.). Typically, a valuation first looks at the market value of the assets first.

Only two people are potentially responsible for the obligations: you, as the current owner, or the future buyer. If you take the responsibility, then the buyer must give you sufficient resources in the transaction to ensure your ability to make payments. If the buyer takes responsibility, then the net resources given you will be less. In other words, the total value of the business will be split between you as the equity holder and the debt holders who now will look to the new owner for payment.

In brief, while the business's assets are worth an amount that depends on the beholder's perceptions, the value of the assets is reduced by the total obligations to creditors, and the result is net equity value. At this point, the tax man will arrive for his share. You will get the remainder.

What You Should do Next

Let me suggest some actions to take over the coming weeks. First, there is much material you could read about valuations. Very little is good. Valuations are based on fundamental theories in finance. Most popular business books on

valuation attempt to distort an owner's view of value and cause overconfidence. My own skill in the area is based on many years in finance and extensive reading in strategy, operations, finance and economics. If you decide not to read the truly good textbooks on finance, then do the following:

- Approach a finance professor from the local college. Offer to pay him or her a consulting fee to go over some basics of finance. Ask questions. Be sure to let the professor know that you are a rookie and need help. The professor will be objective.

- Ask your lawyer, your accountant and your banker for names of people who are in the merger and acquisition business. Your firm is close to the size that will attract the better names in the business, including even some national players. Get references. Get to know the people. Rely on their expertise if you develop trust for their professionalism. You should concentrate on running the business, not on orchestrating the sale.

- Ask your accountant for a tax analysis of various selling scenarios.

- Recognize that the sale may take up to 12 or 18 months. If you rush, mistakes will occur.

- Finally, look to Mike as an ally in the process. He needs to learn some humility, but I suspect that he would not be working with you if you did not care for him as a son. He has the technical background to help your discussions with other professionals. Explain to him that you want to work together. Make sure that he understands that you want patience. Make sure that he knows that you will not tolerate obstinacy. I think that he will see the benefits of cooperation in this endeavor.

Ben, I hope that this letter has helped answer your questions. Please call me if you would like to discuss any portion of it.

Sincerely,

W. Michael Donovan

You should concentrate on running the business, not on orchestrating the sale.

Chapter 9

"Should I Sell My Business to My Son?"

Donald Reinardy, C.P.A., M.S., and Catherine Stover

David McLimans

Ben Logan, 62, president and C.E.O. of Logan Printing Company, Inc., was having a very polite argument with his wife about going to Bora Bora in April. Yet, for all of the politeness and the hushed tones, the intensity of the conversation made other people at the Maplewood Country Club Christmas party mingle elsewhere.

"Of course Bora Bora is lovely in April," Julia Logan said to her husband. "But that is not the point. We can't just sell the company to Michael in March and pack up and go to Bora Bora in April. He'll need us."

Ben thought, but did not say, *He won't need us if we sell the company to someone else.* But he didn't want to start that again. He knew Julia would never change her mind: she insisted that they sell the company to their son—a 29-year-old kid who wore double-breasted suits and who thought he knew everything about the printing business.

"I know what you're thinking, Ben. You have no desire to sell the company to Michael—"

"Look, Julia," he said, glancing at his watch. "Doesn't it seem as though we've already covered this? We've talked about it non-stop all week. Let's give it a break."

Donald Reinardy is a partner with the CPA/business consulting firm of Smith & Gesteland.

Catherine Stover is the editor of the Small Business Forum.

All I ever wanted to do was to show Dad that I could run Logan Printing as well as he could.

But even while they danced to big band holiday music, Ben could not stop thinking about the future of his firm.

A week ago, he had told Julia that they had three choices: sell the company to American Printing in a six-year earn-out, or sell the company to the employees as an E.S.O.P., or finance the sale of his stock to their son, Michael. Julia wouldn't even discuss the earn-out or the E.S.O.P.—she seemed outraged that Ben would even consider them.

But their argument about Michael was an old argument, really. It was Ben's opinion that Julia had coddled him too much and had given him too much over the years. *Let him fight for himself*, he had said over and over.

It seemed as though she was always defending Mike. "He's too intellectual for football," she had argued during the high school years.

"Be proud of his grades, instead. And his trumpet. He was the only one in the band to go to State and you never even congratulated him."

Now, as Ben and Julia continued to dance, Ben remembered how his own father had never done anything for him. Even when Ben left to fight in Korea, his dad had not taken the time to say goodbye. The old man was tough. And all of his kids had turned out well.

But it seemed as though Michael thought that he deserved to be given money for his college tuition, that he deserved to be given a nice car to drive when he was in high school, that he deserved to be given the company that Ben had built for 33 years.

But as Ben and Julia left the dance floor and walked toward their table, he knew that if he didn't sell the company to his son, this woman would never, never forgive him. That much was clear.

But would she forgive him if he sunk their well-earned retirement money into financing the sale of the stock to Michael—only to see the business fail? Businesses go under all the time. There are no guarantees. True, the boy has an M.B.A. from Wharton, and he did work for that place in Atlanta for three years, and he is doing well with the part of the company that he was managing. But all it would take is one mistake, and the whole company would go under. Investing too much in new equipment, or counting too much on one customer, or not foreseeing changes in the market—one mistake could wipe them out. Could wipe them all out.

As Ben and Julia joined their friends, the Riversons, at the table, David Riverson said, "I hear you're going to Bora Bora this spring. You haven't asked us to join you yet."

"We haven't decided if we're going," Ben said. *But if I could,* he thought, *I'd jump on a plane right now. Bora Bora is looking better all the time.*

Michael Logan, relieved that his parents had gone to a Christmas party, was enjoying a rare evening with his sister, Stephanie, who had flown in from Boston a few hours earlier. Her kids were in bed, and her husband was scheduled to arrive in two days. Mike's wife stayed at their house across town so that Mike and Stephanie could finally have a chance to talk about their dad's retirement.

"Mike, let me assure you that I have no interest in the company. I haven't even been in the building for seven or eight years.

"And I've always felt funny about having that stock. Did you know that they gave it to me for a wedding present? A wedding present! Neither of them have ever said anything to me about joining the firm, even after I became a C.P.A. It was as if they were so relieved that their daughter actually got married to a doctor..." She paused. "I don't think I've ever seen you this uptight. What's the worst part of this whole mess for you?"

"Dad."

Stephanie nodded. "He's always been very protective of his company."

"He thinks I'm going to screw it up. You, on the other hand, well, at least he always carried on conversations with you —"

"Wait a minute. I'm on your side, remember? I'm seven years older. If it seemed like they had conversations that were on an adult level with me, it's because I was an adult."

"I'm sorry. None of this is your fault. It's just that...well, all I ever wanted to do was to show Dad that I could run Logan Printing as well as he could."

"Didn't it ever occur to you that maybe Dad wants to believe that no one can run the company as well as he does?"

Michael paused. "What do you mean?"

"What was your old boss like in Atlanta? Was his ego tied into the business?"

"Alright. You make a good point. But where does that leave us? Will he ever get rid of the company if he thinks that no one can run it as well as he can?"

"To say that Dad is burned out is an understatement. He just wants to take his money and run. If he sells it to you, or if he does the earn-out deal with American Printing, his financial future will depend on how well the company does. Can you see why that wouldn't appeal to a burned-out guy who really just wants out?"

"But Mom wants him to sell the company to me."

Logan Printing Company, Inc.
Analysis of Asset Value
December 31, 1994

Assets	1990	1991	1992	1993	1994
Cash	598,400	515,660	190,509	228,611	487,342
Accounts receivable	991,780	968,047	1,055,754	1,266,905	1,434,335
Inventory	290,330	333,879	383,961	460,753	557,511
Marketable securities	389,781	448,248	0	100,000	263,773
Prepaid expenses	26,400	30,360	34,914	41,897	49,019
Income tax refunds	0	0	152,848	0	0
Property and equipment	4,217,307	4,849,903	5,232,388	5,389,360	5,712,721
Accumulated depreciation	(1,850,692)	(2,128,296)	(2,447,540)	(2,863,622)	(3,207,710)
Cash value of life insurance	37,407	43,018	49,471	59,365	68,270
Receivable from officers	382,987	510,435	242,000	290,400	319,440
Total assets	5,083,700	5,571,254	4,894,305	4,973,669	5,684,701

Liabilities					
Accounts payable	388,278	331,518	611,247	373,756	437,294
Accrued wages and vacations	159,428	183,343	210,844	187,242	187,242
Accrued payroll taxes	37,561	43,195	49,674	34,912	34,912
Accrued profit sharing and 401(k)	34,148	39,270	45,161	23,346	23,346
Accrued interest	14,442	16,609	19,100	14,338	14,338
Other accrued expenses	17,595	20,235	23,270	30,909	33,073
Income taxes payable	149,254	171,642	0	0	29,836
Deferred income taxes	166,300	191,240	0	31,880	88,200
Long term debt	2,238,752	1,999,564	3,449,499	3,342,172	3,197,060
Total liabilities	3,205,758	2,996,616	4,408,795	4,038,555	4,045,301

Stockholders' Equity					
Common stock (10,000 shares, $100 par value)	1,000,000	1,000,000	1,000,000	1,000,000	1,000,000
Additional paid in capital	237,198	237,198	237,198	237,198	237,198
Retained earnings	640,744	1,337,440	(751,688)	(302,084)	402,202
Total equity	1,877,942	2,574,638	485,510	935,114	1,639,400
Total liabilities and equity	5,083,700	5,571,254	4,894,305	4,973,669	5,684,701

Logan Printing Company, Inc.
Analysis of Income

	1990	1991	1992	1993	1994
Sales	4,554,543	5,228,815	5,333,392	6,133,401	7,122,413
Cost of sales	2,342,712	2,660,973	2,873,851	3,362,405	3,765,894
Gross profit	2,211,831	2,567,842	2,459,541	2,770,996	3,356,519
Officer salaries	143,010	150,160	131,900	185,400	210,600
Office salaries	99,807	104,797	109,513	113,346	118,673
Payroll taxes	100,095	105,100	109,829	123,673	138,620
Auto expenses	4,419	4,640	4,848	5,018	7,377
Dues and subscriptions	6,424	6,745	7,048	7,295	7,724
Employee benefits	45,743	48,030	50,192	51,948	54,390
Insurance	38,270	40,184	41,992	63,461	73,288
Repairs and maintenance	33,085	34,740	36,303	199,573	93,373
Office supplies	20,144	21,151	22,103	22,877	33,629
Professional fees	24,343	25,560	326,710	120,335	46,892
Rent	180,000	180,000	180,000	180,000	180,000
Personal property taxes	1,507	1,583	1,654	1,712	1,859
Utilities	41,742	43,829	45,801	47,404	54,684
Advertising	45,222	47,483	49,620	66,987	98,471
Bad debts	34,184	35,893	37,508	50,636	74,435
Sales and travel expenses	27,552	28,929	30,231	81,289	119,495
Pension plan contributions	123,073	129,226	135,041	179,768	214,259
Director fees	10,000	10,000	10,000	10,000	15,000
Officers' life insurance	11,500	11,500	11,500	11,500	11,500
Contributions	2,460	2,583	2,699	2,794	2,925
Cleaning and security	15,487	16,261	16,993	17,588	20,754
Depreciation	320,577	336,826	358,375	387,082	421,839
Total expenses	1,328,644	1,385,220	1,719,862	1,929,686	1,999,787
Net operating income	883,187	1,182,622	739,679	841,310	1,356,732
Other income and expense:					
Interest income	41,182	51,860	17,492	22,956	28,102
Gain on sale of assets	17,287	7,918	86,752	7,250	9,836
Miscellaneous income	12,919	9,483	15,627	18,205	16,078
Interest expense	(199,333)	(188,264)	(270,894)	(383,827)	(294,638)
Miscellaneous expense	(5,436)	(24,848)	(21,873)	(24,408)	(30,182)
Pollution damages	0	0	(3,000,000)	0	0
Total other income and expense	(133,381)	(143,851)	(3,172,896)	(359,824)	(270,804)
Net income before taxes	749,806	1,038,771	(2,433,217)	481,486	1,085,928
Income taxes	249,882	342,075	(344,088)	31,880	381,641
Net income	499,924	696,696	(2,089,129)	449,606	704,287

Logan Printing Company, Inc.
Additional explanation

(1) Real estate owned by Ben Logan and leased to the company on a 5 year lease at $15,000 per month. Market rent is $5 per square foot for the 50,000 square foot building.

(2) Stock ownership: Ben - 40%
Julia - 20%
Mike - 20%
Stephanie - 10%
Jim Webb - 10%

(3)

Officer salaries	1990	1991	1992	1993	1994
Ben	143,010	150,160	131,900	148,320	168,480
Mike	———	———	———	37,080	42,120

(4) Pension and profit sharing plans cover officers and office—production workers are covered by union retirement plans.

(5) Company uses last-in, first-out (LIFO) inventory method.

LIFO reserve	1990	1991	1992	1993	1994
	87,100	103,500	122,800	152,000	189,500

(6) Company paid $3 million in 1992 for cleanup of groundwater pollution as a negotiated settlement of an Environmental Protection Agency lawsuit. The company also bought $350,000 of equipment to prevent future incidents and paid $300,000 in legal fees in 1992 and $80,000 in 1993 in connection with this matter.

"Of course she does. And I honestly think that she has your best interests in mind when she says that."

"Wait. Don't you think it would be in my best interest to get the company?"

"I can only speak from my own perspective. I wouldn't take the company if it were given to me."

"How come?"

"Dad would watch every move and second guess every decision. The employees would grumble about working for the boss's kid. The printing industry is hardly recession-proof..."

"But the printing business is what I know! I don't want to work for someone else all of my life! I don't want to turn into a 'good old Jim Webb, the number two guy.' I've got some great ideas. I want to be a leader in the industry. I don't want to spend the rest of my life working for people who say 'Deming? Who is Deming?' And, 'Soy ink? Why should we bother with that?' and 'Team building? Are you saying you want to bring some cheerleaders in here?' Things could be so exciting if I could be in charge."

"Michael, you are twenty-nine—"

"And how many times have you heard Dad say that when he was twenty-nine, he had already fought in Korea and founded a business?"

"I'm not trying to throw a wet blanket on you. I'm just trying to say that you need to see that there is a downside to taking over Logan Printing. You need to acknowledge that you're not fighting for a dream. You're fighting for a tough way to make a living that will have some very unpleasant sides to it."

"It's what I want. I'm not giving up."

Julia was glad to be home. She hated the idea of going to a party just moments after Stephanie and the grandkids flew in from Boston. But Ben, well, it was as if he was possessed with the idea of getting out of the house. He had never learned how to relax. *What will become of him when he retires?*, she thought. *If he can't go in to the company once in a while, he'll start climbing the walls.*

Julia sighed as she heard the intense voices in the family room. She had hoped that Mike would have gone home by now so that they

To say that Dad is burned out is an understatement. He just wants to take his money and run.

The Three Offers

Jim Webb
E.S.O.P. Proposal

Creation of an E.S.O.P.
The company will establish an Employee Stock Ownership Plan, or E.S.O.P. The E.S.O.P. will serve the primary function of providing retirement benefits to employees of the company. Funds will be accumulated by the E.S.O.P. through annual contributions by the company to the plan, as well as loans from the company and outside sources. These funds are used initially to purchase the company stock from the present stockholders either a small amount at a time or in a large block with an installment payment.

Ownership
Each participating employee has an ownership interest in a certain number of shares of stock which will be repurchased by the E.S.O.P. in the event of their retirement or termination.

Once the E.S.O.P. is fully funded and has purchased all of the outstanding stock, the employees own the company. The value of their benefits continue to grow through additional contributions by the company as well as appreciation of the company's stock.

Conversion of Pension Plan
The present deferred benefit pension plan benefits will be used to partially fund the E.S.O.P. All participating employees will be asked to transfer their pension account balances to the E.S.O.P. This should provide approximately $1.3 million in funding for the E.S.O.P.

Stock Purchase
As soon as funds are available from the pension plan conversion, all stock owned by Ben and Julia Logan, amounting to a 60 percent ownership, will be purchased by the E.S.O.P. for $1.8 million. In addition to the pension funds, the plan will also borrow $500,000 from the bank. The loan will be guaranteed by the company.

In addition, Ben Logan may defer income taxes on the sale of his stock by reinvesting the sales proceeds in qualified replacement stocks.

Additional company stock will be purchased as funds are available in the future from employer contributions or additional loans from outside sources.

Purchase Price
This E.S.O.P. represents an established, available market for the stock of Logan Printing, Inc. The stock purchased by the E.S.O.P. will not be subject to a discount for lack of marketability in the valuation of the stock. The same stock may command a higher price if it is sold to the E.S.O.P. than if it is sold to another buyer.

All transfers of stock will be done using an annual valuation of the stock performed by a competent professional chosen by the board of directors.

Management
Directors and officers will be chosen by action of a management team which is representative of the employee participants in the plan.

Mike Logan
Offer to Purchase

Purchase of Stock
Mike Logan will purchase the stock owned by Ben Logan for a total price of $750,000. Payments will be made over the next 20 years at the rate of $75,000 per year including interest at eight percent.

Consulting Services
Ben Logan will provide consulting services to the company as requested by the company and will remain as an employee of the company in this capacity. All consulting services will be authorized and approved by the company president in advance and will be compensated at the rate of $50 per hour.

Real Estate Purchase

Mike Logan will purchase from Ben Logan all real estate presently being leased by the company for a total price of $1.8 million. Payments of $15,000 per month will be made over a period of 20 years including interest at an annual rate of eight percent.

American Printing, Inc.
Offer to Purchase

Purchase of Assets

Buyer will purchase all assets of Logan Printing Company, Inc., the price to be determined by the future performance of the company. An annual payment will be made equal to 15 percent of the net sales of the company in excess of the base amount for the years 1994 through 1998. The base amount will be $7 million in 1994 and increase with the consumer price index over the remaining five years. In no event will the annual payment be less than $200,000.

In addition, the buyer will assume all liabilities of the seller as they appear on the balance sheet as of December 31, 1994. Any additional liabilities not disclosed on this balance sheet will be the obligation of the sellers.

The purchase of all assets includes, but is not limited to the following items:

- Cash in all depository and investment accounts,
- Accounts receivable from customers and officers,
- Inventory of materials and supplies,
- Work in process,
- Marketable securities and all other investments,
- Prepaid expenses and refunds,
- Property and equipment,
- All other insurance policies and contracts,
- Patents, copyrights and trademarks,
- Goodwill, and
- Customer lists and all business records.

Non-Competition Agreement

Ben Logan and American Printing, Inc. will enter into a non-competition agreement which will preclude Ben Logan from any ownership or management of a printing business for a period of five years within a 100-mile radius. Consideration to be paid to Ben Logan for this agreement will be $50,000 per year.

Transitional Services

For a period of one year from the date of closing, Ben Logan will be employed by American Printing, Inc. in an advisory capacity in order to insure the continuity of business operations and to make all necessary introductions and transitions with present and prospective customers. His salary for these services will be $100,000 per year.

Pension Plan

Ben Logan has provided to American Printing, Inc. certain information concerning the company's present defined benefit pension plan. This information indicates that due to recent increases in interest rate assumptions used by the plan actuaries, the plan is presently overfunded. The present value of the plan assets exceeds the present value of the future plan benefits by some $250,000. As the plan administrator, Ben Logan will provide the buyer with all necessary assistance to terminate the plan, secure single premium annuities to provide retirement benefits to all plan participants equal to their present vested benefits under the terminated plan, and make all excess funds available to the buyer in a segregated depository account.

Real Estate Lease

The buyer will assume all rights and obligations as lessee under the company's present real estate lease with Ben Logan.

Employment Contract

Jim Webb will enter into an employment contract with American Printing, Inc. for a period of five years from the date of closing. He will be paid an initial salary of $50,000 per year and will continue in his present position as production manager.

could postpone their "family time" until the light of day. She saw Ben untie his tie and charge to the well-lit corner of the house, and she followed in his wake.

"Well, well," Ben said. "Still up, kids?"

"I'm on my way up to bed, actually," said Stephanie. She rose and went toward the door.

"Good idea," said Julia. "Michael, why don't you join us for a nice late brunch tomorrow? About ten?"

"No thanks, Mom. I'm going into the office."

"It'll be the deadest Saturday morning of the year, Mike, so why don't you just sleep in?" Ben asked.

"Dad, I've got work to do."

"It can wait."

Mike rose and walked over to his father. "Are you asking me or commanding me to not go into work?"

"That's enough, you two," Julia said. "Can't you ever lighten up? It's midnight. Let's all go to bed."

Ben cleared his throat. "I don't want you to do anything with the Johnson contract until I get in."

"They are expecting our call first thing. If you're not in by nine-thirty, I'm calling them."

"Now wait a minute, young man. It's my contract, and *I* am going to call them."

"Young man? That's the problem right there. You can't take me seriously, can you? I'm the one who negotiated the contract—"

"I'm the one who owns the company."

"Enough!" Julia said. "Why must you two always resort to such childish bickering? It's time to end this conversation."

Stephanie said, "Look, everyone. We have a lot of talking to do, but now is not the time. Let's all get some sleep."

As Ben followed Stephanie out of the room, he said in a half-whisper, "Too bad you don't want the company. I wish I could sell it to you."

Mike stood, shocked, in the family room. Julia put her arm around him and said, "He didn't mean that, honey. Really. Forget about it."

Mike looked at her. "I don't know. Maybe that's what he had in mind all along."

Mike quickly left.

What should Ben Logan do? *We asked a second-generation family business owner, a professor of organizational inquiry, a management consultant, an accountant, and a family business consultant to recommend a course of action.*

Authors' note: *The authors would like to thank Mike Cusak of the Louisiana SBDC for his assistance with this case study.*

Let Michael Earn the Right to Run the Company

James R. Hayes, Ph.D.

Dr. Hayes is the second-generation president of Hayes Manufacturing Group Inc. in Neenah, Wisconsin. He is also a family business consultant and speaker, with academic training in organizational psychology.

Dear Ben:

Your letter was a very pleasant surprise. It's been awhile since you and I compared notes. I don't know if I can help with your present dilemma, but let me share my thoughts with you.

Your decision to sell the business now surprises me. You are the last person I ever thought would retire. I gave up hope long ago of ever getting a golf game with you because you would never leave the office. Now, at 62 and in good health, you are looking at retirement. That doesn't sound like you, Ben.

I may be reading between the lines, but I sense this retirement/business sale talk is really an emotional reaction to the news that your largest customer had just been purchased by an international firm. Most of us might think about retiring under similar circumstances. However, I think you need to take some time to sort through your emotions and the various alternatives you have with the business. I'm not convinced that selling the business is the appropriate response.

Having said the above, let me address the rest of my comments to your question of passing the business on to your son. You obviously feel caught between the proverbial rock and a hard place. Mike and Julia feel the business should go to Mike. You, on the other hand, resent what you feel is Mike's "you owe it to me" attitude. Moreover, you don't really feel Mike is competent at age 29 to run Logan Printing Company. Your family problem is exacerbated by the fact that you have a couple of other attractive deals on the table.

Ben, I really think you should give serious consideration to passing the business on to Mike—*eventually*. Nothing in your letter even suggests that Mike doesn't have the ability or desire to run Logan Printing. To the contrary, Mike has excellent academic credentials, he's gained valuable experience working for another printing company and even you admit he's done a super job with the new venture he started six months ago. You aren't faced with a typical succession problem in family business—namely, an incompetent or unmotivated heir.

I think your uneasiness with Mike will mellow given some time and an effort by both of you to understand the other. You need to understand that Mike is young, the ink on his M.B.A. is barely dry, and he's achieved some early success. His cockiness will be tempered when he gains a little more experience and realizes that he doesn't have all the answers. At the same time, he needs to understand that you are only 62 and are really not ready to face retirement. Like most entrepreneurs, you are a doer and probably not a good teacher. You are impatient and still have some things to prove. If Mike can assume the mind of an entrepreneur for a moment, he'll be a little more sensitive to your position.

While I think that Mike deserves a chance to run Logan Printing, I don't think he's adequately prepared at age 29, nor do I think you are adequately prepared, psychologically, to give up the business. Management succession is an evolutionary process. I suggest you consider the following transition steps:

Hire an interim C.E.O./Mentor. At 29, Mike is not experienced enough in all phases of the business. At the same time, I don't think you have the patience to guide Mike or provide a dispassionate evaluation of his progress. An experienced printing executive can bridge the communication gap between you and Mike and, most importantly, guide Logan Printing while Mike continues to hone his skills. Look for a senior-level executive in a company that is five years beyond where Logan Printing is now—a company that has successfully dealt with the growth problems you are now facing. I suggest you look at a five-year contract with someone. You don't need to offer an equity interest in the company, but you may want to consider a phantom stock or deferred compensation plan. I'm sure your legal and accounting people can help with a compensation package.

Solidify a management team. It's real important that Mike, Jim Webb and a new C.E.O. develop a close working relationship. Mike doesn't have much of a production background. Jim Webb can be very helpful here. You may need to enhance Webb's compensation and even structure a stock buy-back agreement with him over a five-year period. Mike also needs to learn more about the financial end of the business. As I have said earlier, succession is an evolutionary process. Mike should assume the responsibility one step at a time. I think a five-year timeframe is realistic, and both Jim Webb and a new C.E.O. will be ready to retire at that time. This time period also gives Mike ample opportunity to earn the respect of the other employees at Logan Printing.

Hire outside directors. Although you didn't say anything about the make-up of your current board, I assume the board still consists of the shareholders of Logan Printing. You should look at adding three to four outside directors. Stay away from professional advisors, such as bankers, lawyers and accountants. Also stay away from customers, competitors and suppliers. Rather, look for other business owners who have grown businesses that are larger than Logan Printing is today. Pay particular attention to businesses that are recognized for their strong market niche orientation, because it appears that the days of Logan Printing as a full-service printer are numbered. You need to compensate these directors for their time and expertise. In addition to their business acumen, outside directors can serve as buffers between generations in a family business. This is particularly important in succession planning.

Continue as chairman. In addition to the above, Ben, I suggest you stay on at Logan Printing as chairman of the board for at least a year or two. A new C.E.O. will need your assistance. It's important, however, that only the C.E.O. report to you, and you give the new C.E.O. responsibility and *authority* for managing the day-to-day affairs of Logan Printing. The company can afford to pay you a salary during this time. As the new C.E.O. gets comfortable, you should take more time off. As you become more comfortable with the management team, you should relinquish your chairman of the board title and limit your participation to board-level types of decisions as a consultant.

I suggest you hold on to your stock in Logan Printing for right now. You don't need the money, and an emotion-driven sale now may be something you will regret a few years down the road. I also think you should hold on to the real estate, but charge the company the market price for the space. Retaining control of both the company and real estate for now may help in estate planning decisions in the future. If Michael works out as I think he will, you might want to turn the business over to him and leave the real estate to your daughter. My point is, Ben, I just don't think you've given enough thought to the future of Logan Printing. Don't act hastily.

At 29, Mike is not experienced enough in all phases of the business. At the same time, I don't think you have the patience to guide Mike.

Well, if the above makes any sense to you, sit down with Michael and lay out a five-year plan for him to assume control of Logan Printing. This program allows you to maintain harmony with Julia while giving Michael a chance to earn the right to run the company. You can keep an active interest in the company while you begin to enjoy some of the fruits of your labor. At the same time, Michael gets his chance, but he has to earn it.

If I can help in any way, please let me know.

Warm Regards,

James R. Hayes

The Decision Isn't Yours to Make

Dennis T. Jaffe, Ph.D.

Dr. Jaffe is the author of Working With the Ones You Love, *about family business development, and* Take This Job and Love It, *about developing management teams. He is professor of organizational inquiry at Saybrook Institute in San Francisco.*

Dear Ben:

We've talked about your business many times, and I want to share some of the lessons I have learned with my business, and make some suggestions about how you, your family and your business can emerge stronger and closer from this transition period.

You ask me who you should sell your business to, and I think that is the wrong question. This decision is totally unlike any decision you have made before. For what may be the first time, you cannot control the outcome. You have to let go. You have to involve all the relevant people in the decision, and together, you need to find the best way. What seems to have happened in your family is something similar to what happens in many families of entrepreneurs. It even has a name: *Entrepreneur's Disease*, which is when the entrepreneur, who is talented and energetic, has founded a powerful business, and makes all decisions inside his head, trying to keep control, and not opening up the process to others.

There are many stakeholders in your decision, and I have to tell you bluntly, the decision isn't yours to make. Because it involves Julia, Mike, Stephanie, Jim Webb, other employees, and even American Printing, you can't make this decision alone. You need to create a process that brings the key people into discussion of what needs to be done, what are the options, and how to find an outcome where everyone remains close and committed to the business. That means that, maybe for the first time, you have to have open discussions with everyone, and put your cards on the table. You may be surprised to find that this will be a great relief to you, as everybody concerned will try to make the process work. They have information that you need.

Your dilemma is complicated because you are a family as well as a business. When you try to talk with Mike, your history as father and son makes it difficult. Even though they are not employees of the business, Stephanie and Julia are involved in the outcome. The family is paramount: you want to maintain closeness and be fair to everyone. But a strong business is the vehicle by which your family ensures its future, so that needs to be maintained. This seems like a conflict to you, even though everybody would share these dual goals. Therefore, you need to bring your family into the deliberations about the future of the business, and, even though the choice rests with you, you need to bring your family together to look at the options and the issues between you.

Are you sure, for example, that Stephanie doesn't want to be involved in the business? Do you know what Mike wants? Has his performance been evaluated clearly? None of these have happened, because you have difficulty communicating as a family. This isn't terribly uncommon, and it certainly can be cured, although you will have to shift some very old ways of talking to each other, and the changes will have to begin with yourself. Are you ready to try?

I have some bad news for you as well: you've neglected the transition issue for a long time, and the cost to you is that you can't disengage as rapidly as you would like. You can probably find more and more time to be away, but the process of securing the next generation of Logan Printing will take some time. Basically, transition isn't something that happens when you make a decision to sell. You and Mike obviously have been having difficulty talking to each other, and as

You ask me who you should sell your business to, and I think that is the wrong question.

a result both of you distrust the motives and actions of the other. You aren't sure that Mike can run the company, and he doesn't think you will let go. Both of these perceptions have some truth to them. You and he need to talk about the next stage.

Talking with Mike should be your first priority. He needs to know your thinking, and you and he have to talk about your different perceptions of what is happening. You have been directing his behavior, and as happens to any person who is directed, he certainly feels some resentment and does not have room to develop, grow, make decisions, take risks, learn from failure. His lack of performance may be due as much to your way of working with him as to his nature. You need to find ways for you to become his coach, not his boss, giving him the space to learn to develop authority and credibility within the business, and space to show everyone that he can do it himself. So maybe you need to go to Bora Bora, and you need to stop interfering in his decisions. You both need to find a way to communicate without blaming the other or getting angry. It will take some work.

But very soon the whole family needs to get together about the future. You need to talk about your options, and even your concerns. You need to bring Stephanie and Julia into the discussion, as well as Mike. You may get some anger for past decisions, but anger is the surface and love lies below it. The goal of the family get-together is to discuss everybody's future, what they want, what they need, and how the family can support that vision. From those understandings, you then need to talk about not only who will run the business, but who will own it.

There are three areas you need to explore: the family future, the business management, and the ownership of the business. Each of them is separate, although they are interrelated. For example, it might be that the family owns some of the stock, and sells some to an E.S.O.P., or even a key employee, such as Jim Webb. You might hire an outside director. The family would be the Board and retain majority ownership. Discussing your options may lead not to decisions, but they may lead to greater understanding.

You need to be aware of another aspect of the family as well. Like most men of your generation, you have assumed that it will be your son, not your daughter, who will inherit the business and work there. But today, daughters as well as sons, are professionals, have careers, and should be considered. Have

you really talked to Stephanie about her future, and are you sure it doesn't include the business? You know she's educated and talented. Maybe there is a role for her in Logan Printing. Perhaps she adds skills that Mike doesn't have. You know she and Mike are close. Maybe they could work together? Neither you nor I know about this, but why don't you talk to Stephanie and Mike about that?

Business succession is not a decision but a process. Key employees, including family members, need to learn and gradually take on more responsibility. Key employees like Jim need to be involved to prevent them from wanting to find an opportunity elsewhere, or even opening a competing business. Otherwise, you set your successor up for failure. You need to create a management team, consisting of not just Mike, but also some other key managers. They need to know how the succession decision will be made, and what you are considering. They know that you can sell it to Mike, they know about the E.S.O.P., and they know that American Printing is interested, so it's no secret. Why not talk with them about it? You still have the decisions to make, but at least you'll get some help.

If Mike is to buy the business, he may or may not be ready for it. You need to give him a chance to take authority, maybe with other managers participating, maybe alone, and you need to draw back and let him make decisions. You have to learn a new role: teacher, elder statesman. Right now you are involved in every decision. You know the big customers, you talk to the banks, you have your lawyers and advisors. You have to begin to shift these relationships to other people before you go. Have you really let Mike move into some of these areas, or do you do them yourself and then blame Mike for lack of initiative? I suspect the latter.

You need to have a plan for the future for your family, for your business ownership, and for management. It can't be done in a day. There are considerations of taxes, your own retirement income (the business is your nest egg, but this may hinder the opportunity for the business to get capital to grow and develop), and of relationships. A family conference, maybe several, and a series of management or employee meetings has to take place. Roles must begin to shift, and you need to be there to help, but not to make decisions for people, or second guess. You have to become a teacher before you leave. The good news is that a teacher doesn't have to be there every

You both need to find a way to communicate without blaming the other or getting angry. It will take some work.

day. You can pull back, learn to let to, and see what happens. If you have reservations about what happens, don't come in and change things, talk with Mike or Jim or whomever is involved, and as a teacher, help them see how they could do better.

I fear that I've made your life more complicated, and I certainly haven't told you what to do. I can't and neither can anyone else. But you can't make the decision alone, and your problems come because you haven't created the necessary conversations to start the succession process to the next generation. Luckily, there are many people who are family business consultants who know how to help families set up family retreats, and who help with business planning. They won't tell you what to do, or advise you privately. Instead, their task is to help create conversations, and help everyone work together to get to the best decision. You might want some help in this area.

Sincerely,

Dennis T Jaffe

Dennis Jaffe

It is Not Just an Economic Decision

Eric G. Flamholtz, Ph.D.

Author of Growing Pains: How to Make the Transition From an Entrepreneurship to a Professionally Managed Firm, *Dr. Flamholtz is professor of management at U.C.L.A. As the president and founder of Management Systems Consulting Corp., he consults for a wide variety of businesses.*

Dear Ben:

The purpose of this letter is to follow up on our recent discussions about your decision to sell Logan Printing Company. As I see it, you have three important tasks.

First, you need to accept the fact that this decision is not merely an economic decision. Second, you need to involve the family in the decision-making process. Third, you need to prepare both Mike and yourself for the sale.

Not Just an Economic Decision

The single most important issue that you and I have discussed is this: In your situation, the sale of the family business is not merely an economic decision.

Granted, you have obviously worked very hard for the last 33 years. You've built a successful business. You have earned the right to retire comfortably. However, if you approach this decision strictly from an economic standpoint (or from the standpoint of "rewarding yourself" for 33 years of hard work), you may irreparably damage your marriage and your relationships with your children. You can't ignore the significant family issues.

It is often true that founders would like to focus on the economic issues because they don't want to face the family issues, which are usually the hardest to deal with. For example, one such issue that you and I have discussed is your concern about "giving" the business to Mike.

He expected that you would buy him a car to drive when he was in high school; he expected you to pay for his college tuition; and now you seem to feel that he expects you to give him your company. Although your tone was relatively calm when you said this, I detected a note of discomfort or perhaps even anger on your part. You have told me many times over the years that your own father gave you nothing and you turned out just fine.

You have to deal with this. If Mike buys the business from you, you will not be "giving" it to him. If you continue with this attitude after the sale of the company, you will simply set yourself up for a variety of problems with Mike and Julia. You need to do some more thinking about how you really feel about this.

Involve the Family

In our discussions, I have repeatedly proposed that you should get your family involved in this decision. I believe that you should get your family together and reach a family decision about what is best for all concerned. Unless you go through this process, you will run a high risk of jeopardizing your family relationships.

Given the level of emotion involved, I strongly recommend that you have someone serve as an outside facilitator. I can help you myself, or I can recommend other suitable people.

The purpose of the family meeting would be to examine all of the alternatives available to you and your family for the disposition of the

---

It is often true that founders would like to focus on the economic issues because they don't want to face the family issues, which are usually the hardest to deal with.

business. It should be an opportunity for each of you to state your concerns and your objections. The discussion could get a bit touchy. You personally should be prepared to have people say things that you might be a bit sensitive about. Brace yourself for some criticism.

If you are prepared to have such a meeting, then we should sit down and talk about the specific agenda and the issues that need to be resolved. I suspect that the meeting will take at least a day, and perhaps two days.

Three of the key issues that need to be discussed are, of course:

- What are the alternative ways of selling the business?
- What are the advantages and the limitations of each of the alternatives?
- If the business is sold to Mike, what steps will you need to take to make it work?

Prepare Mike and Yourself

A significant concern for you is Mike's readiness to run the business. Because this will factor heavily into your decision, let's devote a little attention to this question: *How could you prepare Mike to successfully run the business?*

Mike has an M.B.A. from a fine institution, he has some business experience, and he even has experience in Logan Printing. However, this is not the same as being prepared to be the C.E.O. of a $7 million-plus company. Let's agree on the fact that you cannot simply turn over the responsibilities and authority one day and leave. That is not an adequate transition.

I believe that Mike should agree to engage someone as an advisor to help him define his role and to help him develop the necessary skills. He should select someone that he is personally comfortable with.

You should not place yourself in a formal position as his advisor. You should certainly be available to counsel him if he asks, but I believe that there are some unresolved conflicts going on between you and Mike that may make this very difficult.

I also think that you should strongly consider appointing either a Board of Directors or a Board of Advisors. During the reasonable transition period, you can serve as a Chairman of the Board of Directors or Advisors. You should occupy this position with a great deal of care. Again, you want to avoid second-guessing Mike. The board should include one or two C.E.O.s of other companies who are not your competitors.

They should be experienced and able to provide seasoned advice and counsel.

What about your role? Knowing you as well as I do, I suspect that even after several rounds of golf and a number of trips to Bora Bora, you will get a bit antsy. There are, of course a variety of alternatives open to you.

Do you want to start a new venture separate from Logan Printing in a totally different business? Or, do you want to serve as Mike's resource?

I am not sure that you are fully prepared to do this. I'm not sure that you have completely thought through it at this stage and are psychologically ready to play a new role.

I recommend that you sit down with an outside facilitator and specify the key areas that you would be involved in. You will also need to discuss the nature of decision-making.

You described an incident a few weeks ago in which you told Mike not to make any decision on a contract until you came into the office, and he in turn stated that, unless you arrived by 9:30 in the morning, he would go ahead without your involvement. Pardon my saying so, but the behavior of both of you is quite inappropriate.

You are used to exercising total authority and power in the business, and he is in some ways rebelling from that. Instead of trying to resolve what should be done in terms of who owns the business, you should instead decide who has the responsibility and authority to make decisions.

You are going to have to get used to the fact that:

- Decisions will be made differently from the way you would have made them.
- Some of the decisions will be wrong.
- Some of the decisions may even be better than the decisions that you would have made.

You will simply have to get used to the fact that it is someone else's turn. On a personal level, this will mean that you will have to get some other interests.

Ben, I will be happy to meet with you or talk by telephone to clarify any of the suggestions and analysis that I have presented here. You have some work to do, and if you think I can help you, please let me know.

Best personal regards,

Eric Flamholtz

Eric G. Flamholtz

Brace yourself for some criticism.

Financial Analysis Reveals Three Competitive Offers

Robert Gruber, Ph.D.

Dr. Gruber has worked with many small-business owners as a counselor for the Small Business Development Center in Wisconsin. He is an assistant professor of accounting at the University of Wisconsin-Whitewater.

Dear Ben:

It certainly was a pleasure to have lunch with you last week, especially since you ended up paying! You are very lucky to have three quality offers for your business.

I'm happy that you have asked me to focus my analysis on the financial aspects of each offer. Accountants aren't used to examining the personal aspects of a decision and these factors are usually more important than "number-crunching" and tax planning we do for a living. Your situation seems especially delicate because you have three quality options and one of them is from your son.

I've organized my analysis into three schedules, one for each offer.

Ben, it would be hard to choose from the first and second offers from a financial perspective. Offer #3 could be the best or the worst, depending on whether you keep the major customer. Let me know when you want to sit down and discuss these options in more detail.

Sincerely,

Robert Gruber

Robert Gruber

Offer #1: E.S.O.P. Proposal

Jim's offer consists of a $1.8 million purchase price for 60 percent of Logan Printing Company's common stock, and a five-year rental agreement of $15,000 per month for the land and the building owned by you.

The sale of your stock will provide you with approximately $1.5 million, after the appropriate income and capital gain taxes have been paid. Let's not forget that your $319,440 loan from the company needs to be repaid out of this sum. The present value of the after-tax cash flows from the rental revenue is approximately $510,000, if we use an 8 percent discount rate. Therefore, the value of this offer is about $1.7 million, as summarized below:

Tax Computations

Sale price for the common stock owned by Julia and Ben Logan (60 percent)	$1,800,000
Cost basis of the common stock [($1,237,198/10,000) 6,000 shares]	(742,319)
	1,057,681
Accumulated earnings to be treated as dividend income (60 percent of $402,202)	(241,321)
Capital gain	816,360
Tax on the capital gain (28 percent rate)	228,581
Tax on the accumulated dividend income (31 percent)	74,810
Total tax due	303,391

Summary

Proceeds from sale of common stock	$1,800,000
Present value of the rental revenue [$15,000(1-.31)49.318]	510,446
Taxes due from sale of stock	(303,391)
Repayment of personal loan from company	(319,440)
Net proceeds	$1,687,615

The possibility exists to minimize your tax liability if you are willing to reinvest in qualified replacement stock.

Offer #2: Sale to a Relative

Unlike Jim, Mike only wants 40 percent of the outstanding shares of common stock; i.e., your shares! If you want to get completely out of the business (or conversely, if Mike wants to eliminate your authority in the company), this proposal will have to be renegotiated to include Julia's shares.

Mike's offer is also different in that he wants to purchase the land and buildings from you rather than rent them on a monthly basis. Finally, Mike's offer leaves the financing of the deal in your hands. This allows us to use the installment method of recognizing any capital gains, but it also doesn't get you out of the business. We've just changed the nature of your involvement. Mike's offer has a present value slightly under $2.0 million; $500,000 from the sale of your stock and $1.5 million from the sale of the land and buildings. These are summarized below:

Common Stock

Purchase price of 40 percent of the common stock	$750,000
Basis in the common stock (4,000 shares X $123.72)	(494,880)
Capital gain	225,120
Installment method:	
Recognized gain [(255,120/750,000) X 75,000]	25,512
Capital gains tax (28 percent)	(7,143)
Net proceeds	18,369
Ordinary income [(75,000-25,512)(1-.31)]	34,147
Total	52,516
Present factor (20 years, 8 percent)	9,818
Present value of sale of common stock	$515,610

Land and Building

Purchase price	$1,800,000
Personal Basis	(400,000)
Capital gain	1,400,000
Installment method:	
Recognized gain [(1.4m/1.8m) X 15,000]	11,667
Capital gains tax (28 percent)	(3,267)
Net	8,400
Ordinary income [15,000-11,667)(1-.31)]	2,300
Net monthly proceeds	10,700
Present value (360 months, 8 percent)	136,28
Present value of land and building purchase	1,458,196
Total value of offer #2 [515,610 + 1,458,196 - 319,440]	1,654,366

We also can't forget the tax advantages of selling to a son/daughter. Much of the capital gain can be avoided by reinvesting the proceeds in the appropriate places. We can talk more about that possibility later.

Offer #3: Sale to American Printing

This offer is interesting because it contains several benefits not found in the other two offers. First, it has a one-year transitional salary of $100,000 [Present value of after tax cash flow is $66,102 (100,000) (1-.31) (.9580)]. Second, it has a five-year, not-to-compete agreement worth $50,000 per year [Present value of after tax cash flow is $179,672 (50,000) (1-.31) (3.993)]. Third, and like the first offer, the rent of your land and building is worth $510,446 today. Finally, the future sales performance of the company will determine, at least in part, your final sales price. As you'll recall, you'll receive a guaranteed $200,000 per year for five years plus 15 percent of the gross sales above an index base amount. If your major customer continues to buy from Logan Printing, then American's offer is worth $1,939,993. This then is the highest offer, and from a financial perspective, is the best offer. If your major customer does not continue buying from Logan Printing, then American's offer is only worth $1,107,635. If that's the case, then Jim Webb's E.S.O.P. offer is higher, and from a financial perspective, is the better offer. These amounts are supported below:

Sales Forecasts with a 12 percent sales growth):

Year	Base Amount	CPI (est.)	(without customer) Budgeted Sales	(with customer) Budgeted Sales
1995	$7,000,000	1.045	$6,121,000	$7,977,000
1996	7,315,000	1.050	6,856,000	8,934,000
1997	7,680,750	1.050	7,679,000	10,006,000
1998	8,064,783	1.055	8,600,000	11,207,000
1999	8,508,351	1.055	9,632,000	12,552,000

If the major customer leaves, then the payments for the stock will generate the following cash receipts:

Present Value of Offer #3 if Major Customer Leaves Logan

Year	Minimum	Bonus	After-Tax	Present Value
1995	$200,000	—0—	$138,000	$127,777
1996	200,000	—0—	138,000	118,311
1997	200,000	—0—	138,000	109,546
1998	200,000	80,282	193,395	142,151
1999	200,000	168,547	254,297	173,070
			Total	670,855
		Transition Salary		66,102
		Not-to-Compete Agreement		179,672
		Rental Agreement		510,446
		Loan Repayment		(319,440)
		Total		1,107,635

If the major customer does order from you, then the payments for the stock will generate the following cash receipts:

Present Value of Offer #3 if Major Customer Stays With Logan

Year	Minimum	Bonus	After-Tax	Present Value
1995	$200,000	146,500	239,120	221,407
1996	200,000	242,850	305,567	261,974
1997	200,000	348,788	378,664	300,596
1998	200,000	471,332	463,219	340,480
1999	200,000	606,547	556,517	378,756
			Total	1,503,213
		Transition Salary		66,102
		Not-to-Compete Agreement		179,672
		Rental Agreement		510,446
		Loan Repayment		(319,440)
		Total		1,939,993

Let's Work to Prevent Common Family-Business Problems from Developing

John L. Ward, Ph.D.

Author of the best-selling text on family business continuity, Keeping the Family Business Healthy, *Dr. Ward is the Ralph Marotta Professor of Private Enterprise at Loyola University of Chicago, a consultant to family businesses, and the owner of two business enterprises.*

Dear Logan Family:

Thank you for the opportunity to meet with you all and for your trust. It takes a lot of courage to share your family concerns with an "outsider." I hope that I can help, especially because (as you each said) "What's at risk here is our family—the most important part of our life."

Ben, you were correct when you commented that your situation is not unique. You face many of the same dilemmas and anxieties that most business owners face when they prepare for succession and retirement.

However, we can work together to prevent many of the common family-business problems from developing. If we continue to take the time and the considerable effort to sort things out, to talk frankly with each other, to make clear decisions and clear plans.

Let me emphasize once again that you all have much more going for you than most families:

- Few successors are as well educated, well prepared and dedicated as Mike.
- The business is strong. It earns better than 20 percent ROI and is growing nicely.
- Future ownership is not complicated because Stephanie has assured us that she truly has no interest in helping to operate the business.

During our discussions, we have addressed many issues. I'd like to summarize our work to date by answering five of the most difficult questions that, as a family, you need to answer: (1) How can Ben and Mike get along better? (2) How should Julia and Stephanie handle the bickering between Mike and Ben? (3) How vulnerable are Julia and Ben if the business takes a bad reversal? (4) What is fair for Stephanie? (5) How content will Ben really be if he leaves the business? Let's take it from the top.

1. How can Ben and Mike get along better?

There is a lot of friction between the two of you. Like most business owners, you, Ben, have tremendous ambivalence about turning the business over to a successor. The situation is always harder when the successor is your son. You wonder if Mike will let you down—or if he will outshine you.

To me, the biggest challenge of all is for you two to learn how to work through your personal relationship. It is very normal for each of you to feel as though you don't get full appreciation. Entrepreneurial dads are famous for undersupporting and undercommunicating with their sons. Sons of entrepreneurs are famous for acting on their impulse to do their own thing and to be their own master—especially as they near their 30s. There is no question about it—making this transition is not going to be easy.

We have discussed ways to prevent major problems from developing. Here are some of the steps we have agreed you will take:

Make clear plans. The greatest material gift that parents with a family business can give their children is a clear, definitive ownership and leadership succession plan. Responsible business leaders clarify for the entire organization these future plans—and the certainty of them and demonstrate commitment to them.

You need to spell it out. You need to let everyone know. You need to make the plan irreversible. Yes, irreversible change is very frightening. But it's critical.

I would like to help you prevent what is (from my experience) perhaps the most painful possible future scenario of all: "The return of the dad." Many, many semi-retired business owners have a change of heart two or three years after leaving the business. They find some excuse—any excuse—to come back into the business and seize control.

When that happens, there is permanent family havoc. The relationship between father and son is deeply torn. The mother and the siblings are almost certainly drawn in.

A top priority should be to prevent that by turning over the control irrevocably.

Define Ben's role. But should Ben be out of the picture all together? No. There's no doubt that Ben still has tremendous experience and insight to offer.

We have discussed two ways for Mike to be able to tap Ben's expertise. The first way is for you two to have lunch together (or something

> *To me, the biggest challenge of all is for you two to learn how to work through your personal relationship.*

equivalent) at least once a week. That way Mike can ask Ben's counsel, but, of course, Ben shouldn't always expect it to be heeded.

The second way is to include Ben (as well as Mike) on a Board of Advisers or Directors. This group of respected peers—not personal friends—can help Mike, and can also help assure the security of any future payments to Stephanie, Julia or Ben. I think that Ben should be a part of the board for two or more years. Mike would be in charge of the agenda. I can't recommend this "insurance policy" strongly enough.

Consider counseling. What if the bickering and disappointment continue—even after the plans are made and the roles are clarified? You may wish to seek counseling—together, preferably. You have some very deep, very personal issues to sort out, and an outside perspective may be able to help you.

2. How should Julia and Stephanie handle the bickering?

I recommend that Julia and Stephanie continue to do what they are doing now: reflecting the arguments back to the two men, rather than mediating and trying to solve the problem. When the bickering appears, tell father and son to go and work it out, on their own, face to face, now. The point is that you, Julia and Stephanie, should not be drawn into a "triangle." Don't become involved and don't assume any personal responsibility.

Mike and Ben, will it be hard for you to resist drawing the women into the battle? Of course it will be. I realize that this is another "easier said than done" situation. But the family will be better off if you do not expect Julia and Stephanie to participate in your arguments.

3. How vulnerable are Ben and Julia if the business takes a bad reversal?

It seems very possible for Julia and Ben's financial situation to be secure and independent of the business' situation. With real estate worth nearly $2 million, there is a nest egg.

We have all agreed that, first and foremost, you should structure the final purchase deal so that Ben and Julia have personal financial security. We will work out the particulars of the deal in our future meetings.

4. What is fair for Stephanie?

It's important to begin the buyout of Stephanie, too. She's generous enough to realize that being a small minority owner in a business run by someone else isn't very viable, in the long term. So in fairness to her, and to help Mike reach the ultimate goal of total ownership, that buyout process should begin soon.

Julia and Ben, when you write your will, you should make up to Stephanie for any special deal that you offer to Mike so that he can afford the business. That arrangement in your will should be explicitly communicated to all.

5. How content will Ben really be if he leaves the business?

Some wise psychologists assert that no entrepreneurial business owner can "give up the business baby" to someone else. Too much of their identity is tied up in the business. They have to have substitutes for their energy, for their quick minds and for their pride.

The most likely alternative is to design a new venture or role for you, Ben, to keep active in business. It may be something related to and supportive of Logan Printing, Inc.—but it can't be running Logan.

Some psychologists even suggest counseling for departing business owners because it is difficult to adjust to the loss that occurs when selling or turning over the company.

The point that I've tried to make in our discussions is that Ben will reach a point when he will need a satisfying outlet for his energy. That may be hard to accept now, because he exhibits many symptoms of burnout, but I believe the day will come when he needs to return to the business world.

As I've already discussed in this letter, we need to make sure that Ben doesn't decide to return to the world of Logan Printing. You have many other options—and many ways to explore them.

I would like to end this letter by congratulating you all once again for reaching out and for your willingness to make plans. You have so much to cherish and so many good years ahead of you. Enjoy.

All my best,

John L. Ward

John L. Ward

> *Many, many semi-retired business owners have a change of heart two or three years after leaving the business.*

Resources for Small Business

Upstart Publishing Company, Inc.

These publications on proven management techniques for small businesses are available from Upstart Publishing Company, Inc., 12 Portland St., Dover, NH 03820. For a free current catalog, call (800) 235-8866 outside New Hampshire, or 749-5071 in state.

The Business Planning Guide, 6th edition, 1992, David H. Bangs, Jr. and Upstart Publishing Company, Inc. A manual that helps you write a business plan and financing proposal tailored to your business, your goals and your resources. Includes worksheets and checklists. (Softcover, 208 pp., $19.95)

The Market Planning Guide, 4th edition, 1994, David H. Bangs, Jr. and Upstart Publishing Company, Inc. A manual to help small-business owners put together a goal-oriented, resource-based marketing plan with action steps, benchmarks and time lines. Includes worksheets and checklists to make implementation and review easier. (Softcover, 180 pp., $19.95)

The Cash Flow Control Guide, 1990, David H. Bangs, Jr. and Upstart Publishing Company, Inc. A manual to help small-business owners solve their number one financial problem. Includes worksheets and checklists. (Softcover, 88 pp., $14.95)

The Personnel Planning Guide, 1988, David H. Bangs, Jr. and Upstart Publishing Company, Inc. A 176-page manual outlining practical, proven personnel management techniques, including hiring, managing, evaluating and compensating personnel. Includes worksheets and checklists. (Softcover, 176 pp., $19.95)

The Start Up Guide: A One-Year Plan for Entrepreneurs, 2nd edition, 1994, David H. Bangs, Jr. and Upstart Publishing Company, Inc. This book utilizes the same step-by-step, no-jargon method as *The Business Planning Guide,* to help even those with no business training through the process of beginning a successful business. (Softcover, 176 pp., $19.95)

Managing By the Numbers: Financial Essentials for the Growing Business, 1992, David H. Bangs, Jr. and Upstart Publishing Company, Inc. Straightforward techniques for getting the maximum return with a minimum of detail in your business's financial management. (Softcover, 160 pp., $19.95.)

Building Wealth, 1992, David H. Bangs, Jr. and the editors of *Common Sense.* A collection of tested techniques designed to help you plan your personal finances and how to plan your business finances to benefit you, your family and employees. (Softcover, 168 pp., $19.95)

Buy the Right Business—At the Right Price, 1990, Brian Knight and the Associates of Country Business, Inc. Many people who would like to be in business for themselves think strictly of starting a business. In some cases, buying a going concern may be preferable—and just as affordable. (Softcover, 152 pp., $18.95)

Borrowing for Your Business, 1991, George M. Dawson. This is a book for borrowers and about lenders. Includes detailed guidelines on how to select a bank and a banker, how to answer the lender's seven most important questions, how your banker looks at a loan and how to get a loan renewed. (Hardcover, 160 pp., $19.95)

Can This Partnership Be Saved?, 1992, Peter Wylie and Mardy Grothe. The authors offer solutions and hope for problems between key people in business. (Softcover, 272 pp., $19.95)

Cases in Small Business Management, 1994, John Edward de Young. A compilation of intriguing and useful case studies in typical small business problems. (Softcover, 258 pp., $24.95)

The Complete Guide to Selling Your Business, 1992, Paul Sperry and Beatrice Mitchell. A step-by-step guide through the entire process from how to determine when the time is right to sell to negotiating the final terms. (Hardcover, 160 pp., $21.95)

The Complete Selling System, 1991, Pete Frye. This book can help any manager or salesperson, even those with no experience, find the solutions to some of the most common dilemmas in managing sales. (Hardcover, 192 pp., $21.95)

Creating Customers, 1992, David H. Bangs, Jr. and the editors of *Common Sense*. A book for business owners and managers who want a step-by-step approach to selling and promoting. Techniques include inexpensive market research, pricing your goods and services and writing a usable marketing plan. (Softcover, 176 pp., $19.95)

The Entrepreneur's Guide to Going Public, 1994, James B. Arkebauer with Ron Schultz. A comprehensive and useful book on a subject that is the ultimate dream of most entrepreneurs—making an initial public offering IPO. (Softcover, 368 pp., $19.95)

Export Profits, 1992, Jack S. Wolf. This book shows how to find the right foreign markets for your product, cut through the red tape, minimize currency risks and how to find the experts who can help. (Softcover, 304 pp., $19.95)

Financial Troubleshooting, 1992, David H. Bangs, Jr. and the editors of *Common Sense*. This book helps the owner/ manger use basic diagnostic methods to monitor the health of the business and solve problems before damage occurs. (Softcover, 192 pp., $19.95)

Financial Essentials for Small Business Success, 1994, Joseph Tabet and Jeffrey Slater. Designed to show readers where to get the information they need and how planning and recordkeeping will enhance the health of any small business. (Softcover, 272 pp., $19.95)

From Kitchen to Market, 1992, Stephen Hall. A practical approach to turning culinary skills into a profitable business. (Softcover, 208 pp., $24.95)

The Home-Based Entrepreneur, 1993, Linda Pinson and Jerry Jinnett. A step-by-step guide to all the issues surrounding starting a home-based business. Issues such as zoning, labor laws and licensing are discussed and forms are provided to get you on your way. (Softcover, 192 pp., $19.95)

Keeping the Books, 1993, Linda Pinson and Jerry Jinnett. Basic business recordkeeping both explained and illustrated. Designed to give you a clear understanding of small business accounting by taking you step-by-step through general records, development of financial statements, tax reporting, scheduling and financial statement analysis. (Softcover, 208 pp., $19.95)

The Language of Small Business, 1994, Carl O. Trautmann. A clear, concise dictionary of small business terms for students and small business owners. (Softcover, 416 pp., $19.95)

Marketing Your Invention, 1992, Thomas Mosley. This book dispels the myths and clearly communicates what inventors need to know to successfully bring their inventions to market. (Softcover, 232 pp., $19.95)

100 Best Retirement Businesses, 1994, Lisa Angowski Rogak with David H. Bangs, Jr. A one-of-a-kind book bringing retirees the inside information on the most interesting and most lucrative businesses for them. (Softcover, 416 pp., $15.95)

The Small Business Computer Book, 1993, Robert Moskowitz. This book does not recommend particular systems, but rather provides readers with a way to think about these choices and make the right decisions for their businesses. (Softcover, 190 pp., $19.95)

Start Your Own Business for $1,000 or Less, 1994, Will Davis. Shows readers how to get started in the "mini-business" of their dreams with less than $1,000. (Softcover, 280 pp., $17.95)

Steps to Small Business Start-Up, 1993, Linda Pinson and Jerry Jinnett. A step-by-step guide for starting and succeeding with a small or home-based business. Takes you through the mechanics of business start-up and gives an overview of information on such topics as copyrights, trademarks, legal structures, recordkeeping and marketing. (Softcover, 256 pp., $19.95)

Target Marketing for the Small Business, 1993, Linda Pinson and Jerry Jinnett. A comprehensive guide to marketing your business. This book not only shows you how to reach your customers, it also gives you a wealth of information on how to research that market through the use of library resources, questionnaires, demographics, etc. (Softcover, 176 pp., $19.95)

On Your Own: A Woman's Guide to Starting Your Own Business, 2nd edition, 1993, Laurie Zuckerman. *On Your Own* is for women who want hands-on, practical information about starting and running their own business. It deals honestly with issues like finding time for your business when you're also the primary care provider, societal biases against women and credit discrimination. (Softcover, 320 pp., $19.95)

Problem Employees, 1991, Dr. Peter Wylie and Dr. Mardy Grothe. Provides managers and supervisors with a simple, practical and straightforward approach to help all employees, especially problem employees, significantly improve their work performance. (Softcover, 272 pp., $22.95)

The Restaurant Planning Guide, 1992, Peter Rainsford and David H. Bangs, Jr. This book takes the practical techniques of *The Business Planning Guide* and combines it with the expertise of Peter Rainsford, a professor at the Cornell School of Hotel Administration and restaurateur. Topics include: establishing menu prices, staffing and scheduling, controlling costs and niche marketing. (Softcover, 176 pp., $19.95)

Successful Retailing, 2nd edition, 1993, Paula Wardell. Provides hands-on help for those who want to start or expand their retail business. Sections include: strategic planning, marketing and market research and inventory control. (Softcover, 176 pp., $19.95)

The Upstart Guide to Owning and Managing an Antiques Business, 1994, Lisa Angowski Rogak. Provides the information a prospective antiques dealer needs to run a business profitably. (Softcover, 224 pp., $15.95)

The Upstart Guide to Owning and Managing a Bar or Tavern, 1994, Roy Alonzo. Provides essential information on planning, making the initial investment, financial management and marketing a bar or tavern. (Softcover, 256 pp., $15.95)

The Upstart Guide to Owning and Managing a Bed & Breakfast, 1994, Lisa Angowski Rogak. Provides information on choosing the best location, licensing and what really goes on behind the scenes. (Softcover, 224 pp., $15.95)

The Upstart Guide to Owning and Managing a Desktop Publishing Service, 1994, Dan Ramsey. How to take advantage of desktop computer equipment and turn it into a thriving business. (Softcover, 216 pp., $15.95)

The Upstart Guide to Owning and Managing a Résumé Service, 1994, Dan Ramsey. Shows how any reader can turn personnel, writing and computer skills into a lucrative résumé-writing business. (Softcover, 224 pp., $15.95)

The Woman Entrepreneur, 1992, Linda Pinson and Jerry Jinnett. Thirty-three successful women business owners share their practical ideas for success and their sources for inspiration. (Softcover, 244 pp., $14.00)

Other Available Titles

The Complete Guide to Business Agreements, 1993, Ted Nicholas, Enterprise • Dearborn. Contains 127 of the most commonly needed business agreements. (Loose-leaf binder, $69.95)

The Complete Small Business Legal Guide, 1993, Robert Friedman, Enterprise • Dearborn. Provides the hands-on help you need to start a business, maintain all necessary records, properly hire and fire employees and deal with the many changes a business goes through. (Softcover, $69.95)

Guerrilla Marketing: Secrets for Making Big Profits from Your Small Business, 1984, J. Conrad Levinson, Houghton-Mifflin. A classic toolkit for small businesses. (Hardcover, 226 pp., $14.95)

How to Form Your Own Corporation Without a Lawyer for Under $75.00, 1992, Ted Nicholas, Enterprise • Dearborn. A good book for helping you to discover all the unique advantages of incorporating while at the same time learning how quick, easy and inexpensive the process can be. (Softcover, $19.95)

Marketing Sourcebook for Small Business, 1989, Jeffrey P. Davidson, John Wylie Publishing. A good introductory book for small business owners with excellent definitions of important marketing terms and concepts. (Hardcover, 325 pp., $24.95)

The Small Business Survival Kit: 101 Troubleshooting Tips for Success, 1993, John Ventura, Enterprise • Dearborn. Offers compassionate insight into the emotional side of financial difficulties as well as a nuts and bolts consideration of options for the small businessperson experiencing tough times. (Softcover, $19.95)